FINANCIAL CRISES

UNDERSTANDING THE POSTWAR
U.S. EXPERIENCE

FINANCIAL CRISES

UNDERSTANDING THE POSTWAR U.S. EXPERIENCE

By Martin H. Wolfson

M.E. Sharpe INC. ARMONK, NEW YORK
LONDON, ENGLAND

Copyright © 1986 by Martin H. Wolfson

Available in the United Kingdom and Europe from M. E. Sharpe,
Publishers, 3 Henrietta Street, London WC2E 8LU.

Library of Congress Cataloging in Publication Data

Wolfson, Martin H.
    Financial crises.

m.R   Bibliography: p.
    1. Depressions. 2. Business cycles. 3. Business
cycles—United States. I. Title.
ISBN 0-87332-376-9
ISBN 0-87332-377-7 (pbk.)

Printed in the United States of America

To my parents
Eli and Emma Wolfson

Contents

List of Figures

List of Tables

Acknowledgments

There are a number of people who have helped me in the writing of this book. Both Ray Boddy and Bob Pollin read an earlier draft of the entire manuscript and made numerous useful suggestions. Others who helped in various ways include Bill Charwat, Jacob Cohen, Jim Crotty, Andre Gunder Frank, Ellen Hancock, Sue Headlee, Jeff Keefe, David Kotz, Perry Mehrling, Chris Niggle, Kevin Quinn, Lou Schorsch, Bud Talley, John Willoughby, and Ken Woodward. Of course the responsibility for any errors rests solely with the author.

This book grew out of my Ph.D. dissertation on the same topic, and I would also like to thank the members of my dissertation committee—Ray Boddy, Cynthia Morris, and Robin Hahnel—for their help. Cynthia Morriss's understanding of methodology, organization, and historical perspective was quite helpful, as was Robin Hahnel's insightful analysis. I am especially grateful to Ray Boddy. His theoretical understanding and democratic style were important attributes in his capacity as chairman of the committee, and he has provided much help and advice throughout the long gestation period of this book.

I am indebted to my colleagues at the Federal Reserve Board, who have taught me much about banking and the financial system. In particular I would like to thank Bill Charwat, Tony Cornyn, Ellen Hancock, Jim Houpt, Mike Martinson, and Bud Talley. It should be stressed, however, that the opinions expressed in this book are those of the author. They do not necessarily reflect the views of the Board of Governors or of any other staff member of the Federal Reserve System.

A special word of thanks goes to Ginger Pittman, who typed the manuscript with speed, accuracy, and enthusiasm. I would also like to note the efforts of Dick Bartel, my editor at M. E. Sharpe, Inc. who took over the supervision of this book during a difficult time and has seen it through many twists and turns to publication. In addition, Alfred Eichner, as a reviewer for M. E. Sharpe, Inc., made several helpful comments on the manuscript. Last, but not least, I would like to thank my wife, Linda, for her help, advice, and support—all of which made it possible for me to complete this book.

Over the course of my studies in economics I have had a number of exceptional teachers, in particular Joseph Conard, Frank Pierson, Ray Boddy, Cynthia Morris, and Chuck Wilber. They have paid attention not only to the development of ideas, but also to the communication of those ideas to their students. Even more importantly, they have helped me realize that an understanding of how the economy works is an important first step in changing that economy to benefit the majority of the people. My goal in this book has been to contribute to an understanding of an important aspect of the economy's functioning, i.e., how and why financial crises occur. If the reader's understanding has increased as a result of reading this book, that goal will have been achieved.

FINANCIAL CRISES

UNDERSTANDING THE POSTWAR
U.S. EXPERIENCE

1

Introduction

In the nineteenth and early twentieth centuries, financial crises occurred regularly in the United States, with particularly severe episodes in 1873 and 1893. Closer to the present time were the Panic of 1907 and the banking crises that took place during the Great Depression of the 1930s. In that latter case, faith in the banking system had fallen to such a low level that a national Banking Holiday was declared on March 6, 1933, and all banks in the United States were closed for a period of time.

The severe financial and economic trauma of the Great Depression led to major reforms in the structure of the economy, including important institutional changes in banking and finance. The hope at the time was that these reforms would put an end to the dislocations resulting from financial crises.

For a while after the Great Depression and the Second World War, it appeared that these hopes might be realized. For twenty years after the end of World War II, although certain sectors of the economy suffered financial strains from time to time, events in the financial markets did not resemble those that took place during the financial crises of an earlier era.

During the period immediately following World War II, when financial crises seemed to have disappeared forever from the economic scene, mention of them also disappeared from the economics literature. Nearly an entire generation of economists was trained without ever studying the origins and causes of financial crises. If the prevailing wisdom were true, though, such neglect made sense: why study a phenomenon that no longer existed?

Thus the "credit crunch" of 1966 came as quite a shock. For a period of time during the summer of 1966, the market for municipal securities was "disorganized" by the liquidation of bonds from commercial bank portfolios, and thrift institutions came under strong financial pressure. Events seemed to be developing in the same way as they had during past financial crises.

As it turned out, the crisis was resolved before it caused significant damage to the economy. Though the 1966 crisis was much less intense than the Panic of 1907 or other similar crises, it was nonetheless a shock to observers who had thought financial crises were a thing of the past.

The credit crunch of 1966 was followed by another crisis in 1970. Then the surprise bankruptcy of the Penn Central company threatened the commercial paper market and led to a "flight to quality" (i.e., a preference for safe investments). Corporations that had relied upon commercial paper borrowing scrambled desperately for alternative sources of funds. As in 1966, prompt action by the Federal Reserve Board in its capacity as lender of last resort, and appropriate monetary and fiscal policies, prevented the crisis from developing into a full-scale panic. The downturn in economic activity was relatively mild, but of greater intensity than the growth recession of 1966.

In 1974 an even more serious financial crisis took place when the troubles of the Franklin National Bank, the twentieth-largest bank in the United States, were announced in May. This time the crisis had international implications. Franklin had borrowed heavily in the Eurodollar interbank market and had engaged in substantial foreign-exchange speculation. Both of these markets were threatened by Franklin's difficulties. In addition, the market for bank certificates of deposit in the United States came under increased pressure.

Again, government action prevented the situation from escalating rapidly. At the time, however, it became quite clear that the economy of the United States was susceptible to financial crises.

Silver speculation by the billionaire Hunt brothers again threatened to set off a serious financial crisis in 1980. When the price of silver began to fall in January 1980, the Hunts borrowed on a massive scale—an incredible total of nearly $1 billion—from commercial banks in order to cover their losses. Potential default on this mountain of debt put the banking system under considerable pressure.

A financial crisis occurred again in 1982. Because of the degree of interconnection among the nation's banks, the failure of two relatively small financial institutions—Drysdale Government Securities, Incorporated, and Penn Square National Bank—affected other, bigger institutions and created a crisis of confidence in the banking system as a whole.

In addition, conditions in 1982 pushed two other problems toward crisis proportions: the financial troubles of savings and loan associations and the debt burden of less-developed countries. In September 1982, fear of Mexico's default on its obligations to commercial banks aggravated the banks' problems, set off a capital flight, and required lender-of-last-resort operations on an international scale to manage the crisis.

The problems of financial intermediaries continued past 1982. Weakened significantly by the legacy of bad loans they had purchased from Penn Square, both Continential Illinois and Seattle First National Banks were hit by a run on deposits by large investors. Only an unprecedented government bailout in the summer of 1984 prevented the difficulties at Continental from spreading throughout the banking and financial systems.

The thrift industry also continued to be under financial pressure. During the summer of 1984, a run developed on the deposits of the American Savings and Loan Association, the largest thrift in the United States and a subsidiary of the Financial Corporation of America. In March 1985, the failure of ESM Government Securities, Inc., a small securities dealer in Florida, resulted in the closing of Home State Bank in Ohio. Home State's deposits were insured by a state-backed fund, rather than the federal government. The demise of Home State threatened the solvency of the fund, led to a run on the deposits of all seventy-one state-insured thrifts in Ohio, and eventually led to their closing by the governor of Ohio. A similar crisis developed among state-insured thrifts in Maryland. The image of depositors waiting in long lines to withdraw their money was one that had not been seen in the United States since the Depression.

Despite the reemergence of the phenomena of financial crises in the postwar period, and despite the threat they pose to the financial system, our theoretical understanding of the causes of financial crises has not proceeded apace. As Allen Sinai has noted: "Despite repeated trauma from financial disturbances, systematic study of the financial environment, in the same sense that other topics have been formally analyzed by economists, has been sparse."[1]

In contrast, in the earlier period, when financial crises were associated with severe dislocations of the financial system and deep depressions, economists studied them intently. Theories of financial crises were quite widespread.

One writer who maintained this earlier interest in financial crises was Hyman P. Minsky, a financial economist and monetary theorist. Even before the first financial crisis of the postwar period, the credit crunch of 1966, Minsky was developing models of financial crises and predicting that disturbances of this sort could reappear.[2]

Now that financial crises have in fact reappeared, other economists have begun to follow Minsky's lead. For example, Charles P. Kindleberger has recently published a book entitled *Manias, Panics, and Crashes*.[3] In it he uses a framework similiar to Minsky's to investigate international speculative disturbances dating back to the early eighteenth century. Interest in the topic of financial crises has gradually increased, although it still remains, as Sinai said, relatively sparse.[4]

Moreover, much of the work on financial crises that has taken place recently has proceeded without specific reference to the insights of the theorists who wrote during the time when financial crises were more severe. This book hopes to remedy that defect to some extent by investigating the ideas of those earlier theorists.

Thus Chapter 2 discusses in detail the writings of a variety of theorists who have made contributions to the topic of financial crises. It examines not only theorists from both the earlier and modern eras; it also attempts to investigate theorists from a variety of perspectives. These include Thorstein Veblen, Wesley Clair Mitchell, Karl Marx, Hyman P. Minsky, Allen Sinai, Albert M. Wojnilower, and Milton Friedman.[5]

Despite the widely different theoretical and ideological traditions to which these writers belong, there are certain common approaches among at least a majority of the writers. These approaches taken together do not constitute a theory, but do indicate a certain perspective on how to approach the task of empirically testing the various theories. In addition, they provide a convenient framework that can be used to focus on the particular differences among the theorists, and to highlight specific theoretical questions to be investigated.

Without such a basic perspective it would be difficult to know how to approach the data. As Schumpeter has said, "Raw facts are, as such, a meaningless jumble."[6] One needs to know how to organize the data, what questions to ask, and on what variables to focus. This perspective, it is contended, is basically compatible with the theories of six of the seven writers mentioned above (Milton Friedman's theory is the exception). It consists of two major points.

First, financial crises are the result of the normal functioning of the economic and financial systems over the course of the business cycle. Endogenous processes take place near the peak of the expansion phase of the business cycle, in particular, the deterioriation of the financial condition of the business sector, which set the stage for a financial crisis. This point may be termed the general business-cycle perspective.

Second, the crisis is brought about because of developments in the demand and supply of credit. The key to understanding why the crisis occurs is to be found in the way the supply of credit falls short of the demand. Especially important here is the role of the commercial banks. The crisis itself is a response to these developments which involves a disruption to the financial system. This point is referred to as the credit-market perspective.

With this general orientation, it is possible to approach the data in a coherent way. Our interest is focused on developments in the corporate and banking sectors near the peak of the expansion phase of the business cycle. We can look to see if the financial condition of the business sector deteriorates, and how this development affects the banks and the demand and supply of credit. Finally, we can investigate how these events affect the functioning of the financial system.

However, Milton Friedman rejects the general business-cycle, credit-market perspective, and thus his theory will not be directly evaluated using that approach. Friedman does not place his theory of financial crises within the context of the business cycle, and his focus is on movements in the money supply rather than on developments in the credit markets. His views will be evaluated separately, by focusing specifically on the relationships that he identifies.

For the other six writers, though, as mentioned above, the business-cycle, credit-market perspective provides a convenient way to approach the data. It also serves as a context within which to understand the significant differences among these writers, and therefore focuses attention on the most important theoretical issues (differences) to investigate empirically. These issues have to do with (1) the reasons for the development of financial difficulties in the business sector, (2) the factors influencing the demand and supply of credit, and (3) the defining patterns of a financial crisis.

Let us consider first the reasons for the development of financial difficulties in the business sector. Are these difficulties due only to an increase in interest rates and a consequent escalation of debt payment requirements (Minsky), or are they due also to a decline in profits (Marx, Veblen, Mitchell)?

How do these developments affect the demand and supply of credit? With regard to the demand for credit, do these financial difficulties mean that business has a "necessitous" demand due to an inability to meet fixed payment commitments (Minsky, Marx, Mitchell), or is the significance of the financial difficulties primarily that firms have an increased demand for funds to expand "voluntary" investments and increases in production (Sinai, Wojnilower)? If necessitous, is the demand for credit due to a need to meet debt payment requirements (Minsky, Marx), is it to pay for investment projects initiated at an earlier time (Minsky, Mitchell), or is it for both?

With regard to the supply of credit, the main issue concerns the source of the limitation. All the writers recognize a limitation on the supply of credit due to a conscious tightening of monetary policy by the Federal Reserve Board (for the modern period), or adjustments required by the gold standard (in the earlier period). The key question concerns the reaction of the banks. Do they voluntarily limit credit because of the decreased creditworthiness of their business borrowers (Veblen, Mitchell, Minsky) or do they try to accommodate the increased business loan demand (Wojnilower)? If they try to accommodate the demand for credit, what is the source of the interruption in the supply of credit?

The final set of questions concerns the nature and definition of the financial crisis itself. What is a financial crisis? Is it a gradual liquidation of credit (Veblen), or does it involve a more intense reaction, an urgent demand for money (Marx, Wojnilower)? Does a psychological "panic" reaction play an important role (Mitchell, Marx, Minsky, Wojnilower), or is this reaction less significant (Veblen, Sinai)?

Also, are there regularities in the form the crisis takes? Does it involve the forced sale of assets (Minsky), an intensified effort to borrow (Marx, Mitchell), bank runs (Mitchell), a disruption of financial markets (Wojnilower)?

These theoretical issues are discussed in more detail and compared in Chapter 3, which draws upon the examination of the views of the individual theorists in Chapter 2. The remainder of the study then sets about to resolve these issues and to develop a coherent theoretical understanding of the financial crises that have occurred in the postwar period in the United States.

Part II (Chapters 4–9) is an in-depth examination of these financial crises, including the events in the economy leading up to the crises. The approach to the data is guided by the theoretical business-cycle, credit-market perspective discussed above.

The method employed, dictated by the nature of the subject matter to be investigated, is institutional, dynamic, and historical. It is institutional because the particular institutions of the postwar economy—particularly institutional constraints on bank lending—have played an important role in affecting how financial crises have unfolded and developed. It is dynamic because the events of financial crises, involving uncertainty, psychological reactions, and disruptions to financial markets, cannot be modeled in a static framework. Finally, it is historical because financial crises are due to an evolution of events constantly unfolding in historical time; the concept of financial crises and business cycles underlying the theoretical perspective discussed above is that of a process of endogenous change and perpetual disequilibrium. In the words of Joan Robinson:

> Once we admit that an economy exists in time, that history goes one way, from the irrevocable past into the unknown future, the concept of equilibrium based on the mechanical analogy of a pendulum swinging to and fro in space becomes untenable. The whole of traditional economics needs to be thought out afresh.[7]

The econometric approach, while useful for many applications, has problems in capturing the nature of the process being investigated here. The need to consider historical, dynamic, and disequilibrium phenomena makes econometric modeling difficult. The investigation in Part II is quantitative, however, in the sense that time series data are utilized in connection with the investigation of financial crises. The primary questions to be answered by these data, though, are those concerning timing and the direction and magnitude of change in variables, rather than those involving more formal statistical conclusions.

Chapter 10 of Part III draws out the implications of the investigation of Part II and presents the results in a business-cycle model of financial crises: a model of how endogenous changes near the peak of the expansion phase of the business cycle create the conditions that make financial crises likely. The model is developed by addressing the theoretical issues discussed above.

Some comments about the nature of the model are perhaps in order. It is not a formal, deductive model whose conclusions follow logically from its assumptions; rather, the structure of the model is determined by the nature of the empirical events surveyed in Part II. The model is formulated by linking together conclusions about the theoretical issues into an overall conception of how financial crises develop. The purpose of the model is to aid understanding, rather than necessarily to enable prediction.

However, the model is not a mere statement of an observed sequence of events. It is a theory in the sense that it includes causal statements and propositions about the behavioral motivations of essential economic actors. Nonetheless, it is a carefully limited theory. It is a theory of financial crises, not of business cycles. It does not attempt to address financial developments over the business cycle as a whole, but focuses instead only on developments near the peak of the expansion. Moreover, it does not attempt to explain the behavioral motivations for certain important developments, such as the reason for the decline in profits toward the end of the expansion. It simply observes that profits do fall. Important and complicated questions involved in the theory of investment are only briefly mentioned.

Despite its emphasis on understanding rather than prediction, the model is capable of being evaluated, according to how accurately and consistently it generalizes the postwar history of financial crises. This evaluation is carried out in Chapter 11.

Chapter 12 compares the postwar experience to the theories of financial crises considered in Part I. Chapter 13 takes a broader look at the history of financial crises. It indicates the need to integrate long-term trends and institutional change with the cyclical forces discussed in Chapter 10, in order to obtain a more complete understanding of how financial crises change over time. It compares the recent period with the past, and also considers how financial crises might currently be in the process of change.

PART I

Theories of Financial Crises

2

Theories of Financial Crises

The purpose of this chapter is to set out the main theories and concepts that have been developed to explain the phenomenon of financial crises. No attempt has been made to be exhaustive; rather, the emphasis is on the major theoretical viewpoints of writers from a variety of different perspectives within economics.

Theorists of the late nineteenth and early twentieth centuries have been included, as mentioned in the Introduction. The assumption is that at least some basic processes involved in financial crises are due to the fundamental workings of an industrialized capitalist economy. More contemporary theorists, of course, are also discussed.

Earlier Theorists

Thorstein Veblen

An analysis of financial crises was developed in 1904 by Thorstein Veblen, the founder of the institutionalist approach within economics. His theory of financial crises is based upon the effects of movements in the rate of profit upon the extension of credit.[1]

Veblen stresses the central role of profits. For him, profit considerations dominate business decisions, and the degree to which profits are realized can affect the overall economy: "Times are good or bad according as the process of business yields an adequate or inadequate rate of profits." He distinguishes between two types of credit: (1) "deferred payments in the purchase and sale of goods" (what today we would call trade credit) and (2) "loans or debt—notes, stock shares, interest-bearing securities, deposits, call loans, etc." [2] His view is that credit is necessarily employed in business expansions, and that its use inevitably spreads throughout the economy:

> Whenever the capable business manager sees an appreciable
> difference between the cost of a given credit extension and
> the gross increase of gains to be got by its use, he will seek

> to extend his credit. But under the regime of competitive
> business whatever is generally advantageous becomes a ne-
> cessity for all competitors . . . recourse to credit becomes
> the general practice.[3]

Credit is desired to enhance profits, but it is extended based upon the capitalized value of the assets of the firm which are used as collateral (either explicit or implicit). This capitalized value depends upon the expected future profits to be earned by the assets in question, discounted by the market rate of interest. These assets are the "industrial plant or process" involved in production, but the capitalization of these assets may have to be approximated by creditors on the basis of the market value of the firm's stock on the stock exchange.[4]

During prosperity, two things occur that affect the amount of credit extended: profits increase, and so do expectations of future profits. The increase in actual and expected profitability is based upon a "differential advantage" of the "selling price of the output over the expenses of production of the output," which is due primarily to "the relatively slow advance in the cost of labor during an era of prosperity."[5]

As a result of the increase in expected earnings, the "effective (market) capitalization is increased" and "this recapitalization of industrial property, on the basis of heightened expectation, increases the value of this property as collateral."[6] Thus the amount of credit expands rapidly.

However, the continuation of prosperity eventually leads to a liquidation of this expanded credit:

> In the ordinary course, however, the necessary expenses of
> production presently overtake or nearly overtake the pro-
> spective selling price of the output. The differential advan-
> tage, on which business prosperity rests, then fails; the rate
> of earnings falls off; the enhanced capitalization based on
> enhanced putative [supposed] earnings proves greater than
> the earnings realized or in prospect on the basis of an en-
> hanced scale of expenses of production; the collateral conse-
> quently shrinks to a point where it will not support the credit
> extension resting on it in the way of outstanding contracts
> and loans; and liquidation ensues.[7]

Veblen identifies the crisis as "a period of liquidation, cancelment of credits, high discount rates, falling prices and 'forced sales,' and shrinkage of values."[8] Because of the interdependence of the economy, the liquidation spreads quickly.

Thus, for Veblen, a financial crisis is the process of liquidation of the expanded credit that had been built up during prosperity; it is brought on because expectations of lower profitability lead to a lower capitalization of assets and a restriction of credit.

Wesley Clair Mitchell

The process sketched out by Veblen was considerably developed and expanded by his student, Wesley Clair Mitchell. Mitchell's analysis of financial crises is based upon an elaborate statistical analysis of the movements of economic variables over the course of the business cycle.

Although Mitchell studied business cycles his entire life, his main theoretical results were presented in 1913.[9] The significance of this early work is attested to by Milton Friedman: "Though his subsequent work would alone suffice to give him an unquestioned place in the front ranks of economists, none of it, in my view, rivals in quality or significance the 1913 volume."[10]

In a Bibliographical Note added to the 1941 edition, Mitchell noted that, in his opinion, the theory developed in 1913 was still relevant to an understanding of current economic events, because these events are based upon the fundamental institutions of modern industrial society: private property, a money economy, and the pursuit of profits.[11]

Mitchell's approach to economic theory, influenced by Veblen, focuses on the dynamic, evolutionary process of economic change, and the important role of profits. Mitchell's theory of business cycles traces the process of cumulative change whereby the pursuit of profit transforms one phase of the cycle into the next.[12] An important and integral phase of the business cycle in Mitchell's analysis is a financial crisis. To understand Mitchell's theory of financial crises, therefore, it is necessary to analyze the cumulative changes that create the conditions whereby crises develop.

Mitchell begins his analysis with the legacies from depression. These include a reduction in business costs, inventories, interest rates, and accumulated debt, and a greater willingness on the part of banks and other creditors to lend to business.[13] These conditions restore the basis for profitable expansion. They were the typical result of the depressions that occurred regularly in Mitchell's time.

Once the conditions for expansion are established, the expansion itself begins because of some propitious event or the slow expansion of trade. Once begun, however, it develops rapidly. A lag of costs, especially unit labor costs, behind selling prices boosts profits. The increase in profits also stimulates business confidence, and both contribute to an increase in investment.[14] Expanded investment spending contributes to a process by which profits, optimism, investment, prices, and the volume of trade all continue to expand and produce a cumulative upward spiral.

However, prosperity itself sets in motion contradictory forces. For one thing, costs of construction increase, and interest rates on long-term bonds rise. As a result, businesses rely more heavily on short-term financing, and plans for new construction decline.[15]

Although orders for the construction of new business structures decline, actual spending for investment can remain strong. Mitchell says that, at the same time that industries "find their orders for future delivery falling off . . . for the time being they may be working at high pressure to complete old contracts." "Relief lies in the future, and as a rule it is not felt until after the crisis has occurred."[16]

The demand for financing "is relatively inelastic, since many borrowers think they can pay high rates of discount for a few months and still make profits on their turnover."[17] In addition, often the money obtained from short-term loans is only a fraction of the overall funds already tied up in a particular investment project.

The supply of short-term loans, which "directly or indirectly . . . comes chiefly from banks" is, however, limited by the rigidities of the gold standard.[18] Thus the inelastic demand and limited supply result in increases in short-term interest rates.

As the expansion continues, moreover, businesses find that they no longer can continue to increase selling prices sufficiently to offset increased unit labor costs. The profits of a group of businesses begin to fall off. This decline in profits, along with the increase in interest rates, undermines the expansion and initiates the financial crisis.

As did Veblen, Mitchell viewed the use of credit in the business expansion as based upon optimistic expectations of the capitalized value of future profits. The increase in interest rates, by reducing this capitalized value, begins to question the continued extension of credit. The fall in profits for some businesses worsens the general outlook for prospective profits and causes creditors to fear that they will not be repaid. Hence a liquidation of credit ensues. "And in the course of this liquidation prosperity merges into crisis."[19]

The primary objective for business now is to maintain solvency. As a consequence, the business expansion comes to an end.[20] Also, the process of liquidation of debt spreads rapidly. Mitchell notes that the attempts of debtors to meet their financial obligations can increase the financial pressure upon others. A debtor can demand payment from those who owe him money, or he can dump goods or securities onto the market in order to raise cash. He can also seek easier repayment terms from existing creditors, and he can apply to other creditors. To the extent that he is successful in borrowing from the banks, the supply of loans for other potential borrowers is thereby reduced.[21]

Moreover, the banks are being asked to lend not only to those who must meet immediate demands for repayment, but also to those who anticipate possible difficulties in borrowing to meet payment commitments in the future. Because many borrowers have been shut out of the long-term debt market, they "fall back upon the banks."[22]

The banks at this point are no longer being asked to lend to finance new investment spending. It is more likely that businesses "have bonds maturing" or that they "must raise money to pay for contract work nearing completion."[23] However, this sudden increase in the demand for loans to meet outstanding obligations much more than makes up for the decrease in the demand for loans to finance fresh business ventures. On the other hand, banks are particularly loath to increase loans at such seasons if they can help it.[24] Although the banks are reluctant to lend, their ability and willingness to meet the loan demand placed upon them have important implications for the development of the financial crisis.

Like Veblen, Mitchell identifies the financial crisis with the liquidation of credit: "When the demand for reduction of outstanding credits becomes general, the cycle passes from the phase of prosperity into the phase of crisis."[25] However, unlike Veblen, Mitchell distinguishes between two possible outcomes of the liquidation process. One is a financial crisis which leads to a downturn in the business cycle, "though without a violent wrench . . . there is no epidemic of bankruptcies, no run upon banks, and no spasmodic interruption of the ordinary business processes."[26]

The second outcome is a more severe crisis that turns into a financial panic. The likelihood of a panic depends to a significant degree upon whether or not the banks meet the demands placed on them:

> When the process of liquidation reaches a weak link in the chain of interlocking credits and the bankruptcy of some conspicuous enterprise spreads unreasoning alarm among the business public, then the banks are suddenly forced to meet a double strain—a sharp increase in the demand for loans and in the demand for repayment of deposits. If the banks prove able to honor both demands without flinching, the alarm quickly subsides. But if, as has happened twice in America since 1890, many solvent businessmen are refused accommodation at any price, and if depositors are refused payment in full, the alarm turns into panic.[27]

Mitchell concludes that "the ending of a crisis, whether accompanied by panic or not, is the cessation of intense demand for prompt liquidation." This comes about because "the members of the business community have withstood, on the whole successfully, the test of ability to meet their financial obligations." "The acute stage of liquidation—the crisis—is over, and depression—the dragging stage of the liquidation—begins."[28]

Karl Marx

Karl Marx's theory of financial crises is intimately tied to his theory of industrial crises. Both forms of crisis are situated within the overall framework of the phases of the industrial cycle (although Marx did not systematically analyze this latter topic). He mentions "the cycles in which modern industry moves—state of inactivity, mounting revival, prosperity, overproduction, crisis, stagnation, state of inactivity, etc., which fall beyond the scope of our analysis."[29] Marx's analysis of financial crises also was not fully developed, but it is possible nonetheless to focus on certain of his key ideas which contribute to our understanding of the subject.

For Marx, a financial (or money) crisis occurs whenever there is a crisis in the "real" sector. The possibility of the latter type of crisis is present whenever the purchase and sale of commodities become separated: "If the *crisis* appears, therefore, because purchase and sale become separated, it becomes a *money crisis* as soon as money has developed as *means of payment*, and this *second form* of crisis follows as a matter of course, when the *first occurs*." Moreover, "the second form is not possible *without the first*."[30]

Marx's concept of money as a "means of payment" plays a key role in his explanation of financial crises. Before proceeding further, therefore, it is necessary to explain how Marx uses this term. He distinguishes between money as a means of payment and a means of circulation (or means of purchase). When money acts as a means of circulation, it is exchanged for commodities, thus facilitating their circulation in society. However, money used as a means of payment involves a separation in time between the transfer of commodities and the payment for them. Credit is necessarily involved. The demand for money as a means of payment is a demand for money to pay debts previously contracted. The significance of this demand will become apparent below.

To return to the crisis in the "real" sector: Marx's view is that the separation of purchase and sale provides only the possibility of crisis, not its actuality. "The *general possibility* of crisis is . . . the separation, in time and place, of purchase and sale. But this is never the *cause* of the crisis."[31]

The actual mechanism that brings about the industrial crisis in Marx's system is a fall in the rate of profit. In what follows, we shall assume that the rate of profit falls (at the end of the prosperity phase of the business cycle) and investigate what role this plays in Marx's theoretical explanation of financial crises. Before doing so, however, it is helpful to examine the relationship between the use of credit and the expansion of the productive system.

In Marx's view, credit is "indispensable" for "production on a large scale." He speaks of a "mutual interaction" in which "the development of the production process extends the credit, and credit leads to an extension of industrial and commercial operations."[32] However, credit not only aids the development of production; it is responsible for extending the production process to its absolute limits: "The maximum of credit is here identical with the fullest employment of industrial capital, that is the utmost exertion of its reproductive power without regard to the limits of consumption.''[33]

Now the use of credit sets up a series of fixed payment commitments due to interest and principal that must be met. However, the crisis in the real sector affects the continued ability of firms to meet these commitments:

> The crisis arises and derives its character not only from the *unsaleability* of the commodity, but from the *nonfulfillment of a whole series of payments* which depend on the sale of this particular commodity within this particular period of time. This is the *characteristic form of money crises.*[34]

This analysis, though, is still at the level of the possibility of crisis. The actual cause of the crisis in the real sector, the reason for the unsaleability of the commodity, is to be found in the movement of the rate of profit:

> The *rate of profit* falls. . . . The fixed charges—interest, rent—which were based on the anticipation of a *constant* rate of profit and exploitation of labor, remain the same and in part *cannot be paid*. Hence *crisis*.''[35]

The decline in profits and the resultant inability to fulfill debt payment requirements bring to an end the expansion of credit, although Marx is not specific on the exact mechanism involved. However, he does state that credit ceases abruptly, and that this cessation is responsible for bringing about the financial crisis:

> In a system of production, where the entire continuity of the reproductive process rests upon credit, a crisis must obviously occur—a tremendous rush for means of payment—when credit suddenly ceases and only cash payments have validity.[36]

Marx therefore defines a financial crisis as a ''tremendous rush for means of payment'' brought about by the abrupt cessation of credit. He stresses that the intense demand for money is for the purpose of meeting payment commitments, not undertaking new investment:

> In times of crisis, the demand for loan capital, and therefore the rate of interest, reaches its maximum; the rate of profit, and with it the demand for industrial capital, has to all intents and purposes disappeared. During such times, everyone borrows only for the purpose of paying, in order to settle previously contracted obligations.[37]

Because of the urgent demand for money during financial crises, drastic steps are sometimes taken to avoid bankruptcy. Commodities can be "sacrificed" (i.e., their prices drastically reduced) in a desperate attempt to convert them into the only form of payment that has validity then: money.

> In time of a squeeze, when credit contracts or ceases entire-
> ly, money suddenly stands as the only means of payment and
> true existence of value in absolute opposition to all other
> commodities. Hence the universal depreciation of commod-
> ities, the difficulty or even impossibility of transforming
> them into money.[38]

During Marx's time, the price of commodities often fell precipitously as the result of attempts to sell them at any price in order to obtain money.

However, the policy followed by the banks had an important effect upon the severity of the crisis. If the banks are willing and able to make money available during financial crises, then some of the worst effects of the crisis can be avoided. Moreover, the policy of the central bank can have even more of a decisive effect. In discussing the Panic of 1847, Frederick Engels (Marx's close collaborator) noted that, as soon as legislation restricting the Bank of England's operations was suspended, the Bank rapidly increased the supply of its bank notes in circulation. This increase in the availability of money of unquestioned quality dramatically reduced the Panic.[39]

Contemporary Theorists

Hyman P. Minsky

Hyman P. Minsky's theory of financial crisis is based upon his reinterpretation of the writings of John Maynard Keynes. Minsky contends that the standard inter-pretation of Keynes, the neoclassical synthesis, distorts Keynes's theory. This distortion is due to the neglect of three topics: uncertainty, the business cycle, and finance.[40]

The relationship among these three concepts forms the foundation of Min-sky's theory. A key element linking them together is his theory of investment. Minsky says that "Keynes put forth an investment theory of fluctuations in real demand and a financial theory of fluctuations in real investment."[41] In other words, it is financial variables that mainly determine investment, and the level and changes in investment that determine the overall state of the economy. Moreover, financial variables are strongly influenced by opinions about the fu-ture, which are subject to rapid change. Thus investment decisions are subject to considerable uncertainty.[42]

However, Minsky's "financial instability hypothesis" does not posit wild unsystematic behavior due to constantly changing views about the future. Rather, his theory concerns the endogenous, systematic changes that bring about the stages of the business cycle: "Each stage, whether it be boom, crisis, debt-deflation, stagnation, or expansion, is transitory. . . . Whenever something approaching stability is achieved, destabilizing processes are set off."[43] In particular, Minsky is concerned with the systematic changes that take place during business-cycle expansions. His view is that the expansion is inevitably unstable; processes develop that transform it into a speculative investment boom.[44]

It is during investment booms that Minsky sees the conditions for financial crises developing. Indeed the main emphasis of his entire theoretical structure is on explaining the endogenous process by which these conditions are put in place. Minsky calls this a theory of systemic fragility:

> *Financial fragility* is an attribute of the financial system. In a
> fragile financial system continued normal functioning can be
> disrupted by some not unusual event. *Systemic fragility*
> means that the development of a fragile financial structure
> results from the normal functioning of our economy.[45]

Thus to understand Minsky's theory it is necessary to investigate the concept of financial fragility and the endogenous process by which it develops.

According to Minsky, there are three determinants of the fragility of a financial system. The first is the relative weights of what Minsky calls hedge, speculative, and Ponzi finance. The other two concern the degree of liquidity in the system, and the reliance on debt to finance investment.[46]

The characterization of hedge, speculative, and Ponzi finance is Minsky's way of classifying economic units according to their susceptibility to financial difficulties. The method of classification depends upon the relationship between the cash receipts due to normal operations and the cash payment liabilities due to debt. For a hedge unit these cash receipts are anticipated to exceed substantially cash payment commitments. In contrast, a speculative financing unit expects to have its cash receipts fall short of cash payments for some periods—usually in the immediate future. Typically the shortfall arises because a speculative unit has a significant amount of short-term debt coming due which it expects to refinance. A Ponzi unit is a kind of speculative unit which anticipates that it will be unable to pay even its interest obligations from its cash receipts. Thus a Ponzi unit must continually increase its borrowing in order to pay its interest costs.[47]

With these definitions as a background, let us now investigate Minsky's explanation of the endogenous development of financial fragility. He begins his analysis with the expansion phase of the business cycle, and notes that the use of debt increases profits. The observed profitability from the use of debt increases confidence, allows the use of more debt, and results in expanded investment.[48]

The increase in confidence also affects the stock market positively.[49] It also lessens the need to maintain a high proportion of assets in cash. Thus liquidity declines.

According to Minsky, there are also important incentives for the use of short-term debt. If the yield curve is positive (i.e., short-term interest rates are lower than long-term rates), it may be more profitable to borrow short term. As long as the economy is expanding and confidence is increasing, most businesses do not anticipate any problems in refinancing. Minsky observes that short-term financing has become for many "a way of life."[50] Therefore

> over a period of good years the weight of short-term debt in
> the business financial structure increases and the weight of
> cash in portfolios declines. Thus there is a shift in the pro-
> portion of units with the different financial structures—and
> the weight of speculative and Ponzi finance increases during
> a period of good years.[51]

Thus financial fragility increases as the expansion continues.[52]

Minsky contends that, given the financial fragility of the economy, increases in interest rates can lead to financial crises. Interest rates rise because an inelastic demand for financing runs up against a less than perfectly elastic supply. Let us examine the demand and supply in turn.

The nature of speculative and Ponzi finance is such that units have continually to refinance their debt in order to meet payment commitments. Thus "speculative and especially Ponzi finance give rise to large increases in an interest-inelastic demand for finance."[53]

A second source of inelastic demand for financing originates in the nature of financing of investment. Minsky states that there are two different ways to finance investment. Either the necessary funds can be raised at the beginning of the project (prior financing) or they can be raised as the project proceeds (sequential financing). He argues that sequential financing is the more usual procedure.[54] This method of financing leads to a more inelastic demand for funds; inelasticity in the supply of funds results in sharp increases in interest rates.[55]

Why is there inelasticity in the supply of funds? In the early stages of an expansion the supply of finance is relatively elastic because of the ways that banks in the United States can expand their ability to lend. Minsky contends that the effective quantity of money can be increased by the banks by using time deposits (instead of demand deposits), lines of credit, and by borrowing federal funds.[56]

A tight monetary policy by the central bank obviously makes this process more difficult, as Minsky points out.[57] He argues, though, that interest rates will rise even without a tight monetary policy by the Federal Reserve,[58] because "as lenders and borrowers seek new ways to finance investment, borrowers increasingly, on the margin, will tap sources of funds that value liquidity ever more highly—that is, contract terms on debts will rise."[59] Also, "sharp increases in short-term interest rates lead to a rise in long-term interest rates."[60]

The significance of rising interest rates is the following: "In a fragile financial structure, feedbacks from the rising interest rates of a boom . . . lead to financial crunches and crashes, which in turn threaten to trigger a cumulative debt-deflation."[61] It now remains to trace the process by which rising interest rates initiate a financial crisis.

Minsky says that a rise in interest rates will have three consequences: (1) cash payment commitments can rise relative to cash receipts, (2) the market value of assets can fall relative to liabilities (assuming assets are of longer term than liabilities), and (3) lenders can decide (as a result of the first two consequences) to restrict lending. Minsky also notes that lenders' attitudes can change relatively suddenly.[62]

In other words, "the critical element in explaining why financial instability occurs is the development over historical time of liability structures that cannot be validated by market-determined cash flows or asset values."[63] It is important to note that, according to Minsky, the source of this problem is due to the effect of rising interest rates on a fragile financial structure; he does not specifically mention an independent decline in profit rates. In fact, Minsky does not analyze movements in corporate profits per se; he prefers to use a broader definition of profits called quasi-rents.

He adds gross profits before taxes to interest paid on business debts to arrive at the concept of quasi-rents. Quasi-rents are a measure of gross capital income, and indicate the ability of firms to pay their debts from generated revenue. In Minsky's system, quasi-rents are inadequate to service the debt structure not (necessarily) because profits are falling, or even because quasi-rents are falling, but because quasi-rents grow at a steady rate while debt obligations grow at an accelerating rate:

> The debt base grows at an accelerating rate during a boom.
> . . . Thus, debts require increased servicing as they grow
> and as financing charges increase. Realized quasi-rents
> which ultimately in real terms can grow at only a steady rate
> become in these circumstances an inadequate source of the
> cash that debt servicing requires.[64]

Minsky sees two major scenarios that occur as a result of the rise in cash payment commitments relative to cash receipts, the decline in the market value of assets relative to liabilities, and the revaluation of acceptable liability structures.

In the first scenario, rising interest rates cause a decline in investment. This happens for two reasons. First, "feedbacks from revealed financial weakness of some units affect the willingness of bankers and businessmen to debt finance a wide variety of organizations."[65] When perceived risk (either borrower's or lender's) increases, corporations try to reduce the leverage they have used for investment, and banks refuse to continue to finance investment spending. Second, investment is reduced because investment projects begin to appear increasingly unprofitable. Since investment demand in Minsky's theory is based upon the capitalized present value of the future yields (quasi-rents) expected from investment projects, a rise in interest rates will make some projects untenable.[66]

The decline in investment then leads to a fall in quasi-rents. Minsky here refers to the analysis developed by Michal Kalecki that equates quasi-rents (although here Minsky calls them profits) to the level of investment.[67] Although Minsky recognizes that this equation is an ex post identity given the behavioral assumptions, he insists that the causal relationship runs from investment to profits: "The simple Kalecki relation can be interpreted as meaning that profits are determined by investment."[68]

The decline in profits then exacerbates the problems due to the liability structure, makes continued refinancing unlikely, requires the forced selling of assets to raise cash, and results in sharp declines in the prices of assets.[69] Minsky identifies the financial crisis with these last two developments.[70]

Minsky notes that financial fragility is not restricted to nonfinancial business corporations. Their difficulties also have repercussions on the banks and other institutions that lend to them. The financial position of the banks deteriorates when speculative and Ponzi units are unable to refinance their obligations.[71]

In Minsky's second scenario, rising interest rates in a fragile financial structure first lead to a financial crisis, which is then the cause of a decline in investment:

> The typical problems of a refinancing crisis occur when the 'normal' liabilities cannot be issued either because the borrowers cannot meet the market terms . . . or because a market that has been counted on is not working normally. When this occurs either assets have to be sold or the borrowing unit cannot fulfill obligations to the prior lenders who may seek to withdraw their funds in a 'run.' Such a failure of borrowers to perform in any significant market means that throughout the credit markets a more skeptical view of permissable liability structures and income prospects begins to rule. . . . Such a shift in preferences . . . makes the terms of debt financing . . . more onerous. This leads to a sell off of inventories and to cutbacks in investment, driving the economy towards a recession/depression.[72]

Minsky emphasizes this second scenario less frequently. However, whatever the exact sequence between the financial crisis and the decline in investment (and the resulting recession/depression), Minsky is clear that both occur and that the financial crisis is a necessary element: "Business cycle experience, of the period since the emergence of financial fragility with the crunch of 1966, shows that recessions either are triggered by or they soon lead to a threatened breakdown of some significant set of financial markets—without a crunch no recession takes place."[73]

According to Minsky, our economy is vulnerable to the type of interactive debt-deflation that follows from a severe financial crisis and leads to a deep depression; this debt-deflation process was described by Irving Fisher.[74] However, in the recent experience in the United States since 1966, a severe financial crisis and a deep depression have been avoided. Minsky attributes this success to two factors: (1) lender-of-last-resort interventions by the Federal Reserve Board, which have prevented distress in some financial markets from spreading, and (2) increases in the federal government deficit, which have sustained business profits.[75]

Albert M. Wojnilower

We now turn to two "practical" economists who have studied the financial disturbances of the post-World War II period: Albert M. Wojnilower and Allen Sinai. Each has looked closely at the recent "credit crunch" experience in the United States. Neither has developed the kind of elaborate theoretical structure of Hyman Minsky. Both, however, have important theoretical generalizations based on their empirical investigations that warrant attention. We begin with Albert M. Wojnilower.

Wojnilower's basic views were presented in a significant recent article entitled "The Central Role of Credit Crunches in Recent Financial History."[76] This article is a perceptive history of the credit crunch experience from an "insider's" point of view. Wojnilower describes himself as a trained economist who has spent nearly thirty years in the New York financial community. From the perspective of understanding his views on financial crises, Wojnilower's conclusions can be summarized in four propositions.

First, "the key observation, controversial though it may be, is that the propensity to spend (that is, the demand for nominal GNP) and therefore the demand for credit are inelastic (or at times even perversely positive) with respect to the general level of interest rates."[77] Since Wojnilower states that his focus is on the upper turning points of the business cycle, this statement should be interpreted to mean that the demand for credit is inelastic in the vicinity of the upper turning point—not at all times and places.

However, this proposition is a statement not only about the inelasticity of the demand for credit; it also concerns the relationship between credit and real spending. In Wojnilower's view, the demand for credit is derived from the propensity to spend, so that the funds desired are used to finance real spending. Moreover, what is important for aggregate demand is access to credit, not money per se.[78] The history that Wojnilower describes in his article focuses heavily upon movements in the demand for credit.

Wojnilower's second point is that the growth of credit is determined by the supply of credit.[79] Because, in Wojnilower's view, the demand for credit near the peak of the business-cycle expansion is essentially insatiable at conceivable interest rates, the availability of funds determines how much credit will actually be extended.

The third point is that financial conditions can have a dominant and powerful effect on the course of business-cycle developments because of the rapidity of adjustment of actual to desired financial stocks.[80]

These three propositions taken together imply a fourth: that interruptions in the supply of credit bring on financial disturbances (credit crunches) that are responsible for the business-cycle downturn. Wojnilower's view is not only that credit crunches can cause recessions; it is that a credit crunch is necessary for the recession to take place.[81]

Wojnilower indicates that there may be various reasons for the unavailability of credit. He mentions two in particular: (1) regulations, such as ceilings on interest rates, which affect lenders' incentives, and (2) serious default problems by large organizations, which have the ability to affect financial markets.[82] His article details the particular reasons for the restrictions in credit supply at the postwar business-cycle peaks.

Allen Sinai

Allen Sinai has developed some theoretical generalizations about financial crises from his study of the postwar credit crunch experience in the United States.[83]

Although the term "credit crunch" was first applied to the financial disturbances of 1966, Sinai contends that they are not new. He argues that they occurred in the 1950s, and he suspects that "a money crisis of some sort has characterized the late stages of almost every business expansion."[84] In another paper Sinai goes back to the early financial history of the United States and notes a similarity between financial crises and the credit crunches of recent experience.[85]

Moreover, he asserts that the money crises that have appeared in the late stages of almost every business expansion are part of the systematic processes of the economy: "Financial instability is an endogenous process, rooted in the cyclical evolution of risky balance sheet positions for various decision-making units."[86]

Sinai identifies the postwar credit crunches in the United States with these periods of financial instability. He defines a credit crunch as "a credit crisis stemming from the collision of an expanding economy with a financial system that does not provide enough liquidity."[87] During a credit crunch the liquidity of households, corporations, and financial institutions becomes very low. Interest rates rise, as do the interest-rate premiums on risky investments. Moreover, credit is unavailable for many borrowers, no matter what interest rate they are willing to pay.[88]

The credit crunch itself is the culmination of what Sinai calls a "Crunch Period," the time during which liquidity is gradually reduced for the major sections of the economy. During a Crunch Period, the credit demands of these sectors increasingly exceed the supply of funds from the financial system.[89] These demands for credit are for the purpose of financing real spending, since Sinai notes that during Crunch Periods there is strong activity in consumer durable purchases and capital expenditures.[90]

What are the reasons that the Crunch Period comes to an end and the credit crunch itself begins? Sinai's view is that several factors are important, including the strong demand for funds from the real economy, limits on the supply of funds, and tight monetary policy. The supply of funds is limited not only because of the effect of tight monetary policy in reducing bank reserves, but also because of smaller deposit inflows to financial institutions and reduced savings flows. In addition, the extended period of time during which the above factors are operating contributes to bringing about the credit crunch.[91]

Finally, after each credit crunch there has been a recession. The recession takes place because no economic sector has sufficient liquidity to continue spending.[92]

Milton Friedman

All the theorists that we have discussed thus far have assumed—either explicitly or implicitly—that a financial crisis is a phenomenon of the credit market. They focused their attention on the demand for credit by borrowers (primarily nonfinancial corporations) and the ability and willingness of lenders (primarily commercial banks) to supply the necessary credit. There are important and significant differences among these theorists; all agree, however, on the importance of analyzing changes in credit.

A notable exception to this point of view is Milton Friedman. For him, the important variable is the supply of money, not the supply of credit. Since banking panics are discussed at some length in his important and influential study of the monetary history of the United States (written jointly with Anna Schwartz),[93] it would seem important to investigate how he uses a monetarist perspective to explain financial crises.

A problem in evaluating Friedman's theory of financial crises, though, is that he himself does not set forth a systematic theoretical approach to the subject. A perusal of some of Friedman's major theoretical writings, e.g., his major statement in 1970,[94] his work on money and business cycles,[95] or the theoretical chapter in his most recent book with Anna Schwartz,[96] fails to turn up an explicit general statement of the origins and causes of financial crises.

Thus it will be necessary to present Friedman's theory of financial crises in two stages. One, we will have to infer his theoretical approach by analyzing how he and Anna Schwartz explain the banking panics of the past. Two, we will have to try to investigate whether Friedman considers his analysis to be of broader generality than merely a particular explanation of a historically specific event.

Let us begin by investigating Friedman's approach to the financial crises of the past. In their monetary history Friedman and Schwartz mention a number of banking panics, including those in 1873, 1884, 1890, and 1907. However, by far their most extensive treatment (taking up approximately one-sixth of the book) is of the banking crises that occurred in 1930–33. We will concentrate on this period because of this greater attention, because of the relative proximity to the present of the events in 1930–33, and because Friedman considers that his and Anna Schwartz's "reinterpretation of the Great Depression" was "the most important event" in the revival of interest in the quantity theory "in the scholarly world."[97]

In their monetary history, Friedman and Schwartz pose three questions about the bank failures of 1930–33: "Why were the bank failures important? What was the origin of the bank failures? What was the attitude of the Federal Reserve System toward the bank failures?"[98]

Their answer to the first question is unambiguous:

> If the bank failures deserve special attention, it is clearly be-
> cause they were the mechanism through which the drastic de-
> cline in the stock of money was produced, and because the
> stock of money plays an important role in economic develop-
> ments. The bank failures were important not primarily in
> their own right, but because of their indirect effect.[99]

Of course, the major role of the stock of money, according to Friedman and Schwartz, is that changes in the stock of money, which "often had an independent origin," have had a stable relationship with "economic activity, money income, and prices."[100] They explain the severity of the contraction from 1929 to 1933 by the steep decline in the stock of money during that period. However, they also see an important role for a decline in the stock of money in aggravating the initial bank failures, as we shall see.

Their answer to the second question (the most important one for our purposes) is somewhat less clear. They distinguish between the initial banking crisis beginning in October 1930 and the two subsequent periods of bank failures in 1931 and 1933.

For the first banking crisis, they consider whether or not it was caused by the financial practices of the late 1920s, in particular a deterioration of the quality of bank loans and investments. While they say that there is "some evidence" for this hypothesis, particularly for foreign lending, they conclude that "the evidence is unsatisfactory for loans and investments in general," and "even sparser and more unsatisfactory for the loans and investments of commercial banks in particular.'' Moreover, ''if there was any deterioration at all in the ex ante quality of loans and investments of banks, it must have been minor, to judge from the slowness with which it manifested itself.''[101]

A possible explanation for the initial bank failures, in Friedman and Schwartz's system, might be a decline in the stock of money. They state that the stock of money did decline almost continually since 1927, even during the expansion of 1927–29. The fact that the stock of money ''failed to rise and even fell slightly during most of the expansion'' was ''a phenomenon not matched in any prior or subsequent cyclical expansion.''[102] With regard to the subsequent decline up through October 1930, they say that ''compared to the collapse in the next two years, the decline in the stock of money seems mild. Viewed in a longer perspective, it was sizable indeed.''[103] Although they connect the decline in economic activity with the decline in the stock of money, they stop short of explicitly attributing the October 1930 banking failures to the money decline. The 1930 banking crisis remains largely unexplained by them.

On the other hand, they are quite clear about the causes of the subsequent bank failures. These they attribute to the sharp decline in the stock of money due to the bank failures of 1930. In other words, the chain of events runs from the bank failures of 1930 to a decline in the stock of money, and then to the subsequent bank failures. They say that, although the money stock only fell gradually from 1929 to 1930, it

> was converted into a sharp decline by a wave of bank fail-
> ures beginning in late 1930. Those failures produced 1)
> widespread attempts by the public to convert deposits into
> currency . . . and 2) a scramble for liquidity by the banks.[104]

Because of the attempt to convert deposits into currency, the banks' reserves were depleted. As a result, they had to contract their deposits even further, thus reducing the money supply. Moreover, their attempts to replenish their depleted reserves weakened their own position and thus led to further bank failures. Friedman and Schwartz describe the process as follows:

> The banking system as a whole was in a position to meet the
> demands of depositors for currency only by a multiple con-
> traction of deposits, hence of assets. Under such circum-
> stances, any runs on banks for whatever reason became to
> some extent self-justifying, whatever the quality of assets
> held by banks. Banks had to dump their assets on the market,
> which inevitably forced a decline in the market value of those
> assets and hence of the remaining assets they held. The
> impairment in the market value of assets held by banks, par-
> ticularly in their bond portfolios, was the most important

source of impairment of capital leading to bank suspension, rather than the default of specific loans or of specific bond issues.[105]

Friedman and Schwartz assert that the Federal Reserve Board aggravated the decline in the money supply by their specific policies, that they were not constrained to do so by international or other considerations, and that they had the ability to increase the money supply to any degree had they only chosen to do so.[106] Thus Friedman and Schwartz's answer to their third question—the attitude of the Federal Reserve to the bank failures—is that the Federal Reserve stood back and did not provide the banks with the additional reserves that they needed.

The reason for this inaction is an interesting question, but one that we cannot pursue at length. Friedman and Schwartz's explanation is that the Federal Reserve did not take steps actively to increase the money supply because of a combination of lack of understanding and the death of Benjamin Strong, the governor of the New York Federal Reserve Bank. [107]

Now Friedman and Schwartz come to their main argument: the counterfactual contention that, had the Federal Reserve increased the money supply sufficiently, the economic contraction would not have been so severe, and the banking crises would have either been prevented or been much milder. With regard to the first banking crisis of 1930, they state the following:

> The hypothetical purchase of government securities would have reduced in two ways the likelihood of a banking crisis like the one in the fall of 1930: indirectly, through its effect on the severity of the contraction; and directly, through its effect on the balance sheets of banks.[108]

Note that while Friedman and Schwartz do not directly attribute the banking crisis of 1930 to a decline in the stock of money, they do argue that an increase in the money supply probably would have prevented it.

For the banking crisis of 1931, they state that, had the Federal Reserve increased the reserves of the banks,

> banks would have been freed from the necessity of liquidating securities, and could have reduced their borrowing from the Reserve System, instead of increasing it by $40 million. The bond market would accordingly have been far stronger, bank failures would have been notably fewer, and hence the runs on banks milder if at all appreciable.[109]

Friedman and Schwartz continue their argument about the role of the money supply with another, rather startling, counterfactual hypothesis: had the banks restricted payments (i.e., refused to convert deposits to currency), as they had in 1907, the depression would not have been so severe and the bank failures might have been prevented.

> If the 1907 banking system had been in operation in 1929, restriction of payments might have come in October 1929 when the stock market crashed. If not, it would surely have come at the latest at the end of 1930. . . . Had restriction come then, it seems likely in retrospect that it would have produced an immediate shock and reaction much more severe than the unspectacular worsening of conditions that occurred in the fall of 1930, but would also have prevented the collapse of the banking system and the drastic fall in the stock of money that were destined to take place, and that certainly intensified the severity of the contraction, if they were not indeed the major factors converting it from a reasonably severe into a catastrophic contraction.[110]

This argument is rather unorthodox because, as Friedman and Schwartz state, the standard interpretation of the Panic of 1907 is that "an apparently rather mild contraction was converted into a severe contraction by the banking panic and the associated restriction of payments by the banking system," and that this interpretation "provided the prime impetus for the monetary reform movement that culminated in the Federal Reserve Act."[111] However, the argument is certainly consistent from Friedman and Schwartz's perspective. The key link again is the decline in the stock of money. They contend that restriction of payments would have prevented the decline in the money supply and thus also prevented subsequent bank failures.

The importance of the counterfactual arguments about the money supply from Friedman and Schwartz's point of view is its relevance to monetary policy. For our purposes, though, it is significant because it gives indirect support to our earlier conclusion about their explanation of the causes of the banking crises. That conclusion, it will be recalled, was that the bank failures after 1930 were caused by the decline in the stock of money due to the runs on the banks in 1930. This decline required the banks to sell assets to try to replenish their reserves and resulted in a fall in the market price of those assets, additional pressure on the solvency of the banks, and increased bank failures. The counterfactual arguments support this conclusion by indirectly suggesting that the banking crisis of 1930 might have been caused by a decline in the stock of money as well (although of course this conclusion is not logically necessary).

Thus, by examining the ideas implicit in Friedman and Schwartz's historical discussion of the banking panics of the Great Depression, perhaps we have also found what might be termed the monetarist explanation of financial crises.

Nonetheless, an important question still remains. Since Friedman and Schwartz were talking about events that took place over fifty years ago, what can be said about their views on financial crises in the period since World War II? Can there still be financial crises, in their opinion, or are they a thing of the past? Or, as stated earlier, how general is their theoretical explanation of the specific historical events of the 1930s?

In an article entitled "Why the American Economy is Depression-Proof,"[112] written in 1954, Friedman states that federal deposit insurance has eliminated the basic causes for bank runs, all but eliminated bank failures, and ruled out banking panics. After describing three changes in the U.S. banking system since the Great Depression—federal deposit insurance, the increased importance of government securities in bank portfolios, and the rejection of the gold standard—Friedman states their combined effect is to "eliminate as a practical possibility anything approaching a collapse of the American banking structure. . . . It is hard to see how under these circumstances any sharp *decline* in the stock of money could occur except through deliberate action by the monetary authorities to bring one about."[113] That Friedman still upholds this analysis today is attested to by comments he made in 1980,[114] in which he quotes this earlier analysis verbatim. He also says that, although the "second change in the banking structure—the increased ratio of government obligations to the total assets of commercial banks—proved temporary in form," it was "long lasting in substance" due to the increase in government guarantees of private obligations.[115]

Thus Friedman's conclusion appears to be that a crisis in the banking system in the United States is unlikely today *unless the Federal Reserve acts so as to reduce sharply the stock of money*. Given Friedman's frequent and emphatic criticisms of the Federal Reserve for erratic control of the money supply, one might conclude that his qualification to the likelihood of banking crises is more than an academic logical possibility. Has Federal Reserve mismanagement of the money supply in the post-World War II period replaced runs on banks as Friedman's causal mechanism responsible for a sharp decline in the money supply leading to cumulative bank crises (or at least to incipient crises which are then aborted by Federal Reserve increases in the money supply)?

This interpretation is given credence by other statements by Friedman, e.g., a paper called "Current Monetary Policy," a memorandum prepared for the Consultant's Meeting of the Board of Governors of the Federal Reserve System, June 15, 1966.[116] In this paper Friedman first notes that bank reserves increased rapidly in December 1965, and as a result, banks took on additional commitments. He then adds the following:

> But these commitments became embarrassing when the Fed
> reversed course and drained banks of liquidity in January.
> The result was that banks had to unload investments to meet
> commitments, which depressed security prices, pushed up
> interest rates, and produced many of the symptoms of *financial crisis* in late February. The reversal of Fed policy at the

end of January and the rapid rate of rise in the money stock
in March eased the money market and overcame the crisis.[117]

In this passage Friedman assigns a key role to the same process he emphasized in his analysis of the banking crisis of 1930–33: the forced sale of assets by
banks to replenish reserves, which drives security prices down and interest rates
up, and brings on a crisis. The only difference is that, instead of it being bank runs
that drain the banks of reserves and reduce the money supply, it is the Federal
Reserve itself that performs this function.

Later on in the paper prepared for the Consultant's Meeting at the Federal
Reserve Board, Friedman again refers to financial crises. He asks the Federal
Reserve Board why they had not restrained the growth of the money supply more
than they had. He suspects their answer would be that the consequences of such
restraint would have been "seriously adverse."[118] He then continues:

> It is this answer which baffles me. What are the other conse-
> quences of, say, a 4 per cent instead of a 7.6 per cent growth
> rate in M1 or a 6 per cent instead of a 9.5 per cent growth
> rate in M2 that would have been seriously adverse? *A finan-
> cial panic? Inconceivable if the growth in the money supply
> had proceeded smoothly; entirely conceivable whatever the
> average rate of growth, if it had been highly erratic.*[119]

Given Friedman's earlier discussion of the events from December 1965 to
February 1966, we can safely conclude that what he means by erratic—for the
purposes of financial crises—is a fairly rapid increase in the money supply,
followed by a sharp decline.

This conclusion is reinforced by Friedman's analysis of the growth of the
money supply from April 1965 to April 1966. His view is that the money supply
was allowed to grow too rapidly by the Federal Reserve during this period, even
though inflation was beginning to be a problem. Then, according to Friedman,
the Federal Reserve slowed money supply growth too abruptly in April 1966. His
analysis of the outcome of such action is as follows: "The result was the so-called
'money crunch' in the fall of 1966."[120]

In summary, it appears that we can find a theory of financial crises in Milton
Friedman's writings. Moreover, Friedman's theory is of broader generality than
an explanation of the specific events of 1930–33. It contains hypotheses that can
in principle be tested by the experience of the recent period in the United States.

3

Comparison of Theories of Financial Crises

Having reviewed the major theories of financial crises, we turn to a comparison of these theories in the context of the business-cycle, credit-market perspective discussed in the Introduction. The comparison will attempt to take a more detailed look at how the theoretical issues mentioned in the Introduction flow from the differences in the viewpoints of the theorists considered.

As noted earlier, since Milton Friedman does not share the perspective of the other writers, we will proceed in two stages. First we will discuss the theories of those writers who adhere to the general credit-market, business-cycle perspective on financial crises and evaluate the similarities and differences within this group of theories. Then we will discuss Friedman's theory and contrast it with the others.

The Business-Cycle, Credit-Market Perspective

As mentioned above, most of the theories just reviewed can be understood within the context of the general theoretical perspective discussed in the Introduction. That framework views financial crises as endogenous to the economic process. In particular, it sees financial crises developing at the peak of the expansion phase of the business cycle, due in part to financial difficulties that originate in the business sector. The crisis itself is a disruption of the normal functioning of the financial system and is brought about by developments in the demand and supply of credit.

The differences among the various theorists have to do with their specific interpretations within this overall framework. These differences concern (1) the reasons for the development of financial difficulties in the business sector, (2) the factors influencing the demand and supply of credit, and (3) the defining patterns of a financial crisis. By using the discussion of the specific theorists in Chapter 2, it is possible to explore each of these differences and compare the various theories.

The Development of Financial Difficulties

In the latter part of the business-cycle expansion, financial difficulties occur which lay the groundwork for the subsequent financial crisis. Minsky calls this period the systemic development of financial fragility. It is characterized, according to him, by an increasing number of firms that have difficulty in meeting their debt payment commitments.

According to Minsky, three developments that typically occur towards the end of the expansion are correlated with financial fragility: (1) an increase in the use of short-term debt, (2) a decline in liquidity, and (3) an increase in interest rates, especially short-term rates.

In Minsky's scenario, once the financial environment becomes fragile (toward the end of the expansion phase of the business cycle), further increases in interest rates can cause payment commitments to become greater than the cash flow generated from normal operations, even though capital income continues to grow at the full employment rate. For Minsky, it is the explosive growth of payment commitments due to debt, not a shortfall of profits, that is the cause of the difficulties.

In contrast, for Marx, a decline in profits plays the key role in causing cash receipts to fall short of payment commitments. However, Minsky's assumption of the initiating role for investment in the profits-investment equation means that profits cannot decline in his system without a prior decline in investment. This assumption rules out any major causal role for profits in setting the stage for a financial crisis.[1]

For Veblen and Mitchell, a decline in profits also is the source of the financial difficulties of business firms near the peak of the expansion. Unlike Marx, though, they do not stress the direct role of a decline in profits as the cause of firms' difficulty in meeting debt payment requirements; they stress the indirect role on the suppliers of credit. For them, the main role of the fall in profits is to encourage the liquidation of outstanding debt.

The Demand for Credit and the Supply of Credit

Three theorists (Minsky, Mitchell, and Marx) maintain that developments at the peak of the expansion result in an increased demand for borrowing to meet payment commitments. In addition, firms also resort to other devices to raise cash, such as selling assets.

Marx and Minsky mention a demand for funds to meet debt payment requirements. Minsky and Mitchell also explicitly discuss a lag between the decision to invest and actual spending for investment. This lag means that, even if firms decide to decrease investment spending near the business cycle peak, there still can be an ''involuntary'' demand for funds for investment.

In contrast, Wojnilower and Sinai assume that there is a ''voluntary'' demand for funds for investment right up until the point of crisis.

Thus there are three possible reasons for the demand for funds. Borrowing takes place in order to (1) meet payment commitments due to debt, (2) finance "involuntary" investment, or (3) finance "voluntary investment." The significance of this issue has to do with the relationship of the financial crisis to the business cycle downturn, and the potential disruptiveness of the financial crisis to the economic system.

If businesses are seeking to finance "voluntary investment," then presumably they still see profitable investment opportunities in the context of an expanding economy. In this case the financial crisis, by limiting the supply of credit for these investments, interrupts the expansion and helps to initiate the recession. On the other hand, if the demand for funds is for "involuntary" investment, then presumably most plans for new investment have been discarded, and the economy is already in recession, or quite close to it.

The second point concerns the potential disruptiveness of the financial crisis. If "voluntary" investment is prevented by a limitation in the supply of credit, then plans for new investment would be abandoned, the growth of employment would slow, but the decline of the economy should be relatively mild. However, if firms are unable to meet their legal obligations to repay debts, then bankruptcy is likely, and the effect on the economy would be more severe.

The limitation of "involuntary" investment is perhaps an intermediate case in terms of its potential effect on the economy. Although partially completed investment projects can be abandoned without necessarily incurring bankruptcy, the economic loss from such a course of action could be significant, and could have a major impact.

There are also important differences among the theorists with regard to the role of the suppliers of credit, especially the commercial banks which have been the traditional lenders of last resort to business. These differences concern the reactions of these suppliers of credit to the demand for funds from their business customers.

Veblen and Mitchell see the financial crisis coming about as a direct result of this reaction. Their view is that the financial problems of business lead to a revaluation of the acceptable amount of credit to be extended. The deteriorating financial position of the companies and their reduced outlook for future profitability cause creditors to refuse to extend additional credit and to seek actively to liquidate existing credit outstanding. This liquidation of credit is identified as the financial crisis by both Veblen and Mitchell.

Minsky also sees the liquidation of credit playing a major role, but he stresses in addition some other important developments. In his view, the liquidation of credit is mainly responsible for the inability of business to debt-finance investment. The decline in investment then leads to a fall in profits, which aggravates the financial difficulties of the firms and forces them to sell assets in order to raise cash. The forced selling of assets leads to sharp declines in price,

THEORIES OF FINANCIAL CRISES COMPARED   37

which Minsky identifies as the financial crisis.

Wojnilower, on the other hand, has a different view of the attitude of the commercial banks toward lending. He assumes that the banks do not voluntarily restrict their lending because of the financial condition of businesses. On the contrary, his view is that the banks make every effort to come up with funds to meet the business loan demand despite the obstacles placed in their way by the tight monetary policy of the Federal Reserve Board. Moreover, in his opinion, the demand for loans is for "voluntary" investment purposes, not for paying debts.

Wojnilower examines the ways in which the banks have used liability management to avoid the restrictions placed on their lending by the Federal Reserve. In his scenario, financial crises, or "credit crunches," come about when the banks finally come up against restrictions on their lending which they cannot circumvent.

Sinai is also of the opinion that the banks do not voluntarily restrict their lending because of concerns over the financial condition of the corporations. The supply factors that he mentions as being responsible for the credit crunch include a restrictive monetary policy and a shortage of loanable funds due to reduced savings flows, slowed deposit inflows, and tighter bank reserves.

The difference between the views of Wojnilower and Sinai, as indicated earlier, concerns the nature of the supply limitation. According to Sinai, the credit crunch occurs as the end result of a slow process of restriction of credit. Wojnilower sees (as does Marx) the crisis coming about due to an abrupt cutoff of funds.

The Financial Crisis

We turn now to the financial crisis itself. First of all, it is important to realize that the various authors do not necessarily mean the same thing when they refer to financial crises.

To Veblen and Mitchell, the financial crisis is the process of gradual liquidation of the credit that had been built up in the preceding expansion. Sinai identifies the crisis with the culmination of this process.

In contrast, Marx and Wojnilower consider the crisis to be more intense, resulting from a sudden cutoff of funds. The difference between these two theorists, as noted earlier, is that Marx sees the demand for money to be for the purpose of repaying debt obligations, whereas Wojnilower considers the demand to be for the purpose of expanding production. Mitchell recognizes this intense reaction, but in his terminology it is called a financial panic.

The issue of abrupt versus continuous change raises another important issue concerning financial crises—that of psychological reactions to economic events. There is an assumption in almost all of the theories discussed above of a psychological element associated with financial crises. There is an element of

sudden panic that comes from a desperate scramble for liquidity. Nearly all the
theorists identify this reaction, with the exception of Sinai and Veblen.

Thus whether or not such a psychological element can be shown to play a
significant role in financial crises would be one way to evaluate this aspect of the
theories of Sinai and Veblen. Moreover, where this psychological aspect appears,
if it does, would enable us to distinguish among the other theories, because each
theorist has a somewhat different view of where and when it emerges.

Mitchell, for example, sees the element of panic appearing when the process of liquidation of credit hits a weak link and the bankruptcy of some "con-
spicuous enterprise" spreads "unreasoning alarm." In this situation the banks
experience a sharp increase in the demand for loans and the repayment of deposits.

Marx identifies the psychological element with the intense demand for
money to meet payment commitments arising from an abrupt cessation of credit.
Wojnilower focuses primarily on the disruption of financial markets caused by the
abrupt cutoff of funds, whereas Minsky sees the element of panic appearing when
there are sharp drops in the price of assets sold to raise cash to meet payment
commitments. These differences represent different emphases, however, rather
than fundamental disagreements.

Milton Friedman's Theory of Financial Crises

As mentioned earlier, Milton Friedman's theory of financial crises differs sharply
from those of the other writers we have considered. One way of appreciating the
contrast is to see how Friedman himself describes the differences. In an article on
Henry Simons,[1] Friedman goes into detail about his differences with Simons on
the reasons for financial crises. (Friedman focuses his argument on the banking
panics of the Great Depression, but as we have seen in the previous chapter, his
arguments about the Depression era can be translated into an appropriate form for
the current period.) Since Simons's theory, as described by Friedman, contains a
number of elements in common with some of the theories described above,
Friedman's discussion of his differences with Simons is a convenient way of
contrasting Friedman's theory with these theories.

According to Friedman, Simons held that loans by banks to business were
based on the state of confidence, which in turn depended on business earnings.
The credit thus extended was capable of stimulating aggregate demand by substituting for money and increasing velocity. When earnings fell, though, the process
was reversed, confidence fell, loans were contracted, there was a scramble for
liquidity, and banks failed.[2]

Friedman feels that Simons's "vision undoubtedly was derived from the
1929–33 crash," and that the "keystone of Simons's interpretation of 1929–33
was that the trouble originated with business earnings and the shock to business
confidence, documented or perhaps initiated by the stock-market crash."[3]

Friedman criticizes Simons's interpretation on two important points: the relationship between confidence and the liquidation of bank assets, and the reasons for the liquidity and solvency problems of the banks.

On the first point, Friedman says that it was not a decline in earnings and a shock to business confidence—as "documented or perhaps initiated by the stock-market crash"—that led to a demand for liquidation of bank loans and a decline in the money supply.[4] On the contrary, he contends that it was the prior decline in the stock of money that forced the banks to liquidate their assets and that affected confidence.

On the second point, Friedman says that the liquidity problems of the banks were not due to a defaulting of commercial loans or an attempt by the banks to contract risky loans. Rather, they resulted from the pressure on bank reserves from two sources: runs on the bank by the public, and the Federal Reserve's refusal to expand the money supply to compensate. The banks' attempts to sell bonds in their portfolios to replenish their reserves resulted in drastic price declines and affected their solvency.

Thus, as we saw above, for Friedman, a financial crisis is a situation in which banks are forced to sell assets in order to obtain needed reserves. This forced sale of assets reduces their price, raises interest rates, threatens bank solvency, and reduces the state of confidence.

In some respects, this description of the crisis itself resembles Minsky's; both emphasize the fall in security prices and the increase in interest rates that are due to the forced sale of assets. Minsky, however, sees the dumping of assets taking place in both the financial and nonfinancial sectors, primarily the latter.

Also, of course, the two theorists disagree on the reason for the need to sell assets. For Minsky and the other theorists, it is the endogenous processes that occur in the late stages of the business cycle expansion, in particular, the development of financial fragility in the nonfinancial sector and the relevant developments in the credit markets. For Friedman, it is a sharp decline in the stock of money by the Federal Reserve after a previous expansion.

An important aspect of this difference is that financial crises for Friedman do not necessarily have to occur at any particular stage of the business cycle. We should expect a financial crisis to develop any time that the Federal Reserve's control of the money supply is erratic in the downward direction. Likewise, we should not necessarily expect a financial crisis to occur at the peak of the business cycle. Obviously, if financial crises occur only at the peaks of the business cycle, this would be evidence against Friedman's theory (assuming that declines in the money supply occur at other times); if financial crises occur at other times (associated with money supply declines), this would be evidence for Friedman's theory.

* * *

The purpose of this chapter has been to clarify the main theories of financial crises and the important differences among the various writers. These differences cannot be settled by theoretical argument, however. A close look at how the financial system actually works, as reflected in the operation of financial institutions and practices in the context of the actual historical record, is necessary. Thus it is to an investigation of the financial crises in the postwar U.S. economy that we now turn.

PART II

Financial Crises in the Postwar U.S. Economy

For twenty years after World War II, it appeared that the nation's banking and thrift institutions, and the financial system in general, had become immune to the disruptive financial crises of the past. It seemed that the startling events of the panic of 1907 or the banking crises of the Great Depression were mere historical curiosities. Subsequent events, beginning with the "credit crunch" of 1966, challenged this thinking. Although in intensity the 1966 "crunch" did not compare with some of the earlier crises, in form it was remarkably similar. Moreover, it was followed by other periods of financial crisis which posed a greater threat to the stability of the financial system. As Henry Kaufman has noted, these crises contained all the ingredients that had fueled the financial debacles of old: "How close we came to disaster . . . no one will ever accurately record. It was a frightening period. . . ."[1]

In what follows, the postwar financial crises in the U.S. economy will be analyzed in detail. The investigation will focus on the questions highlighted by the theoretical issues discussed in the Introduction. Specifically, for each crisis period, we will attempt to answer the following questions:

1. Did financial difficulties develop in the corporate sector near the peak of the business-cycle expansion?

2. If so, what was the cause of these difficulties?

3. How did the corporations attempt to raise funds to meet their financial needs?

4. What was the response of the commercial banks to the corporate loan demand?

5. How was the financial condition of the banking system affected?

6. What was the cause of the disruption to the normal functioning of the financial system?

7. What form did the financial crisis take?

8. How was it resolved?

At times when it is relevant, the financing demands and the supply of funds from all four primary sectors—household, government, corporate, and foreign—will be examined. Mostly, though, the analysis will focus on the corporate sector. There are two reasons for this emphasis. First, the theories of financial crises being investigated concentrate primarily on the corporate sector. Second, financial difficulties and defaults on obligations of large business corporations can threaten the financial system with crises. (This is an important reason why the various theories focus on the corporate sector.) The federal government can avoid a default on its obligations, and defaults by individuals do not involve systemic risk.

4

The Credit Crunch of 1966

The first financial crisis in the postwar period was called the "credit crunch" of 1966, as noted above. It came about when commercial banks were suddenly prevented from funding a strong demand for loans from the corporate sector. To understand how this crisis came about, it is necessary to understand conditions in the economy prior to the crisis in August of 1966.

As the year 1966 began, the U.S. economy was experiencing a strong surge in investment spending. Investment in plant and equipment by nonfinancial corporations, which had been quite low in the late 1950s and early 1960s, accelerated sharply in 1964 and 1965. Nonfinancial corporations financed this growth in investment through 1965 by relying mainly on internal funds, and, as a result, corporate borrowing through 1965 exerted little upward pressure on interest rates. In an unprecedented performance equaled neither before nor since in the postwar period in the United States, the bank prime rate remained constant, at 4.5 percent, for over five years (from 1960 to December 1965). Moody's AAA corporate bond rate also remained stable at slightly under 4.5 percent.

An increasing proportion of total debt through 1965 consisted of short-term debt. However, given the relatively low amount of total debt, the short-term ratio had less significance for overall corporate financial strength. Moreover, the total amount of short-term debt outstanding through 1965 was relatively low.

The liquidity ratio of nonfinancial corporations did decline steadily from 1963 through 1965. However, this level too was still relatively high for the period since 1961.[1] Thus, corporate balance sheets appeared not to have suffered too much damage from the surge in spending for investment in plant and equipment—at least through 1965. However, in addition to strong investment spending by business, government defense purchases of goods and services expanded sharply in 1965, particularly in the fourth quarter.

This rapid increase in spending in 1965 put pressure on the economy's scarce resources. The capacity utilization rate for manufacturing reached 91.6 percent in March 1966, the highest level in the entire postwar period; the unemployment rate fell in February 1966 to 3.8 percent. Compensation of employees in nonfinancial corporate business increased throughout 1965, and rose sharply in the first quarter of 1966. Prices also started to escalate.

The favorable financial conditions of 1965 deteriorated rapidly in 1966 under the sustained pressure of the overheated economy. Interest rates started a sharp rise as 1966 began, and profits, which had grown steadily since 1961 and remained at a high level in 1965, peaked in the first quarter of 1966. These developments had important implications for the level of internal funds, the ability of nonfinancial corporations to pay their debts, the growth of investment in plant and equipment, and the financing gap between capital expenditures and internal funds. Let us consider each in turn.

Since profits make up a significant portion of internal funds, the decline in profits had an important influence in slowing the growth of internal funds. Of the components of internal funds, earnings received from abroad held fairly steady during the first three quarters of 1966, while dividends paid out dropped only slightly. A small increase of $1.5 billion in depreciation allowances was negated by the $2.3 billion decrease in profits. As a result, internal funds of nonfinancial corporations stopped increasing and held quite steady during the second and third quarters of 1966, actually declining slightly in the third quarter. The significance of this development for the financing of investment will be discussed below.

The decline in profits and the increase in interest rates put more pressure on nonfinancial corporations attempting to meet debt payment commitments. The interest coverage ratio for nonfinancial corporations is a useful way to measure this pressure. It measures the sum of net interest paid, domestic profits before tax, and earnings received from abroad, divided by net interest paid. Thus it indicates the ability to pay interest on debts out of capital income. After increasing from 1961 through the first quarter of 1965, this ratio declined slightly through the first quarter of 1966 and dropped sharply after that (although it still remained relatively high).

The total payments due to debt consist of principal coming due as well as net interest charges. Thus the total need for funds to meet debt payment requirements is larger by the amount of outstanding debt maturing in the given period of time. Unfortunately, the data necessary to assess accurately this total magnitude for all liabilities are not available. We can conclude, though, that the decline in interest coverage increases the need to come up with additional funds to meet debt payment requirements, even though the magnitude of this need is uncertain. Some corporations presumably would have to try to sell assets (liquid assets if possible) or borrow additional money to pay their existing debts. Corporations unable to raise these funds might be forced into bankruptcy.

Turning now to investment in plant and equipment, we would expect an increase in interest rates to decrease investment demand because the discounted present value of future profits from new investment is thereby reduced. Moreover, to the extent that movements in profits today are interpreted as indicative of future trends in profitability, then the decline in profits in 1966 could be expected also to have reduced investment demand.

The stock market—which reflects the opinions of market participants about future profit trends—peaked at the beginning of 1966. And indeed the growth rate of investment dropped sharply from what it was in 1965. Investment by nonfinancial corporations increased only slightly in 1966, even though it remained at a high level.

However, there are two reasons why one should be careful about concluding that the increase in interest rates and decline in profits caused the slowdown in investment which followed. First, although the timing relationships are supportive of such a conclusion, the demand for investment is a complex topic which we cannot pursue thoroughly here; other influences are important in affecting demand, such as the capacity utilization rate. This rate remained quite high in 1966, which would indicate a continuing demand for further investment in plant and equipment. Secondly, the amount of investment spending is determined not only by the demand for investment, but also by the supply of available funds, which will be discussed below.

One indicator that could be used to gauge corporate plans for investment, though, is the data on contracts and orders for plant and equipment (COPE). This series did not peak until September 1966, which might mean that corporations had more plans for investment than they were able to realize.

Regardless of the underlying motivation, the important point for our purposes right now is that actual spending for investment in plant and equipment did level off in 1966. Both internal funds and plant and equipment spending held relatively steady. However, inventory investment jumped sharply in 1966. Thus in the first part of the year preceding the crisis point in August, nonfinancial corporations had a strong demand for funds for investment that could not be met from internal funds.[2]

Thus, to sum up the above discussion, the increase in interest rates and the decline in profit margins at the beginning of 1966 meant that nonfinancial corporations had financial difficulties of two sorts. They had more difficulty in meeting their debt payment commitments, and they had a high level of capital expenditures which could not be met out of internal funds.

How did the corporations go about obtaining the funds to meet their needs for capital expenditures and debt payment commitments? And how did their efforts affect financial markets and financial institutions?

Flow of funds data for the nonfinancial corporate business sector can help answer the first question. The flow of funds tables do not give any information about the extent to which corporations were forced to borrow to pay maturing debts, because only figures for the net increase in liabilities are given. However, flow of funds data are useful in understanding how corporations funded the financing gap between internal funds and total capital expenditures.

The data indicate that corporations met this need for external funds for capital expenditures in the first quarter of 1966 primarily from long-term debt (of which nearly four-fifths was corporate bonds) and loans from banks. In the second quarter, to fund an even greater financing gap, corporations increased their loans from the banks. However, in the third quarter of 1966, in which the crisis occurred, the net credit market borrowing of nonfinancial corporations fell by 25 percent from the second quarter pace. It was off by 44 percent in the fourth quarter.

Thus the nonfinancial corporate sector appears to have been shut out from external sources of funds in the last half of 1966, particularly from the commercial banks. Bank loans dropped precipitously from their peak in the second quarter. Yet capital expenditures remained high throughout 1966. They hit their peak in the fourth quarter, reflecting an unusually high level of (probably unintended) inventory accumulation. To compensate for their restricted access to external markets, nonfinancial corporations were forced to sell liquid assets in both the third and fourth quarters.

Assuming, therefore, that the corporations had needs for funds that were not met by the banks and other creditors, what was the reason that their borrowing was restricted? One possibility is that the nonfinancial corporate sector was "crowded out" of the markets by other sectors of the economy. However, this was not the case. Federal government borrowing as a percentage of GNP remained at quite low levels through 1966. Moreover, the share of credit market borrowing by the household sector decreased in the fourth quarter of 1965, just as the share of the corporate sector was getting ready to accelerate.

There are two other possible scenarios that will be considered. The first is that the banks and other creditors restricted their lending to the corporations because the corporations' creditworthiness had deteriorated and they were afraid of making bad loans. The second is that the banks attempted to meet the loan demands of their corporate customers, but that they were prevented from doing so by outside influences, the most important of which was the monetary and regulatory policy of the Federal Reserve Board. Which of these explanations more accurately fits the available information about the period, and what role did these developments play in bringing about the financial crisis in August of 1966?

To access the first scenario, we can examine two pieces of information that would be relevant in understanding how the banks assessed corporate creditworthiness. The first is the rate of business bankruptcies. The number of failures (per 10,000 concerns) did increase sharply in the third quarter of 1966. However, they increased only to a level that had already been recorded in 1965, and in the context of a declining trend throughout the 1960s. Thus the significance of this increase could be questioned.

The second source of information consists of the amount of poor quality (nonperforming) loans, and the amount of losses (net charge-offs) that banks suffered on their loans because of defaults by their corporate borrowers. Unfortunately, we do not have data going back to 1966 on nonperforming loans, and no data for the period that separate loan losses by category of loan (i.e., commercial and industrial loans, real estate loans, consumer loans, etc.). The evidence for total loan losses, though, indicates a slight increase in 1966, in the context of a relatively low level overall: net loan charge-offs as a percentage of average total loans for the banking system increased from 0.16 percent in 1965 to 0.19 percent in 1966. Thus it appears that the creditworthiness of the corporate sector did decrease in 1966 but not significantly enough to warrant a sudden cutoff of funds from the banks.

To analyze the second scenario, it will be necessary to examine Federal Reserve policy and the responses of the commercial banking sector. In late 1965, in response to the rapidly expanding economy, the Federal Reserve Board decided to tighten monetary policy. The Board raised the discount rate applicable to member bank borrowing from 4 percent to 4½ percent in December 1965. The operating target of the Federal Reserve at the time—money market conditions, i.e., money market interest rates and the net borrowed reserves of member banks—showed considerable tightening during the first part of 1966.

However, while the Federal Reserve was forcing banks to come to the discount window, it was also supplying the increased borrowed reserves that the banks desired. As a result, the monetary and credit aggregates continued to expand.[3] As measured by the aggregates, monetary policy was still quite loose through April.

At its April meeting, though, the Federal Open Market Committee (FOMC) concluded that "additional stabilization policy measures would be desirable in light of present and prospective inflationary pressures."[4] The policy directive was changed to state that growth in the reserve base, bank credit, and the money supply should be "restricted" rather than "moderated" (as the March directive stated).

The FOMC still used money market conditions as the operating guide to implement and measure this policy. However, at the May meeting, a significant "proviso clause" was inserted for the first time into the directive. The instructions to the Federal Reserve Bank of New York stated that System open market operations should be "conducted with a view to attaining some further gradual reductions in net reserve availability, *and a greater reduction if growth in required reserves does not moderate substantially.*"[5]

Reserve and money supply growth slowed during the April-June period. However, even though bank reserves increased by only 0.9 percent and the money supply by only 0.7 percent, bank credit continued to expand rapidly at a 9.1 percent annual rate. Business loans increased even more rapidly, at a 20.5 percent pace. To understand why, it is necessary to look more closely at developments in the nation's commercial banks and other financial intermediaries.

Investments in securities and nonbusiness loans did not increase nearly as rapidly as business loans did at commercial banks. Thus banks were able to step up their lending to business by cutting back on investments and loans to other sectors.

However, bank credit overall could expand so much faster than bank reserves because of the banks' efficient use of these reserves. Even though demand deposits decreased, banks used their new tool of liability management—large negotiable certificates of deposit (CDs)—to increase their time deposits. Because time deposits have lower reserve requirements than demand deposits, the growth of bank CDs could support a larger volume of bank lending. In addition to large CDs, banks began aggressively to sell small (under $100,000) CDs to individuals. These, too, enabled the banks to use their reserves more efficiently.

The banks' ability to bid for small time deposits, however, was at the expense of other financial intermediaries, particularly the savings and loan (S&L) associations. The loss in deposits to the banks intensified the squeeze on the S&Ls that had been going on throughout the year. The rise in open market interest rates since January had subjected the S&Ls to disintermediation, i.e., depositors withdrew their funds and invested them directly in the money market. Unlike the banks, the S&Ls were not able to compensate by issuing CDs. Advances to the S&Ls by the Federal Home Loan Bank Board increased sharply in the second quarter of 1966.

The Federal Reserve Board became increasingly concerned about the intensifying squeeze on the S&Ls and the threat of inflation from the continuing expansion of business loans by the commercial banks. Towards the end of the second quarter, they began to take steps to bring both problems under control.

In June, the Board raised from 4 to 5 percent the reserve requirements against time deposits in excess of $5 million at member banks. In July, they lowered the maximum rates payable on small time deposits. The purpose of both actions was to make it more difficult for the big banks to bid for deposits, thus relieving some of the pressure on the S&Ls and slowing down the expansion of bank loans.

In addition, the Board actively limited access to the discount window by member banks. In May, the federal funds rate began to increase rapidly, but the discount rate was left in place (it remained at 4.5 percent throughout 1966). Thus it would have been less costly for banks to borrow at the discount window than in the market for fed funds. The fact that discount window borrowing increased less rapidly from May through August than it did in the beginning of the year indicates that the banks were prevented by administrative action from tapping this source of funds.

The Board also did not raise the maximum Regulation Q ceiling rate on large negotiable certificates of deposit. In June, the rate in the secondary market for CDs of six months or longer maturity rose up through the Regulation Q ceiling. In July, the rate on shorter maturity CDs did the same thing. As the Board Annual Report noted: "As the summer progressed, commercial banks found that negotiable time CDs, with interest rates limited by the 5½ percent ceiling, were no longer competitive with other short-term market instruments . . . banks were unable to roll over all maturing CDs after mid-August, and their holdings of such deposits began to decline."[6]

Finally, monetary policy continued to tighten sharply. Bank reserves declined by 2.7 percent from June through August, and the money supply dropped by 2.4 percent. The National Bureau of Economic Research designated June 1966 as the peak of the expansion and the beginning of a "growth" recession.

Now the commercial banks began to feel the squeeze. With their reserves declining, their access to the discount window cut off, and their ability to raise funds from time deposits diminished, they had to cut back on the growth of bank credit. The rate of increase of bank credit (on an annual basis) dropped from 11.3 percent in the April-June period to only 2.5 percent in June-August. However, business loans continued to increase during the June-August period at a 15.1 percent annual rate. The reason that the banks could do this was because they decreased their investments by 2.3 percent during this same period.

The banks had already sold off a part of their portfolio of U.S. government securities, and a good part of the remainder was pledged as collateral against the deposits of state and local government units. Thus the commercial banks also began to liquidate their investments in municipal securities in order to come up with the needed funds.

Because the market for municipal securities is relatively thin, the sell-off by the banks had a large impact. The market became "disorganized" during the latter part of August. According to the 1966 Annual Report of the Board of Governors:

> The tax-exempt market . . . became by far the most unsettled of all the markets during August. . . . Several large commercial banks . . . were making very sizable sales of tax-exempt issues in order to ease some of the pressures on their reserve positions. On a nationwide basis, commercial banks' holdings of securities other than Governments (a balance sheet category that in fact includes mostly tax-exempt issues) fell by $200 million in August. With commercial banks acting as net sellers rather than in their normal role of net buyers, and with other investors and dealers generally discouraged, it was difficult to find bidders for offerings of tax-exempt issues even at sharply reduced prices and higher yields. By the end of August the Bond Buyer's index of yields on 20 seasoned tax-exempt bonds had risen to 4.24 percent, a full 1/2 of a percentage point above the level prevailing around mid-June.[7]

Although the municipal securities market was the most unsettled, other financial markets felt the strain as well. Market participants were apprehensive about the ability of the markets to meet the heavy demands for credit, given the still-weakened condition of the thrifts, the squeeze on the banks, and the continuing tight monetary policy of the Federal Reserve. (Fiscal policy at this point was still quite expansive, putting the entire burden of fighting inflation on Federal Reserve policy.)

The Federal Reserve Annual Report stated that the June-August

> . . . period was marked by progressively deepening gloom in all financial markets. Indeed, by late August—before official policy actions succeeded in restoring a degree of calm in early September—there were even some fears being expressed that a financial crisis might be near at hand. Although such fears were not borne out, the feeling of apprehension led a number of borrowers to accelerate their capital market offerings, and this in turn added to an already congested market situation. At the depths of the gloom in the second half of August, conditions in the market for tax-exempt securities were on the verge of disorder, and yields throughout short- and long-term markets were at the highest levels in more than 40 years.[8]

To prevent the financial crisis from developing, the Federal Reserve took two important actions. First, at its meeting on August 23, 1966, the Federal Open Market Committee changed its operating instructions to the Federal Reserve Bank of New York from "maintaining about the current [tight] state of net reserve availability and related money market conditions" to "supplying the minimum amount of reserves consistent with the maintenance of orderly money market conditions and the moderation of unusual liquidity pressures."[9] Thus it concluded that its tight monetary policy would have to be abandoned as long as intense demands for liquidity existed in the financial markets.

Second, and perhaps even more important for heading off a serious financial crisis, the Federal Reserve Board sent out a letter to each member bank. The letter essentially stated that the banks should stop liquidating municipal securities and reduce their business loans, and that the discount window would be open to those banks that did so. Excerpts from this letter as it appeared in the Annual Report are as follows:

> The System believes that the national economic interest would be better served by a slower rate of expansion of bank loans to business within the context of moderate over-all money and credit growth. Further substantial adjustments through bank liquidation of municipal securities or other investments would add to pressures on financial markets. Hence, the System believes that a greater share of member bank adjustments should take the form of moderation in the rate of expansion of loans, and particularly business loans.
>
> Accordingly, this objective will be kept in mind by the

Federal Reserve Banks in their extensions of credit to member banks through the discount window. Member banks will be expected to cooperate in the System's efforts to hold down the rate of business loan expansion—apart from normal seasonal needs—and to use the discount facilities of the Reserve Banks in a manner consistent with these efforts. It is recognized that banks adjusting their positions through loan curtailment may at times need a longer period of discount accommodation than would be required for the disposition of securities.[10]

This letter went a long way toward relieving the mounting feeling of crisis in the financial markets. Market participants were also reassured by an announcement on September 8th that the U.S. government would cut back on low-priority federal expenditures, temporarily suspend certain tax incentives for business investment, and curtail federal agency borrowing in the capital markets.

Monetary policy eased during the rest of the year, and so did pressures in the financial markets. The nonfinancial corporate business sector reduced its borrowing from banks. Although it funded a large involuntary inventory investment in the fourth quarter by selling both U.S. and municipal securities, the household sector bought the securities and allowed prices in these markets, especially the threatened municipals market, to stabilize. Fears of a serious financial panic subsided, and continued high military spending probably kept the subsequent economic downturn relatively mild.

The first financial crisis of the postwar period, the credit crunch of 1966, had passed.

5

1970: Penn Central

In June 1970, the surprise announcement of the bankruptcy of the Penn Central Railroad sent shock waves through the commercial paper market. The fear of a financial crisis—of larger proportions than the events of 1966—developed among market participants. To understand the background to this crisis, we will again trace developments in the corporate and banking sectors and in Federal Reserve policy.

The expansion of the economy resumed in 1968 after the growth recession that occurred from June 1966 to October 1967. Investment in plant and equipment contributed strongly to the expansion, beginning in mid-1968.

In addition, government defense spending continued at a high level. Because of these spending increases, and because the slowdown in the economic expansion in 1966–67 was relatively mild, the pressures on the economy during 1966 resumed relatively unabated in 1968. A 10 percent income tax surcharge that was passed in June 1968 did not slow the economy in the way that many had expected. The unemployment rate fell to 3.6 percent in 1968, and the capacity utilization rate was a high 87.1 percent. Compensation of employees in nonfinancial corporate business increased by 12.7 percent in 1968, and prices continued to rise.

Profits (as a percentage of the domestic income of nonfinancial corporations) continued to decline in 1968, as they had ever since 1966. In 1969, though, profits of nonfinancial corporations fell even further, dropping sharply and continuously throughout the year. The level of internal funds declined in 1969 as profits fell, dividends and foreign earnings held relatively steady, and depreciation increased slightly.

The decline in internal funds combined with an increase in capital expenditures to cause an increase in the financing gap of nonfinancial corporations during 1969. Investment in plant and equipment in dollar terms increased continuously from the third quarter of 1968 through the end of 1969, and inventory investment generally remained high. The financing gap rose steadily throughout the year, peaking at 18.6 percent of capital expenditures in the fourth quarter.

Given our earlier discussion regarding the expected effect of profits and interest rates on investment, it might be wondered why plant and equipment investment continued to increase in 1969, given the sharp decline in profits, and the fact that stock prices started to fall in 1969 and interest rates increased sharply. The Federal Reserve Bank of New York suggested several possible reasons in their Annual Report for 1969. These included the expectations of further price increases in capital goods and continued high interest rates, the spur to labor-saving capital equipment from sharp increases in wages, and the limitations of existing plant capacity.[1]

However, another possible explanation is that at least part of the investment that was actually carried out in 1969 was involuntary, i.e., due to previous commitments, because contracts and orders for new plant and equipment peaked in April 1969. Moreover, the ratio of inventories to sales rose strongly in 1969 to a level higher than that obtained in the fourth quarter of 1966. Thus the high level of inventory investment in 1969 may also have been at least partly involuntary.

In any event, capital expenditures remained strong during 1969, whereas internal funds declined and the financing gap increased. How did nonfinancial corporations go about meeting their need for external funds?

Although net funds raised in external markets increased gradually in 1969, debt took a declining share of this total. Funds raised from the sale of equity and liquid assets increased proportionately.

Clearly, nonfinancial corporations were under pressure in 1969, particularly in the second half of the year. They sold stock at a time when stock prices were generally down, and they sold liquid assets even though their level was already dangerously low.

In many respects the situation in 1969 was similar to that of 1966. In both instances internal funds fell and nonfinancial corporations were forced to fund a growing financing gap at a time when monetary policy was tightening significantly (see the discussion of Federal Reserve Board policy below). However, in 1966, credit market borrowing dropped off sharply, whereas in 1969 the decline was very gradual. As a matter of fact, it is significant how well bank loans held up. While funds raised in the bond market dropped sharply from the first quarter to the fourth, bank loans fell only gradually. Two important additional sources of debt in the last three quarters were loans from finance companies and borrowing in the rapidly expanding commercial paper market.

Of course, it is true that the funds raised in the last half of the year purchased less in real terms because prices were moving up strongly. Indeed, real investment in plant and equipment declined in the fourth quarter even though it increased slightly in dollar terms. Thus it might be said that additional funds were needed because of inflation. While this is certainly true, it is also true that inflation increased the nominal level of internal funds. It is the difference between investment and internal funds, not their absolute magnitudes, that is significant for an analysis of the demand for external funds by nonfinancial corporations.

Let us now examine monetary and financial policy, and the flow of funds for the commercial banking sector, in order to explain how banks were able to prevent their lending to nonfinancial corporations from dropping as drastically as it did in 1966.

During 1969 the Federal Reserve Board adopted what they described as a "very restrictive monetary policy" in order to "slow the expansion of aggregate money demands in the economy and to dissipate deeply rooted expectations of continuing inflation."[2] The Federal Reserve raised the discount rate in December 1968, and then again in April 1969. As the System increased its open market sales, net borrowed reserves increased sharply in the first half of 1969. In contrast to the first part of 1966, however, the Federal Reserve this time offset member bank borrowing by further reducing nonborrowed reserves. Total member bank reserves decreased slightly in the first half of 1969, after having increased sharply in the last half of 1968. The monetary aggregates and bank credit also slowed their rates of growth.

In addition, the Federal Reserve Board increased reserve requirements against net demand deposits at all member banks by 1/2 percent in April. However, this action was not intended to further reduce bank reserves (since that result could easily be obtained by further open market sales). It was aimed at directly influencing inflationary expectations by sending a clear signal of the Federal Reserve Board's intention to tighten monetary policy.

The Federal Reserve Board also took another significant step at the end of 1968 by again refusing to raise the Regulation Q ceiling rate on large negotiable certificates of deposit. Secondary market rates again rose above the ceiling rate and remained above it throughout 1969. Once more the commercial banks were unable to market new issues and faced a runoff of outstanding CDs. The runoff during 1969 was of even greater magnitude than that of 1966.

The banks, however, learned from the experience of 1966 and were better prepared to adjust to a loss of CDs. They tapped a number of relatively new sources of funds. To compensate for the large and continuing drains during 1969 in large time deposits, the banks dramatically increased their borrowing from foreign banks. Most of this borrowing was by U.S. banks from their overseas branches, which were able to tap the Eurodollar market for funds.

In addition, banks raised a significant amount of money (indirectly) in the commercial paper market. Because of the adoption by many large banks in the late 1960s of the one-bank holding company form, bank holding companies were able in 1969 to sell commercial paper and transfer the funds to their banks by purchasing loans originated by the banks. Thus the banks' funds were replenished for further lending. The banks also raised funds by borrowing federal funds and utilizing security repurchase agreements.[3]

As they did in 1966, commercial banks also cut back on other components of bank credit in order to use their available funds for loans to business. The growth of nonbusiness loans slowed down during 1969, investments in U.S. Treasury securities dropped dramatically, and other securities showed no growth.

Although state and local governmental units were under strong pressure during 1969, there were no reports of crisis conditions developing in the market for municipal securities. Apparently market participants were better prepared this time for the fall-off of commercial bank purchases. Also, the banks did not withdraw as precipitously from the market as they did in 1966.

By using sources of funds other than CDs and by restricting other components of bank credit, commercial banks were able to increase their business loans in the first half of 1969 by 16.2 percent. To counter this growth in credit and also because inflation showed little sign of decreasing, the Federal Open Market Committee (FOMC) intended to maintain the existing monetary restraint upon the economy. Its operating instructions to the Federal Reserve Bank of New York remained essentially unchanged from June to December 1969. It directed that

> System open market operations be conducted with a view to maintaining the prevailing firm conditions in money and short-term credit markets, with provision for modification of operations depending on the course of bank credit developments.[4]

Judged by the policy targets then in use by the FOMC—money market conditions—monetary policy remained unchanged throughout the year. The federal funds rate remained close to 9 percent, and net borrowed reserves decreased only slightly. Nevertheless, as judged by the monetary aggregates, monetary policy was becoming tighter in the second half of 1969. Although bank reserves showed a slight increase from their first half decline, the narrow and broad measures of the money supply and total bank credit slowed dramatically. Real GNP growth turned negative in the fourth quarter of 1969 and the recession of 1969–70 began.

Two of the Federal Reserve Board governors—Sherman J. Maisel and George W. Mitchell—contended that the policy of maintaining unchanged money market conditions was in fact producing an overly restrictive monetary policy (as judged by the monetary aggregates). They dissented from the policy directive of the FOMC of August 12, 1969 for this reason.

The debate over the appropriate way to analyze monetary policy continued into 1970. Governors Maisel and Mitchell apparently were persuasive in their arguments, because the FOMC mentioned money and bank credit as policy targets for the first time in its directive for January 1970. Thus the FOMC now expressed its objective in terms of the monetary aggregates and bank credit. However, it still focused on money market conditions as the variables to manipulate in order to obtain the desired growth in the aggregates. Thus, as Sherman Maisel expressed it in his book on his experiences as a member of the FOMC, "the FOMC changed its target, but not its operating guide."[5]

Therefore, if we judge monetary policy by the aggregates, policy was growing more restrictive during the second half of 1969. In addition, the Federal Reserve Board took steps to close off the alternative sources of funds of the commercial banks. The largest of these sources of funds was Eurodollar borrowings from foreign branches. It has been estimated that (before the Federal Reserve actions) "large New York banks, which had the best developed access to the Eurodollar market, were able to replace their CD losses almost dollar for dollar with such borrowings."[6]

On July 24, 1969, the Federal Reserve Board amended Regulation D to require that member banks count outstanding drafts due to Eurodollar transactions as demand deposits subject to reserve requirements. Also, on August 13, the Board amended Regulations D and M to place a 10 percent marginal reserve requirement on net borrowings of banks from their own foreign branches. Also, the Board amended Regulations D and Q on July 24th to make funds obtained from repurchase agreements subject to reserve requirements.

The form of these actions is important. Apparently the Board wanted to avoid the abrupt cutoff of funds that occurred in 1966. By imposing reserve requirements, the Board did not eliminate Eurodollar borrowing as a source of funds; rather, it reduced the total amount of expansion of bank credit that a dollar of such borrowing could support. The banks could obtain additional funds if they were willing to pay the increased interest cost necessary to obtain them. The avoidance of an abrupt cutoff of funds may have been the reason why a repeat of the 1966 financial crisis did not happen in 1969. Nonetheless, the tight monetary policy and the actions to subject other sources of funds to reserve requirements had its effect, as the expansion of bank credit slowed in the second half of 1969 and the economy headed into recession.

Albert M. Wojnilower has an interesting alternative interpretation of the events of 1969. He contends that there was, in fact, a sudden cutoff of lending even if there was no sudden cutoff of funds to the banks. The reason for the cutoff, according to Wojnilower, was congressional reaction to an increase in the prime rate of one percentage point in June 1969. This reaction made further increases in bank lending rates politically impossible. It therefore made bank lending unprofitable, in Wojnilower's view, because short-term rates "continued to escalate to year-end." Thus the "growth in bank credit virtually halted."[7]

This explanation has a certain appeal, although evidence of this sort is hard to come by. However, there are some inconsistencies with the proposed scenario. For one thing, all other short-term rates did not escalate rapidly during the second half of 1969. The three-month Treasury bill rate increased, but not before November, and the commercial paper rate remained stable through November. The discount rate and the federal funds rate also remained stable throughout the second half of the year. Perhaps even more to the point, the rate on Eurodollar deposits, after rising sharply in the first half of the year to 11.10 percent in June, did not go any higher during the rest of the year. It fluctuated between 10 percent and 11 percent and closed out the year at 11.09 percent in December.

Second, although it is true that "growth in bank credit virtually halted," it was not because the growth in loans virtually halted. Bank credit slowed because banks reduced their investments while continuing to expand their loans, especially their loans to business (as we saw earlier).

On the other hand, the rate of growth of business loans did decline, from 16.2 percent in the first half of 1969 to 9.1 percent in the second. Presumably the tight monetary (and fiscal) policy affected the *ability* of the banks to expand business loans. Did a deterioration of the financial condition of the business sector also influence the *willingness* of the banks and other creditors to continue their lending? An examination of the creditworthiness of the corporate sector may shed some light on this question.

We have already seen that profits fell quite sharply in 1968 and 1969, and that interest rates for corporate borrowing were at record highs by June 1969. The use of debt by nonfinancial corporations reached, in the fourth quarter of 1968, the peak of 3.7 percent of GNP attained in the second quarter of 1966. The use of debt declined in 1969; however, the debt-equity ratio increased in 1969, particularly the ratio measured by total debt outstanding divided by the market value of equity (partly because of the decline in stock prices).

Other aspects of corporate financial conditions deteriorated as well. An increasing portion of the debt used by nonfinancial corporations in 1968 and 1969 consisted of loans and short-term paper; the ratio of outstanding loans and short-term paper to total debt outstanding kept climbing. Thus corporations became increasingly vulnerable to adverse conditions in the financial markets (such as higher interest rates), as their debt had to be renegotiated more often. Moreover, the growth of short-term liabilities outpaced the ability of nonfinancial corporations to add to their liquid assets, and the liquidity ratio continued to fall.

That nonfinancial corporations had more difficulty in servicing their debt is evident by the decline in the interest coverage ratio. This ratio fell sharply and continuously during 1968–69 (and also during 1970). Again, lacking adequate data on the total amount of debt repaid during this period, we are unable to determine how much corporations had to borrow merely to repay debt. Judging by the decline in the interest coverage ratio, however, it probably was significant.

We would expect that the deteriorating financial condition of the corporate sector would adversely affect the quality of bank loans to business. Indeed, net charge-offs as a percentage of average total loans jumped sharply in 1970. Since loans are charged off only after their quality has deteriorated for some time, the high level of charge-offs in 1970 probably means that there was a high level of past-due and nonperforming loans in 1969 (the data to measure this hypothesis directly do not exist).

Thus, although there are imperfections in the data, there does seem to be some reason to think that banks restricted credit to the business sector during the second half of 1969 because of the worsening financial condition of nonfinancial corporations.

We could perhaps look at other creditors of the corporations for additional evidence. Trade debt is a form of credit that is often extended automatically when a sale is made. However, when suppliers need funds or when they doubt the creditworthiness of their customers, they may restrict their terms somewhat. Trade debt as a percentage of sales declined steadily from the third quarter of 1969 through the fourth quarter of 1970.

Despite a restriction of credit, however, the economy survived 1969 without the threat of a financial crisis. The same cannot be said for 1970.

As 1970 began, the FOMC moved to make credit conditions somewhat easier. In its economic policy directive of January 15, 1970, the FOMC noted that "real economic activity leveled off in the fourth quarter of 1969 and that little change is in prospect for the early part of 1970." They were concerned, however, that "prices and costs . . . are continuing to rise at a rapid pace." Accordingly, the instructions to the trading desk spoke of a "modest growth in money and bank credit" and "maintaining firm conditions in the money market."[8]

The directives for February through May spoke of "moderate" growth in money and bank credit. In fact, growth in the aggregates over this period did increase somewhat over the last half of 1969. The increases were not dramatic, however; the FOMC was trying to ease up somewhat while still maintaining pressure on bank lending.

Nonfinancial corporations were still in need of funds as 1970 began. Although plant and equipment spending had leveled off in dollar terms, and inventory investment had fallen in the first quarter, internal funds also fell. Nonfinancial corporations had a $19.9 billion financing gap plus an unknown (but certainly large) demand for funds to pay off maturing debt.

They continued to sell liquid assets and issue new equity in the first quarter of 1970, as bank loans (and also finance company loans) declined. Nonfinancial corporations raised additional funds from corporate bonds. Also, they sharply increased their borrowing in the rapidly growing commercial paper market.[9]

Interestingly, issuance of commercial paper by nonfinancial corporations got a boost in response to the credit crunch of 1966:

> In the latter part of the 1960s activity in the [commercial paper] dealer market expanded sharply as increased numbers of nonfinancial corporations began issuing paper. . . . The initial impetus for growth during the second half of the 1960s occurred in 1966. . . . In the final three quarters of that year many companies found it difficult to obtain bank credit as loans were being stringently rationed. . . .
>
> Under these circumstances commercial paper became an important source of financing for large, well-known firms, and a substantial number of companies—especially utilities and industrial concerns—began to issue such paper.[10]

The Penn Central Co. was one such corporation that relied heavily upon commercial paper for its financing. Penn Central had about $200 million worth of commercial paper outstanding at the end of the first quarter of 1970. Along with other nonfinancial corporations, Penn Central was having earnings difficulties, but its situation was particularly severe. It reported a $63 million loss in the first quarter, and began to experience increasing difficulty in marketing its commercial paper.

When Penn Central filed for reorganization (bankruptcy) on June 21, 1970 and indicated that it could not pay its outstanding commercial paper obligations, fear spread to the holders of other companies' commercial paper. The risk premium incorporated into commercial paper interest rates (as measured by the spread over Treasury rates) increased sharply.

The usual situation in the commercial paper market is for borrowers to maintain backup lines of credit from their banks. Thus if holders of commercial paper were to refuse to roll them over—and the average finance company paper at the time had a maturity of twenty-five days—corporations could place potentially enormous demands for funds upon the commercial banking system.

The Federal Reserve Board and the FOMC were aware of the demand for liquidity and the possibility that banks would be unable to meet the financing demands of corporations with commercial paper coming due. In that event, further bankruptcies and a generalized financial crisis could well develop. They acted to forestall such a possibility.

At their meeting on June 23, 1970, the FOMC determined that open market operations should be "conducted with a view to moderating pressures on financial markets" because of "market uncertainties and liquidity strains."[11] In fact, the FOMC had also loosened monetary policy in May because of unsettled conditions in the securities markets arising from the Cambodian invasion.

The potential financial crisis following the Penn Central bankruptcy, however, required further action:

> In recognition that pressures might pyramid in the commercial paper market after a major railroad filed for reorganization in mid-June, the authorities supplemented their efforts to ameliorate market strains through open market policy with other policy measures. It was made clear that the Federal Reserve discount window would be available to assist banks in meeting the needs of businesses unable to roll over their maturing commercial paper. Also the Board of Governors moved promptly to suspend maximum rate ceilings on large-denomination CD's with maturities of 30 to 89 days.[12]

Banks in all Federal Reserve districts were informed on Monday, June 22nd, that the discount window was open to them. On the next day, June 23rd, the Board suspended Regulation Q interest rate ceilings on short-term large-denomination certificates of deposit.

After Penn Central failed, outstanding nonbank commercial paper declined by approximately $3 billion. As companies shut out of the commercial paper market turned to the banks, borrowing from the discount window by the banks increased rapidly. According to Thomas M. Timlen, an officer of the Federal Reserve Bank of New York:

> Discount window borrowings hit a peak of almost $1.7 billion nationwide during July, more than 2½ times borrowings immediately preceding the Penn Central failure. . . . Finally, with the lifting of Regulation Q ceilings, $10 billion in time deposits flowed into the banks.[13]

The banks were thus able to meet the demands for funds from corporations shut out of the commercial paper market. Since money was readily available, the crisis soon dissipated.

1974: Franklin National

The threat of a financial crisis developed again in 1974. The crisis was precipitated mainly by the effective failure of Franklin National Bank, at the time the twentieth largest bank in the United States.

This time the crisis had international ramifications. Franklin had large Eurodollar liabilities, and its difficulties were followed by the failure of a German bank, Bankhaus I.D. Herstatt; both banks had financed unsuccessful foreign-exchange speculation by heavy borrowing in the Eurodollar interbank market. The Federal Reserve acted as a lender of last resort to prevent instability in foreign as well as domestic financial markets. Such activity to protect markets overseas was a significant expansion in the use of lender-of-last-resort activities.

Before discussing the crisis itself, however, it is necessary again to follow the developments in the economy, and especially in the corporate and banking sectors, that created the conditions in which the crisis developed.

The 1970 recession ended in November, but the growth of the economy in 1971 was disappointing. Real GNP recovered strongly in the first quarter of the year from its low point in 1970, but growth in real GNP for the rest of the year averaged only 2.9 percent. Such low growth is atypical for the first year of recovery from a recession.

In addition, the capacity utilization rate increased only slightly from its low point of 75.9 percent in November 1970, and the unemployment rate averaged close to 6 percent for most of the year. Despite this evident slack in the economy, prices continued to increase at a 5.8 percent rate during the first half of the year.

These domestic developments, however bad, were nonetheless overshadowed in 1971 by the continuing balance of payments deficits of the United States and the difficulties of the dollar. The dollar came under increasing attack from speculators in 1971, and foreign central banks were forced to take in increasing amounts of dollars to maintain the system of fixed exchange rates.

The pressure became too much in late summer; President Nixon announced a New Economic Policy (NEP) on August 15th to try to address the domestic and international difficulties. The NEP suspended convertibility of the dollar into gold, instituted a 10 percent surcharge on imports, froze wages and prices for ninety days, and proposed tax legislation designed to spur economic recovery.

The ninety-day freeze was replaced with Phase Two of the wage and price control program, which aimed at holding price increases to no more than 2.5 percent. The President's tax legislation became law in December 1971. Fiscal policy in general became highly expansionary in 1972, as did monetary policy. The high employment budget was in deficit throughout the year, and the monetary aggregates increased rapidly.

On December 18, 1971 the Administration agreed to devalue the dollar by raising the dollar price of gold from $35 an ounce to $38. It was the first change in the value of the dollar since the $35 per ounce price was established at the Bretton Woods Conference at the end of the Second World War.

The stimulative monetary and fiscal policy, the devaluation of the dollar, and the wage and price controls combined in 1972 to produce rapid economic growth at stable prices. Most of the price stability came during the first three quarters of the year, however. Prices increased during the first three quarters of 1972 at an annual rate of only 2.9 percent, but by the fourth quarter they were increasing at a 5.1 percent rate. Towards the end of 1972 pressures on the economy increased, and the period of noninflationary growth came to an end.

The capacity utilization rate climbed steadily throughout 1972. The unemployment rate declined slowly from January to October 1972, and then plunged to 4.9 percent by January 1973. Investment in plant and equipment began to increase sharply in the fourth quarter of 1972. Profits of nonfinancial corporations peaked in the first quarter of 1973, but investment demand remained strong. The decline in profits, however, was responsible for a decline in internal funds.

Thus, with investment in plant and equipment spending rising sharply, with inventory investment increasing in 1973, and with internal funds falling, the financing gap for capital expenditures rose to high levels in 1973. In the two earlier periods that we have discussed, nonfinancial corporations sold liquid assets at times when the financing gap widened. However, by 1973 their stock of liquid assets was relatively low, and they could not use them as a source of funds. In fact, in 1973 nonfinancial corporations were net purchasers of liquid assets rather than net sellers.

How, then, did nonfinancial corporations meet their growing need for funds in 1973? For the most part they relied heavily on bank loans. In the first quarter of 1973 alone, nonfinancial corporations borrowed the huge sum of $47.8 billion (at an annual rate) from the banks. This amount was 76.5 percent of the total external funds raised by nonfinancial corporations in the first quarter. Part of the explanation for this extraordinary bank borrowing has to do, however, with price controls.

In early 1973 the Committee on Interest and Dividends, as part of the overall effort to limit price and wage increases, put pressure on the banks to hold the prime rate down despite the general upward pressure on rates at the time. The commercial paper rate was not subject to controls. Although the commercial paper rate had been below the bank prime during 1971 and 1972, it rose above the prime in February 1973. Since commercial paper had become the major alternative source (other than the banks) of short-term funds for many large corporations, the switch in relative costs made bank financing much more attractive. As we have seen, bank lending to the corporate sector increased dramatically, although at a reduced spread for the banks.

The administrative pressure to hold down the prime rate was eased in April, and the prime rate rose sharply through August. Although bank loans decreased from their record-setting rate in the first quarter, they still remained high in the next two quarters. Part of the reason is that the prime rate still remained slightly below the commercial paper rate through September, but part of the reason also has to do with banks' sources of funds.

Banks during this period were able to rely heavily on large time deposits (primarily large negotiable CDs) to meet the heavy loan demand from the corporate sector. In previous periods of strong corporate loan demand—1966 and 1969—banks experienced a runoff of large CDs because of Regulation Q interest rate ceilings.

However, in 1973, although Regulation Q ceilings did threaten the banks' reliance on CDs, the Federal Reserve Board chose not to leave the ceilings in place. On May 16, 1973 the board voted to suspend interest-rate ceilings on large CDs with maturities of ninety days or more. Thus there were no longer any ceiling rates on CDs of any maturity, as the Board had previously suspended interest-rate ceilings on large CDs with maturities of eighty-nine days or less in June 1970 (in response to the Penn Central crisis, as discussed above).

At the same time, however, the Board amended Regulation D to increase the reserve requirements on large time deposits by 3 percent, to a total of 8 percent. The increased reserve requirements took effect on June 21, 1973. The Board attempted to limit the use of CDs by making them more expensive (as it did with Eurodollar borrowing in 1969) rather than abruptly cutting off their supply. Also, on May 21st, the Board sent a letter to all member banks asking them to resist excessive credit demands and to exercise prudence in issuing large-demonination certificates of deposit and in borrowing from nondeposit sources. Since the net increase in large time deposits at commercial banks jumped from (an annual rate of) $27.5 billion in the second quarter to $69.9 billion in the third, these actions do not appear to have had any immediate effect.

The Board's actions to limit loan growth should be considered in the context of its overall efforts to tighten monetary policy. As economic activity, loan demand, and prices began to accelerate towards the end of 1972, the Federal Open Market Committee voted to restrain the growth of the economy. The policy directive issued on December 19, 1972 to the Federal Reserve Bank of New York spoke for the first time in 1972 of "slower" growth in the monetary aggregates. The directives of January through August 1973 (with the exception of April) also directed the trading desk in New York to achieve slower growth of the aggregates.

The growth of the monetary aggregates did slow during this period, but prices continued to increase rapidly. Contributing to inflationary pressures in 1973 were materials shortages and capacity bottlenecks in several industrial sectors, a second devaluation of the dollar, and worldwide shortages in the supplies of energy and agricultural products. (A good part of U.S. agricultural production was used for export in 1973—to meet the worldwide food shortage and to improve the U.S. balance of payments.)

The demand for funds from the corporate sector continued at a high level. Business (commercial and industrial) loans at commercial banks increased by 27.9 percent from December 1972 to August 1973. Nonbusiness loans increased by 19.3 percent. The strong demand for funds, combined with the tight monetary policy and inflation, drove interest rates to new highs.

However, the rate of growth of real GNP slowed sharply in the second quarter of 1973. Short-term market rates fell during the rest of the year and into the first part of 1974, as the economy slowed further. The National Bureau of Economic Research declared November 1973 to be the beginning of a recession.

Short-term interest rates began to rise again in mid-February. Moreover, corporate loan demand and commercial bank issuance of certificates of deposit, which had fallen off in the fourth quarter of 1973 and in the beginning of the first quarter of 1974, began to increase again. Industrial production also declined after the recession began and picked up again in February.

This unusual behavior is explained by the cause of the economic decline in November 1973. Most observers now attribute this decline to the effect of the oil embargo which was imposed in October. Speaking of developments in 1974, the Federal Reserve Bank of New York stated that "largely as a result of the energy shortage, weakness had emerged in the domestic economy early in the year. . . . It was not until the final months of the year that a classic recessionary pattern, including substantial declines in industrial output and sharply rising unemployment, set in."[1] This second stage of the recession began in September.

Monetary policy had eased in response to the supply-induced recession, but it began to tighten again once the oil embargo was no longer disrupting the economy. The combination of tight monetary policy, inflation, and heavy loan demand again put financial markets and interest rates under increased strain. According to the Federal Reserve Board:

> During the early part of the year, when the economy was still being depressed by the Middle East oil embargo, the System continued the posture of lessened monetary restraint that had been initiated in late 1973 when dislocations from the embargo began. . . .
>
> By late February, however, it was becoming evident that all the monetary aggregates were again expanding at rapid rates. Therefore—once a lifting of the oil embargo had been

assured—the System moved to counter this accelerating growth of the aggregates. In the months that followed, the combination of increased monetary restraint, continuing rapid inflation, and ballooning business credit demands produced a sharp, general tightening of credit markets. Interest rates rose well above earlier historical highs.[2]

The heavy loan demand and conditions in the financial markets put further pressure on corporate balance sheets. The heavy use of debt had sent debt-equity ratios to historic highs. Moreover, as we have seen, a large fraction of this debt was short-term, mostly bank loans. (The increased use of short-term debt was partly due to corporate borrowing to finance "anticipatory" inventory-building in advance of future price increases and to avoid shortages. The "stockpiling" of inventory was reflected in a large increase in the ratio of inventories to sales.)

Although not all bank loans are short-term debt (with maturities of less than one year), by 1974 a significant fraction of bank loans to business were being made with floating interest rates. (Exact data on the percentage of loans made with floating rates are not available until 1977.) Thus the sharp increase in interest rates resulted in rapidly increasing interest costs for nonfinancial corporations. Also, pretax profits of nonfinancial corporations (after adjustment for artificial inventory profits) fell, and the interest coverage ratio of nonfinancial corporations sunk to new lows in the first part of 1974.

Further financial pressure was put on corporations in this period because of the tax treatment of reported profits. Due to the accounting treatment of inventories at historical cost, reported profits of corporations were overstated in 1974, when inventory prices were increasing rapidly. Yet corporations paid increased income taxes on these artificially high reported profits.

Finally, the liquidity ratio of nonfinancial corporations also declined to new lows in 1974. As we noted above, corporations were not able to finance spending needs in 1974 by drawing down their stock of liquid assets.

As a result of this pressure on corporate balance sheets, the rate of business bankruptcies increased sharply in 1974. Thus in addition to borrowing from the banks to finance capital expenditures and other needs, corporations also had to borrow from the banks to meet their outstanding obligations.

In addition to the corporations, there was another group of borrowers who had large needs for short-term loans in this period: the Real Estate Investment Trusts (REITs). As of the second quarter of 1974, the REITs had $9.666 billion in bank loans outstanding, $7.406 billion of which was short-term.[3]

The REITs had experienced rapid growth in the early 1970s as they profited from the expansion of the real estate market. The majority of REITs made loans for construction and development, which is generally considered to be the riskiest area of the real estate business. In addition, in order to expand, the REITs often made loans which the banks (the major lender in this area) refused to make because of excessive risk. The REITs also made loans at below-market interest rates.

Despite these problems, the banks encouraged the growth of the REITs. The banks profited from the fees they charged the REITs for investment advice. Quite a number of banks also set up their "own" REITs. The best known of these, and the largest REIT in mid-1974, was the Chase Manhattan Mortgage and Realty Trust.

In 1971 the REITs began to borrow heavily in the commercial paper market. For the most part their borrowings were backed up by unused lines of credit at commercial banks. As long as the real estate market was booming, the REITs had ready access to cash. But as difficulties developed in this market, the fortunes of the REITs took a turn for the worse.

The difficult economic conditions made many housing development projects unprofitable in 1973. The increasing prices and interest rates during this period rapidly escalated costs for developers. Moreover, the shortages of materials that characterized 1973 meant that many projects were subject to costly delays. The unavailability of mortgage money meant that many developers could not obtain "takeout" (permanent mortgage) financing for their projects. An increasing number of developers had difficulty paying their loans to the REITs; the REITs, in turn, began losing money.

The failure in December 1973 of the Kassuba Development Corporation, one of the largest developers of apartment buildings in the country, highlighted the problems of the REITs. Apparently about twenty REITs had made loans to Kassuba. Its failure put the difficulties of the REITs into the glare of public attention.

As a result, the auditors of the REITs, now under some pressure, required the REITs to increase their provisions for loan losses and to stop counting as income interest payments that had accrued but that had not been received (and probably would not be received). Both actions had a negative impact on earnings.

Lenders in the commercial paper market became increasingly reluctant to lend to the tottering REITs. To replace the estimated $4 billion they had borrowed in the commercial paper market, the REITs turned in early 1974 to the banks. Without loans from the banks, quite a number of REITs doubtless would have failed. The outcome of this mini-crisis was detailed by one observer as follows:

> By spring it was apparent that some trusts would be unable
> to roll over their paper, and the specter of "another Penn
> Central" loomed. Had it not been for the Herculean efforts
> of some major banks . . . a number of the very largest
> REITs might have toppled.[4]

It might be added that some of the major banks also wished to avoid the failure of REITs that were associated with the banks (because of the same name or because the banks were prominent investment advisers).

Although the troubles of the REITs were managed for the time being (and a possible crisis prevented), the "solution" of increased bank loans only added to the difficulties of the banks. During the same time period that they were lending to the REITs, the banks were also increasing their already large loan exposure to the corporate sector. From February to April 1974, bank loans to nonfinancial corporations increased by 38.3 percent. This increased lending had several negative implications for the banks.

The intense loan demand in 1974 came on top of strong loan demand during most of 1973. Since monetary policy had remained tight throughout all of this period, except for the brief respite during the oil embargo, the banks' liquidity came under increasing strain. The ratio of liquid assets to total liabilities for large weekly reporting banks fell during most of 1973, improved slightly during the few months when monetary policy eased in late 1973 and early 1974, and declined again in 1974. The low liquidity levels and the slow growth of core deposits in this period meant that the banks had to increase their reliance upon expensive "purchased funds" to fund the large loan demand. In the second quarter of 1974, the commercial banking system sold large time deposits at an annual rate of $71.5 billion.

The increase in loans also had negative effects on bank asset quality. The banks increased their lending to the REITs and to nonfinancial corporations at a time when both were experiencing increasing financial difficulties. Net charge-offs as a percentage of average total loans increased in 1974 and even more in 1975. Since loans are charged off only after a period of time during which they are nonperforming, we can safely conclude that many of the loans on the banks' books in 1974 were not earning the interest income that they should have.

It might be asked why the banks made these loans if the creditworthiness of their borrowers had deteriorated significantly. For the loans to the REITs, we saw that the banks were trying to avoid the failures of some of the larger REITs (some of them associated directly with their bank sponsors). In addition, the REITs had established lines of credit upon which they drew.

For loans to the nonfinancial corporate sector, the use of loan commitments is of special significance. The use of loan commitments (which are promises by the bank to lend up to a specified amount) developed after the credit crunch of 1966, when the banks were forced to limit their business loans by the Federal Reserve Board. By 1974 commitments were widely used, although formal data did not become available until the Loan Commitment Survey was initiated by the Federal Reserve Board in 1975.

Presumably the banks in early 1974 limited loans they made to business borrowers without loan commitments so that they could satisfy the increased demands for takedowns of outstanding commitments. According to the quarterly survey on changes in bank lending practices conducted by the Federal Reserve Board, 37.9 percent of the 124 banks surveyed indicated that between February and May 1974 they adopted a "much firmer policy" for loans to new nonfinancial business customers.[5] Only 2.4 percent of the banks did so for established customers. Moreover, the value of the borrower as a depositor became more important for 63.7 percent of the banks surveyed.

Thus despite apparent efforts to limit loans for which there were no outstanding commitments (and a sharp increase in the prime rate), banks increased their loans to nonfinancial business at a rapid rate in this period. However, the accompanying reliance on expensive purchased funds and the loan-loss difficulties affected commercial banks' income adversely. Net income as a percentage of average total assets for all commercial banks declined in 1974.

The strong increase in loans and the poor earnings performance negatively affected bank capital. Capital ratios for all banks declined in 1974, but the ratio for large banks declined even faster, and to a lower level. Since it is capital that protects a bank in danger of bankruptcy, the low capital ratios for the large banks meant that the risk of bankruptcy of a large bank was increased.

In December of 1973 the U.S. National Bank of San Diego, with $932 million in deposits, failed. However, the biggest shock by far to the financial system came from the difficulties and eventual failure of the Franklin National Bank in 1974. At the end of 1973 Franklin was the twentieth largest bank in the United States, with deposits of $3.7 billion.

Franklin in the early 1960s was a regional Long Island bank. It had grown rapidly on Long Island and was looking to expand further. It was finally granted permission in 1964 to expand into the New York City market. In 1969 it established a branch in London in order to enter the field of international banking.

In both of these arenas Franklin was a relative latecomer. In addition, it was competing in both places against the biggest and most powerful banks in the world. To attract business, Franklin made loans to poor credit risks, often at lower interest rates than other banks were charging.

Franklin funded this rapid loan growth by heavy reliance on purchased funds, especially large CDs and federal funds. It also was a heavy borrower in the Eurodollar interbank market.

Although bank fortunes in general took a turn for the worse in 1974, Franklin was particularly hard hit. In its frantic rush to expand, it had made more bad loans at lower profit margins than had most banks, and had relied more heavily on purchased funds. Franklin's rate of return on assets was just over two-fifths of that achieved by other large banks in 1973, and in June 1974 its problem loans had climbed to 177.4 percent of its total equity capital.[6]

In addition to the problem of domestic banking in 1974, there were international problems as well. Joan Edelman Spero, in her study of Franklin National Bank, notes that rapid expansion of the Eurodollar market in the late 1960s and early 1970s put strong competitive pressures on the banks that participated in it.[7] Again, as a relative latecomer to the Eurodollar market, and one intent on rapid growth, Franklin fared especially poorly.

In an attempt to recoup its declining fortunes, Franklin turned to speculation in foreign exchange. However, it suffered losses rather than gains, and by the spring of 1974 it was in dire shape.

Although Franklin's problems were known to a few market participants relatively early (Morgan Guaranty apparently had stopped selling fed funds to Franklin in the fall of 1973),[8] they became known to the markets as a whole and to the general public in May 1974. On May 1st the Federal Reserve Board turned down Franklin's application to acquire the Talcott National Corporation, a large diversified financial institution. The Board stated that Franklin should attend to its internal problems rather than expand further. On May 10th Franklin announced to the public that it would not be able to pay its quarterly dividend. It also announced that it had requested the Securities and Exchange Commission to suspend trading of its stock. Franklin had great difficulty borrowing money after these announcements.

In addition, in the third week of June, Franklin announced that it had lost $63.8 million during the first five months of 1974, $46.8 million from foreign-exchange transactions. On June 26th, Bankhaus I.S. Herstatt, a private bank in West Germany, went bankrupt due to heavy foreign exchange losses. According to Andrew Brimmer:

> These events sent shock waves through both the domestic and international money markets. As uncertainties spread, depositors become extremely risk conscious and were more and more reluctant to deal with any bank except the handful of large institutions whose stability appeared to be beyond question.[9]

The domestic market for large negotiable certificates of deposit was disrupted; internationally, the crisis affected the foreign-exchange and Eurodollar markets.

In the market for large CDs, a tiering developed in which banks of greater perceived risk had to pay a higher rate in order to sell their CDs. This tiering, however, was based solely on bank size, . ot objective measures of profitability.[10] The differential between CD rates and risk-free Treasury bills widened dramatically.

Similar problems developed in international markets as well. The Eurodollar market stopped growing, and the foreign branches of U.S. banks faced a contraction of their deposits. Eurobanks had to pay a premium for dollars, compared with banks in the United States. Tiering within the market also developed, and "for two or three weeks many [banks] were unable to obtain funds."[11]

Thus the immediate consequences of public knowledge of Franklin's difficulties were threefold. First, Franklin no longer had access to new borrowing in the money markets. Second, holders of Franklin's liabilities in the domestic CD market, in the Eurodollar interbank market, and in foreign-exchange contracts became quite apprehensive about the safety of their funds and tried to withdraw what they could (by the end of July Franklin had lost 71 percent of its domestic and foreign money-market resources). Finally, the markets as a whole became increasingly nervous, and a flight to safety and liquidity developed.

Keep in mind that the above were consequences of Franklin's difficulties, not its actual failure. Had Franklin actually failed in May or June, and had investors lost money because of nonpayment of Franklin's liabilities, the situation would have been far worse. Spero describes the possible consequences to the international banking and financial system:

> On May 3 Franklin's foreign branches held $926 million in deposits from other banks, an estimated half of which were from foreign branches of American banks. These deposits were entirely uninsured and quite volatile. Had Franklin failed precipitously, all or part of these deposits could have been lost or "blocked." The loss of confidence in Franklin could then easily have spread to weaker banks having important deposits in Franklin, to weak banks in the system generally, and even to strong but less well-known small and medium-sized banks. . . .
>
> Because of banking and other forms of economic interdependence, such an international financial crisis would have had potentially deeper and broader effects than earlier international financial panics such as the 1931 Credit-Anstalt crisis.[12]

Franklin's abrupt failure was a consequence to be avoided. However, because of its previous heavy reliance upon borrowed funds, Franklin's inability to borrow after May mortally damaged its continued viability. It could have been declared insolvent in May; its eventual failure on October 8, 1974 was a foregone conclusion. One might wonder, then, how it managed to survive from May until October.

The answer is that it was propped up by massive loans—totaling $1.7 billion—from the Federal Reserve discount window. In acting to prevent Franklin's abrupt failure, the Federal Reserve sought to forestall a potential financial crisis. In the opinion of Andrew Brimmer, who was a governor of the Federal Reserve Board at the time, the Federal Reserve knew that Franklin would eventually fail; nonetheless, it lent money to Franklin in order to protect financial markets which would have been threatened by Franklin's collapse. These markets included the domestic market for bank certificates of deposit, the Eurodollar market, and the foreign-exchange market. A large portion of Franklin's borrowing from the discount window went to replace deposits lost by Franklin's branch in London. In addition, the Federal Reserve Bank of New York acquired $725 million of Franklin's foreign-exchange liabilities.[13]

The Federal Reserve also encouraged other banks to lend to Franklin in order to bolster confidence in the domestic money markets, which had been weakened by Franklin's difficulties. This lending, which consisted of a daily average of $300 million of fed funds, was guaranteed by the Federal Reserve.[14]

Granted that the Federal Reserve wanted to avoid a financial crisis, why was it necessary to extend aid to Franklin for so long? The shock from the announcement of Franklin's difficulties had worn off by late May. Since it failed eventually in October anyway, why wasn't it allowed to fail in late May?

Apparently this plan would have been acceptable to the Federal Reserve Board.[15] However, the reason it was not implemented was that Franklin could not have been closed in May in the way it was in October. By October the Federal Deposit Insurance Corporation (FDIC) had arranged for another bank to purchase Franklin's assets and to assume its liabilities. Thus no holder of Franklin's liabilities suffered any loss due to its failure, and therefore a further shock to investor confidence was avoided. Apparently such a purchase and assumption (P&A) transaction was not possible in May.[16]

The events of 1974 posed more of a threat to the financial system than had any previous crisis in the postwar period. In addition, the 1974 crisis threatened, for the first time since the 1930s, the international financial system. Prompt action by the Federal Reserve Board again prevented the full consequences of the crisis from developing.

This crisis was also significant in that it involved an important expansion in the concept of a lender of last resort. Both the protection of Franklin's Eurodollar liabilities and the assumption by the Federal Reserve Bank of New York of Franklin's foreign-exchange commitments were unprecedented. In fact, Brimmer concludes that the Franklin experience was unique in that it involved an expansion of the traditional responsibilities of the central bank in the United States. That expansion consisted of the "clear and explicit acceptance" of the use of the resources of the Federal Reserve to help stabilize financial markets overseas.[17]

Despite this expansion of the Federal Reserve Board's role, lender-of-last-resort operations did not have to be coordinated among more than one central bank. This coordination would soon be required, however—to overcome the problem posed by Mexico's potential default on its loan obligations in 1982.

7

The Silver Crisis of 1980

The financial crisis of 1974 was the most far-reaching and the severest of any that had previously occurred in the postwar period. Moreover, the recession, which ended in March 1975, was the deepest of any since the Great Depression. As a result, although balance sheet ratios improved during the recession, both the corporations and the banks turned their attention in 1975 and 1976 toward a further rebuilding of their liquidity and balance sheets.

Capital expenditures of nonfinancial corporations declined, and debt ratios improved. The balance sheets of commercial banks also improved during this period, due to the weak loan demand and a desire on the part of the banks to reduce their loan exposure following the 1974 crisis.

These favorable financial developments in the corporate and banking sectors began to change in 1977, however. They turned negative in 1978 under the pressure of an expanding economy.

Real investment in plant and equipment by nonfinancial corporations posted strong gains in both 1977 and 1978. Moreover, this investment was no longer financed primarily out of internal funds. Credit market borrowing as a percentage of investment, which was abnormally low in 1975 and 1976, rebounded strongly in 1977 and 1978.

An increasing proportion of the debt used to finance investment spending was short-term. As a result, the maturity ratio of total debt outstanding, after improving in 1975 and 1976, again began to deteriorate in 1977 and 1978. In addition, the liquidity ratio for nonfinancial corporations peaked in the last quarter of 1976 and the debt-equity ratio increased in 1977 and 1978.

By the second quarter of 1978 economic activity was expanding strongly. The unemployment rate fell to under 6 percent in 1978, and the capacity utilization rate climbed to 87.1 percent by December. The GNP price deflator increased by 14.7 percent during the year, and compensation of employees in nonfinancial corporate business jumped by 15 percent. At the same time, productivity growth slowed sharply. After increasing at an average of 2.6 percent per year from 1975 through 1977, the output per hour of all employees (in 1972 dollars) in the nonfinancial corporate business sector slowed to only a 0.9 percent increase in 1978.

The profits of nonfinancial corporations began to come under pressure in 1978. Profits peaked in the third quarter of 1977, at 8.7 percent of total domestic income of nonfinancial corporations. After increasing briefly in the second quarter of 1978, profits continued to fall steadily through the first quarter of 1980 (although the sharp decline did not begin until 1979).

Despite the fall in profits, internal funds remained relatively constant during 1978 because of a relatively rapid increase in depreciation allowances. Since the capital expenditures of nonfinancial corporations continued to expand, the financing gap began to widen. Increases in inventory investment were at a relatively high level in 1978 (averaging $23.5 billion for the year as a whole), and investment in plant and equipment continued its upward growth. In addition to capital expenditures, nonfinancial corporations also used funds in 1978 to acquire liquid assets and to increase their net trade credit outstanding. Nonfinancial corporations financed their needs for external funds in 1978 almost entirely by debt.

In addition, debt of the household sector reached record levels in 1978. Mortgage debt increased moderately, but the sharpest jump was recorded in consumer credit.

Prices rose rapidly in 1978, as noted above. The increased price level adversely affected the foreign exchange value of the U.S. dollar, which came under increasing pressure during the year.

Thus in order to slow the sharp rise in prices and the expanding credit demands, and to protect the value of the dollar abroad, the Federal Open Market Committee (FOMC) and the Federal Reserve Board, beginning in April 1978, moved to tighten monetary policy.

The operating procedure that the Committee used then was to target the federal funds rate within a certain range in order to influence its policy variables, the monetary aggregates. Accordingly, the FOMC progressively increased the federal funds rate from 6.9 percent (monthly average) in April to 10.0 percent in December. In addition, from mid-May to the end of the year the Federal Reserve Board increased the discount rate six times.

The increasing interest rates again threatened the depository institutions, especially the thrifts, with disintermediation. In response, the Federal Reserve Board, the Federal Deposit Insurance Corporation, and the Federal Home Loan Bank Board authorized a six-month "money market certificate" to be issued by the depository institutions. The minimum investment was $10,000, and the maximum interest rate that these certificates could pay varied with the rate on Treasury bills. For banks, the ceiling was set equal to the average yield in the weekly Treasury auction; the thrifts were allowed to pay an additional one-fourth of a percentage point.

Now, for the first time, relatively small depositors were being offered a market rate of interest. For the thrift institutions, especially the savings and loans, the certificates were quite successful in controlling the outflow of deposits.

Small time and savings deposits at all savings institutions jumped by more than $10 billion (at a seasonally adjusted annual rate) in the third quarter of 1978.

The certificates were less successful for the commercial banks; their small time and savings deposits declined slightly by the end of the year. However, their loss was more than made up by increased reliance on purchased funds. In the fourth quarter the banks raised $86.5 billion (again, at a seasonally adjusted annual rate) from large time deposits, fed funds and repurchase agreements, and commercial paper. This total included $54.7 billion alone from large time deposits.

The banks used this purchased money to fund the strong loan demand. Thus although the FOMC was successful in slowing the monetary aggregates, the expansion of credit continued. In the April to December period total loans at commercial banks increased at a 17.7 percent annual rate, whereas total investments increased by only 2.1 percent. Nonbusiness loans increased particularly rapidly at a 19.2 percent annual rate; this increase reflected the strong growth in consumer borrowing. Investments in U.S. Treasury securities, on the other hand, decreased at an 8.3 percent annual rate.

In response to the increased use of purchased funds by the banks to expand credit, the Federal Reserve Board announced on November 1st an amendment to Regulation D which established a supplemental reserve requirement of 2 percent on all time deposits of $100,000 or more (the increase in required reserves became effective November 16th). In addition, the Board announced a series of other measures on November 1st which were designed to slow the expansion of bank credit and to improve the foreign-exchange value of the dollar (which had fallen at a rapid pace in October).

The discount rate was raised by a full percentage point on November 1st, the largest increase in 45 years. Also, the FOMC authorized, by a special vote on October 31st, an increase in the federal funds target rate from 9.5 to 9.75 percent. Finally, the Federal Reserve Board and the Treasury announced a series of actions which were designed to increase U.S. holdings of foreign currencies so that exchange-market interventions to protect the value of the dollar could be carried out more effectively.

The immediate effect of these actions was a sharp rise in the exchange value of the dollar. Although this increase was reversed in the latter part of 1979, it did serve to moderate the steep slide in the dollar's value. On the other hand, the Board did not have as much success in restraining the growth of bank credit. In the period from December 1978 to June 1979 bank credit increased at an annual rate of 13.9 percent. However, this increase in credit took place in a much different economic setting.

In early 1979 the economy of the United States was hit by the second oil shock. Oil supplies were disrupted and the price of oil escalated rapidly. The effects on the economy were negative, as they were during the first oil shock of 1973-74. The oil price increases and shortages at the same time depressed economic activity and increased inflationary pressures: the growth of real GNP slowed in the first quarter and turned negative in the second, even as the GNP price deflator was increasing by more than 8 percent.

Productivity slowed even further from its 1978 pace, and unit labor costs increased. Profits dropped sharply, as did the interest coverage ratio.

Particularly hard hit was the automobile industry. The increase in the price of gasoline, combined with gas shortages, caused car sales to drop sharply. The Chrysler Corporation suffered the most damage. It lost $120 million in the first quarter and $207 million in the second and was on the verge of bankruptcy.

However, unlike the experience of Penn Central in 1970, Chrysler's troubles did not come as a shock to the financial markets. It had had financial troubles in the past, and its market share had been declining ever since 1970. A study conducted by Data Resources, Inc. in mid-1979 concluded that a bankruptcy by Chrysler would have had only mildly negative effects on the financial markets.[1] The fate of Chrysler was debated throughout the year, and the company was finally granted a government loan guarantee of $1.7 billion in January 1980.

The slowdown in economic activity and the decline in profit share for nonfinancial corporate business was accompanied by a deceleration in investment. Real investment in plant and equipment grew at only a 1.8 percent annual rate in the first half of 1979. Contracts and orders for plant and equipment peaked in March 1979.

Although investment in plant and equipment slowed down in the first half of 1979, involuntary inventory investment increased. The ratio of inventories to sales increased sharply in the first half of 1979. Moreover, internal funds stopped growing and the financing gap widened.

Thus, although economic activity slowed, the nonfinancial corporate sector increased its borrowing in the first half of 1979. Since long-term interest rates were relatively high, and since a recession was expected imminently, corporations were reluctant to borrow long term. Business (commercial and industrial) loans at commercial banks increased at an annual rate of 22.1 percent in the first two quarters.

Consumer and other loans also increased rapidly during this period, although the growth of these loans slowed from the record pace of the April-December 1978 period. Borrowing by the household sector as a percent of GNP began to decline.

The net funds borrowed by the federal government in the credit markets, although increasing somewhat during the year, fell to quite low levels in 1979. This development was due primarily to a reduction in the budget deficit for the year.

Although economic activity slowed due to the oil shock and the tightening of fiscal policy, the Federal Open Market Committee did not move to ease monetary policy in this period, due to continuing concern over inflation and the strength of the dollar. On the other hand, they did not try to tighten policy because they (along with most forecasters) expected that the economy would soon slide into recession. The federal funds and discount rates were held steady.

Those forecasters predicting recession in 1979 were surprised in the third quarter. As the impact of the oil shock receded, economic activity rebounded strongly. Real GNP increased by 4.7 percent in the third quarter. Both investment and consumer spending increased rapidly.

The rate of growth of the monetary aggregates began to accelerate. The FOMC raised the federal funds rate in an effort to slow the growth of the aggregates, but with relatively little success. The report of the Manager for Domestic Operations of the Federal Reserve System Open Market account stated that

> the markets were depressed by the System's inability to slow the rapid growth of money even as money market rates rose. . . .
> In the late summer, speculative forces gathered strength in many markets as participants lost confidence in official efforts to deal with inflation. The dollar came under renewed attack in the foreign exchange market. . . . In the futures markets, prices of commodities advanced rapidly.
> . . . The price increases reinforced fears that inventory building and consumer buying binges would set off a further round of escalating prices.[2]

In an effort to get inflation and the growth of the monetary aggregates under control, and to stop the growing speculation and the decline of the dollar, the Federal Reserve Board announced three actions on October 6, 1979. First, the Board raised the discount rate a full percentage point again, from 11 percent to 12 percent. Second, it announced that the operating procedures for monetary policy would be changed.

Under the new procedures, although there would be no change in the policy variables that the Federal Reserve System was trying to influence (the monetary aggregates), the operating target was changed—from the federal funds rate to nonborrowed reserves. It was thought that, in a time of inflation, the federal funds rate had become an unreliable guide, and that by manipulating nonborrowed reserves instead of the federal funds rate, the System could obtain better control over the movement of the aggregates.

The new procedures thus opened the door to much greater variability in interest rates. If nonborrowed reserves were to be kept on a targeted path, control would have to be relinquished over the federal funds rate. Indeed, in the wake of the announcement on October 6th, the federal funds rate jumped sharply. In addition, day-to-day movements in the rate were quite volatile, although this volatility probably also reflected the newness of the procedures to some extent.

The third action announced on October 6th was the imposition of reserve requirements on the managed liabilities, or "purchased" funds, of large banks. The Board put into effect a marginal reserve requirement of 8 percent on net increases above a base-period level (September 13 to 26, 1979) on the following liabilities: (1) large (over $100,000) certificates of deposit with maturities of less than one year, (2) Eurodollar borrowings, (3) security repurchase agreements, and (4) federal funds borrowing from nonmember institutions. These reserve requirements applied to all member banks that had over $100 million in total of the four nondeposit sources of funds. In addition, the requirements applied to Edge corporations and to the U.S. branches and agencies of foreign banks whose foreign parents had worldwide banking assets over $1 billion.

The marginal reserve requirements were designed to stop the large banks from managing their liabilities so as to avoid the impact of tight monetary policy. The policy met with apparent success in the fourth quarter. Bank credit increased at only a 3.9 percent annual rate, as all the managed liabilities of the banks showed low or negative growth. The Federal Reserve Board's Senior Loan Officer Opinion Survey on Bank Lending Practices indicated that, as of November 15, 1979, banks had tightened their price and nonprice terms of lending.[3] In addition, M_1 grew at only a 3.1 percent annual rate in the fourth quarter.

Inflationary expectations, however, were more difficult to eradicate. Although the rate of growth of the GNP price deflator slowed slightly in the fourth quarter, the growth rate of the consumer price index increased. Moreover, energy prices rose due to a further increase in the price of oil. The Soviet invasion of Afghanistan and the Iranian hostage situation raised the possibility of a defense buildup and kindled inflationary expectations. They also increased uncertainty and fueled additional speculation in the commodity futures markets in November and December.

As 1980 began, inflation began to accelerate further. The consumer price index increased by (an annual rate of) almost 17 percent in January, and the GNP price deflator jumped sharply. What was especially significant about these price increases, though, was that they were broadly based. Unlike 1979, they were not due primarily to special circumstances resulting in increases in the prices of food, energy, and real estate.

Also, at the beginning of the year, the Administration announced a $16 billion deficit for the coming fiscal year. Since a deficit had not been expected, this announcement added to inflationary fears. Moreover, the recession that had been anticipated in 1979 did not seem to be materializing.

All these developments combined to create a situation in which fears of inflation were building rapidly. The Federal Reserve Bank of New York summarized the situation succinctly: "Early in 1980, inflationary expectations exploded."[4]

The inflationary fears led to a marked increase in borrowing in anticipation of further price increases. Borrowing also increased dramatically to finance silver speculation (see below). In addition, as profits continued their sharp decline and as expenditures for plant and equipment increased, the financing gap increased. In the first quarter of 1980 it reached (an annual rate of) $62.7 billion, its highest level since the second quarter of 1974.

Bank credit, which had decelerated to a 3.9 percent annual rate of growth in the fourth quarter of 1979, increased to a 10.6 percent annual rate in the first quarter of 1980. Moreover, total loans grew at an 11.6 percent rate, and business loans at 15.7 percent.

The monetary aggregates began to increase rapidly in February, despite tight control over nonborrowed reserves by the Federal Open Market Committee. In the December 1979 to March 1980 period, M_1 grew at a 6.2 percent annual rate, even though nonborrowed reserves declined at an annual rate of 17.0 percent.

In this situation banks were borrowing heavily at the discount window. Borrowings rose sharply in the first quarter of 1980. On February 15th, the Federal Reserve Board again increased the discount rate a full percentage point—from 12 to 13 percent.

In the environment of inflationary expectations and heavy demands for credit, interest rates rose to unprecedented levels. It was not only short-term rates that increased sharply; long-term rates also shared in the general rise.

The dramatic increase in interest rates played havoc with the financial system. Investors in the bond markets faced enormous potential capital losses on their holdings and became quite reluctant to commit any further funds long-term.

For example, the life insurance industry, which is one of the main suppliers of funds to the mortgage and corporate bond markets, was caught in a serious bind. At the same time that the value of its long-term bond portfolio was declining, it was having to pay increased costs for its liabilities. Policyholders were deserting their traditional whole-life insurance policies in droves for lower-cost term insurance, and investing the difference in high-yielding money market certificates at depository institutions or in money market mutual funds. The liabilities which the life insurance industry had considered to be stable and long-term were becoming short-term and very expensive. In addition, policyholders were taking advantage of below-market rates that were fixed by regulation on policy loans. In some cases life insurance companies suffering from liquidity problems had to sell long-term bonds at a loss.

In addition, some institutions and individuals who had speculated on lower interest rates got badly burned as rates increased dramatically in early 1980. One of the biggest losers was the First Pennsylvania Bank, which had invested heavily in long-term bonds and had financed its investments with short-term purchased funds.[5] In April, First Pennsylvania was the recipient of loans from the government and a group of banks; this aid was significant in helping First Pennsylvania to survive.

The savings and loan associations (S&Ls) also ran into trouble because of a mismatch between long-term assets and short-term liabilities. However, the troubles of the S&Ls were not due to speculation, but to an asset-liability structure arising from a commitment to financing home ownership that was not designed to cope with an environment of high and volatile interest rates.

The problem of disintermediation faced by the thrifts in earlier periods of high interest rates had been eased somewhat this time by the use of retail money market certificates (which had been introduced in 1978). However, the high cost of this source of funds led to large operating losses for many S&Ls. (See the next two chapters for more discussion of the problems of the thrifts.)

The commercial banks did not have the same problems as the thrifts with low-yielding, long-term assets. However, the cost of their purchased funds was escalating rapidly. Also, as interest rates on consumer loans bumped into ceilings established by state usury laws, consumer lending became less and less profitable.

Charge-offs of loans by commercial banks, which had been falling ever since the 1974–75 recession, began to increase in 1980. The decline in asset quality reflected the troubles that high interest rates and declining profitability had inflicted upon both the consumer and business sectors. Consumers ran into trouble when real disposable personal income failed to keep up with the rapid increase in debt. Similarly, in the nonfinancial corporate sector, high interest rates and declining profitability sent business bankruptcies up and interest coverage ratios down.

Many firms, in need of funds and apprehensive about their ability to obtain them in the extremely volatile environment that existed in early 1980, sharply increased their loan commitments at commercial banks. Total bank commitments for commercial and industrial loans increased by 45.9 percent from January to March 1980.

Thus, in March, the financial environment appeared to be deteriorating rapidly. On March 14, 1980 the administration announced a program designed to arrest the unfavorable developments. The most significant aspect of the program was the authorization by the president for the Federal Reserve Board to restrict and control the extension of credit. This authority was granted by the Credit Control Act of 1969, which the president used for the first time.

Accordingly, the Federal Reserve Board took a number of actions on March 14th. First of all, it increased the marginal reserve requirements on managed liabilities to 10 percent from the 8 percent level which it had established in October 1979. In addition, it extended these requirements to nonmember banks, which had not been covered under the October regulations. The Board also established a 3 percent surcharge to the discount rate on frequent borrowings at the discount window by large member banks (those with deposits of more than $500 million).

To restrain the increase in consumer credit, the Federal Reserve Board required lenders to meet a special deposit requirement of 15 percent on all consumer credit extended through credit cards, check-credit overdraft plans, unsecured personal loans, and secured credit when the proceeds are not used to finance the collateral. These regulations were applied to all consumer lenders, not just depository institutions. Money market funds were also required to maintain special deposits equal to 15 percent of the net increases in their assets after March 14, 1980.

Finally, a very important part of the Federal Reserve Board actions was a voluntary credit restraint program. Under this program banking institutions and finance companies were asked to limit their lending to U.S. borrowers in 1980 to an increase of between 6 and 9 percent (consistent with the FOMC's targeted ranges for 1980 for M_2 and bank credit). They also were asked to avoid lending for speculative and purely financial purposes (but not to place special restrictions on credit for small businesses, farmers, homebuilders and homebuyers, and auto dealers and buyers).

The banks' response to these actions was to decrease their lending sharply. New loan growth quickly dried up, and for the second quarter as a whole, total loans decreased by 6.5 percent. Business loans fell by only 4.6 percent, though, as banks attempted to maintain lending relationships with their best customers and to honor requests for takedowns of existing loan commitments.

Consumer loans were more severely restricted, however. Since specific restrictions on consumer credit were included in the Federal Reserve Board's regulations, and since state usury laws had made much consumer lending unprofitable in any event, there were definite incentives for the banks to limit their credit in this area.

The abrupt cutoff of consumer credit helped to throw the economy into a tailspin. Real GNP declined at an annual rate of 9.4 percent in the second quarter, after increasing at a 1.9 percent rate in the first quarter. The National Bureau of Economic Research dates the beginning of the 1980 recession in January, but the rapid decline in production and employment did not begin until March.

Another aspect of the Federal Reserve Board's announcement on March 14th had important implications for the financial system: its request that banks refrain from making loans for speculative purposes. Although a similar injunction had been made a part of the Board's actions in October 1979, it had been largely ignored by the banks. This time it was clear that a good deal more leverage would be applied by the Federal Reserve if its "voluntary" guidelines on credit were not followed.

The limitation on lending to finance speculation was an important step in a complicated series of events that led to a financial crisis centered around the silver futures market in late March 1980. The Securities and Exchange Commission summarized the situation as follows:

> For six days late in March 1980 it appeared to government
> officials, Wall Street and the public at large that a default by
> a single family on its obligations in the plummeting silver

market might seriously disrupt the U.S. financial system.[6]

However, to understand these events it is necessary to trace some of the history of the involvement of Bunker and Herbert Hunt in this market prior to March 1980.

The Hunt brothers, Bunker and Herbert, are sons of the late H. L. Hunt. They first became interested in silver in 1973, although their involvement accelerated rapidly in 1979. As Herbert Hunt told Congress in 1980:

> I began purchasing silver futures contracts and silver bullion
> in 1973. At that time, New York spot prices for silver for
> the year 1973 averaged $2.55 per ounce. . . .
>   In early 1979, I became convinced that the economy of
> the United States was in a weakening condition. This rein-
> forced my belief that investment in precious metals was
> wise, and because of the rampant inflation, I felt the value of
> soft currency was in jeopardy. I did invest substantially in
> silver futures contracts.[7]

The Hunt brothers did indeed invest substantially in silver futures contracts, and also other silver-related assets. Information subpoenaed by the House Committee on Government Operations indicates that, as of August 1, 1979, Bunker Hunt owned directly 20.9 million ounces of silver bullion and silver coins, and 9,228 silver futures contracts. Since each futures contract was for 5,000 ounces of silver, the 9,228 contracts enabled him to control an additional 46.1 million ounces. His brother Herbert also owned 20.9 million ounces of silver, and an additional 4,391 futures contracts.[8]

The Hunts were able to control this vast amount of silver with a relatively small investment. With silver selling for approximately $9 per ounce at the beginning of August, each futures contract allowed a purchaser to buy $45,000 worth of silver at a specified date in the future. Yet the holder of the futures contract did not have to put up anywhere near this $45,000. All that was required was an initial payment, called "margin," which at the time was only $2,000 per contract. The margin payment is deposited with the speculator's broker as a kind of insurance payment in case the speculator suffers losses.

The trouble comes, however, if in fact price movements do go against the holder of futures contracts. Then he is subjected to "margin calls." These are additional payments to cover the potential losses. For example, suppose someone had a contract to sell silver at $9 an ounce and the price increased to $10 an ounce. He would be subject to a potential loss of $5,000 and also would be subject to a margin call from his broker, since his initial margin would not be sufficient to cover the loss. These additional payments must be made every day, because the broker must "clear" his accounts every day and is responsible to the clearing-house for his customers' losses.

In the case of the Hunts, however, the increase in the price of silver made additional profits for them, since they had contracts to buy silver. When the holder of a contract to sell silver met his margin call, his broker would give his payment to the clearinghouse which would then credit the account of the Hunts' broker. In this way the Hunts were able to pyramid their holdings and to increase their position substantially without additional investment. Although they did take delivery on some silver, for the most part they "rolled their position forward," i.e., they took their profits on their contracts and used the proceeds to buy additional futures contracts.

The Hunts' practice of always holding more contracts to buy than to sell silver is what is called a net "long" position in the market. Those who held more contracts to sell than to buy took a net "short position." Generally, dealers in silver bullion, and producers, distributors, and processors of silver who maintain substantial stocks of silver will go short in the futures markets in order to hedge their supplies of silver against a decrease in price. On the other hand, speculators like the Hunts are in the market hoping to profit by correctly predicting the future movement of the price of silver. Although speculators can go short if they expect the price to fall, the Hunts always maintained a long position, reflecting their belief that the price of silver was going to continue to increase.

Of course, the massive purchases of silver and silver futures contracts by the Hunts influenced the price in an upward direction. In addition, there is evidence to indicate that the Hunts, by August of 1979, had convinced a number of wealthy Arab investors to buy heavily in the silver futures markets.[9] This Saudi Arabian money entered the market in the late summer and early fall of 1979 and helped to drive the price of silver up. From the beginning of August to the third week in October the price of silver went from $9 an ounce to over $17 an ounce.

In addition, in July 1979 a new corporation, named International Metals Investment Co., Ltd. (IMIC), began buying silver futures contracts. By the end of August, IMIC had a net long position of 8,400 futures contracts. On September 24, 1979 Bunker Hunt confirmed to the staff of the Commodity Futures Trading Commission (the government agency responsible for regulating the commodity futures markets) that he and his brother owned interests in IMIC and participated in its trading decisions. The other owners were two Saudi Arabians, Sheikh Ali Bin Mussalam and Sheikh Mohammed Aboud Al-Amoudi, and the Profit Investment Company, a recently formed Delaware corporation owned by the Hunts.[10]

On October 25, 1979, the staff of the Commodity Futures Trading Commission (CFTC) estimated that the Hunts owned "perhaps as much as half" of the silver stocks being traded on the two major exchanges—the Commodity Exchange in New York (Comex) and the Chicago Board of Trade (CBOT).[11] This estimate did not include the silver controlled by the Hunts' Saudi Arabian allies.

It began to appear that the Hunts were trying to "corner" the silver market. In this type of maneuver, a speculator, or group of speculators, owns so much silver bullion and so many long future contracts that there is not enough silver for the "shorts" to obtain in order to meet their contractual obligations to sell silver.

For the "shorts" to obtain silver, they must then buy it from the speculator who has cornered the market and who is in a position to dictate the price.

Such attempts at manipulating the market are illegal. Nonetheless, the CFTC did not take action in 1979 because the commission members were divided over whether or not the Hunts were trying to corner the market and they felt that such an assertion could be very difficult to prove.[12]

The two exchanges are also supposed to regulate the actions of market participants. They were also reluctant to interfere with the market, but they did raise margin requirements. For example, at the Chicago Board of Trade margins were increased, in a series of steps, up to $30,000 (for more than 250 contracts) by the end of October; margin was raised to $50,000 at New York's Comex.[13] These actions, however, while protested by the Hunts, did not significantly affect them. Although they did borrow more money to finance the higher margin payments, profits from their long contracts generally enabled them to pay the initial margin on new contracts. Also, they were not subject to any margin calls as long as the price of silver kept going up.

On October 25, 1979 the Chicago Board of Trade established position limits of 600 contracts for each trader. This action meant that no individual could hold more than 600 net futures contracts; any excess had to be liquidated by April 1, 1980. Although the CBOT's new rule did affect the Hunts, they responded by moving more of their business to New York. Comex did not set position limits in October.

After remaining fairly stable in November, the price of silver began an extraordinary rise in December. On November 30, 1979 it was at $18.77 per ounce; by January 3, 1980, it stood at $38.40 per ounce.[14] By the end of December the CFTC was very worried about the rise in price and the amount of silver controlled by the Hunts. Their report states the following:

> The Commission was concerned that the cash and futures positions of these few large speculators had become too large relative to the size of the U.S. and world silver markets. Commissioners noted that futures markets were neither designed nor intended to be substitutes for the cash market for a commodity and that the futures market—and perhaps even the world cash market—might no longer be capable of supplying the large quantities of physical silver then being demanded.[15]

Under the increasing pressure, the Comex established position limits of 500 contracts on January 7, 1980. This rule change put more pressure on the Hunts and their allies. However, they responded by opening more accounts under different names and by preparing to take delivery on some of their silver contracts. The price of silver kept on rising.

One transaction that the Hunts undertook in this period was an "exchange of futures for physicals" (EFP) with the Engelhard Mineral and Chemicals Corporation. Under the terms of this deal, the Hunts agreed to buy 19 million ounces of silver at $35 an ounce from Engelhard, and to cancel 3,800 of their long futures contracts with a like number of Engelhard's short contracts.

This transaction was advantageous for both parties. Engelhard, a bullion dealer, had large stocks of silver which it had hedged in the futures market by going short. It was in dire straits on January 14th, when this transaction was undertaken, because the increasing price of silver had subjected the company to continued margin calls. When their short contracts were canceled, the pressure on them was relieved. The Hunts also benefited by being able to buy even more bullion at an attractive price (silver was trading at $42.50 an ounce on January 14th). The deal was to be completed on March 31, 1980.

By Friday, January 18, 1980, the price of silver went over the $50 mark. It reached $50.36 an ounce on Comex and $52.50 an ounce on the CBOT. On Monday, January 21, 1980 the Comex delayed its opening until 1:30 p.m. and announced that from then on, trading would be for liquidation only. On January 22nd the CBOT took similar action. These drastic steps meant that the Hunts could no longer continue to increase their long position in futures contracts. There were no longer any buyers; the wild increase in the price of silver had come to an end.

The price of silver began to fall. It fell primarily because of the rule change, but also because the dollar had strengthened in foreign-exchange markets and because the high price of silver had encouraged compensating shifts in supply and demand. Industrial users of silver looked for alternative processes that could employ substitute materials, refineries increased their production of silver, and individuals began selling silver possessions for their cash value.

From its peak on January 18th, the price of silver slumped sharply in late January and early February, to approximately $35 an ounce. It stabilized briefly and then began to fall sharply again in mid-March.

As the price went down, the Hunts had to meet margin calls. Given their immense holdings of futures contracts, the total amounts were staggering, even for people as wealthy as the Hunts. The Hunts could have reduced their margin calls by selling off their futures contracts, but they resisted this course of action. They also showed no interest in selling their vast hordes of bullion. Of course, such selling would have driven the price of silver down even further, but in January and February it was still at such high levels that they probably could have counted their profits in the billions of dollars.

Moreover, the Hunts did not try to squeeze, or "corner" the silver futures market in December 1979, although they probably were in a position to have done so. The Hunts contended that they never had an interest in manipulating the silver market, that they were interested in silver only as an investment. On the other hand, Stephen Fay suggests that the Hunts tried to hold on to their silver and did not attempt to corner the silver market because they had bigger goals in mind: to create a worldwide silver cartel and permanently control the price of silver, i.e., to control silver itself.

> To attempt to corner the silver market means, I suppose, that you are greedy enough to be quite unconcerned by the disruption of a worldwide market. To wish to corner silver itself suggests a new dimension to our concept of greed.[16]

In any event, the Hunts chose to hold on to their silver and to borrow in order to cover their growing margin calls. The Federal Reserve Board has estimated that, by the end of March 1980, the Hunts' silver-related obligations amounted to the incredible sum of $1.765 billion. Not all of this total was from the banks, but a good part of it was. The Federal Reserve Board's estimates of bank lending are as follows:

> Looking just at *bank credit*, it appears that total bank credit associated with the episode probably peaked at $1.0 to $1.1 billion level in late March or early April. . . . The major increases in domestic bank credit occurred in early February when such loans rose by $350 million and between March 16 and April 1 when the aggregate domestic loans rose by more than $250 million. For the months of February and March combined, the use of domestic bank credit in connection with this situation increased by $800 million. By contrast, total business loans and total bank loans rose by $6.2 billion and $9.3 billion on a nonseasonally adjusted basis, respectively during this two month period.[17]

These figures mean that, in a period when the Federal Reserve Board was trying to control the increase in bank credit and the use of bank credit for speculative purposes, approximately 13 percent of all business loans were going to fuel the Hunts' speculation in the silver market.

It is instructive to take a closer look at this enormous borrowing. As the Hunts' primary broker, the brokerage firm of Bache Halsey Stuart Shields was responsible for paying a major share of the Hunts' margin calls. By virtue of financial information subpoenaed by the House Committee on Government Operations, the extent of the Hunts' borrowing from Bache has been made public. In these documents Nelson Bunker Hunt listed $186.8 million as the amount that he borrowed from Bache in February 1980. The total amount of borrowing that he and his brother did from Bache between October 1979 and February 1980 was $233 million.[18]

In turn Bache borrowed this $233 million from ten banks. The largest lender by far was the First National Bank of Chicago, which lent Bache $75 million.[19] Also, the Chicago bank had lent the Hunts directly an additional $50 million.[20]

The Federal Reserve Board's tough new credit controls announced on March 14, 1980 made the continuation of this enormous borrowing more difficult. Accordingly, as the price of silver continued to drop in March, the Hunts had difficulty meeting their margin calls. Finally, on March 25th the Hunts indicated to Bache that they could pay no further margin calls. The inability of the Hunts to pay their margin calls put Bache in a very tenuous position. The CFTC reported the following:

> On the morning of March 26, the Commission's Office of the General Counsel received a telephone call from an attorney who stated that he represented a client involved in the futures markets in New York (which later was identified as Bache). The attorney warned of the possible existence of a market emergency and requested that the Commissioners remain available all day. The Commission and most of the senior staff members were appearing at Senate appropriation hearings that morning. Bache apparently had also been contacting other senior officials in Washington, including Chairman Paul Volcker of the Board of Governors of the Federal Reserve System (''FRB''), who requested an urgent meeting with Chairman Stone that afternoon.
>
> The Commission's Division of Trading and Markets was informed at approximately 1:15 p.m. that the Hunts had failed, for the first time, to meet their margin calls at Bache. On the evening of Tuesday, March 25, 1980, Bache advised Mr. W. H. Hunt that additional margin of $135,000,000 was required. Mr. Hunt reportedly advised Bache by telephone that he was unable to meet the margin call and acquiesced in the Bache position that it would begin immediately to liquidate collateral held for the Hunt accounts. Bache informed the Division that the Hunts' activity and positions in silver futures were so substantial that daily margin calls in excess of $10,000,000 had been commonplace.[21]

Bache indicated to the CFTC and to Chairman Volcker of the Federal Reserve Board that the silver futures markets should be closed. They feared that, if they were forced to liquidate the silver holdings of the Hunts in order to meet their margin calls, they would be faced with the prospect of bankruptcy. The reasons were explained by the Federal Reserve Board as follows:

As the amount of Hunt obligations became apparent to the
Federal Reserve late in March, the immediate concern of the
Federal Reserve and that of other government agencies related to the potential implications of the situation for the financial markets generally. Those concerns reflected not only the
situation in the silver market but the uneasiness that characterized markets in general at that time. While all of these obligations were secured, the collateral in most cases was silver. And, as the price of silver declined, the margin on such
loans became very thin and in some cases the value of the
collateral actually fell below the amount of the loans. Thus,
in the extreme, the creditors were faced with the prospect of
recouping their funds by forced liquidation of silver that
could, from their viewpoint, further undermine the value of
the collateral and accentuate their risk. And, in these circumstances, there was always the threat that a localized problem
could quickly spill over to affect other institutions and markets. [22]

Bache was perhaps the broker in the most trouble, but the failure of the
Hunts to pay their margin calls would put pressure on other brokers as well.
Moreover, the situation also had implications for the banking system. In view of
the large exposure of the First National Bank of Chicago to both Bache and the
Hunts, and in view of the difficulties of the bank stemming from interest-rate
mismatches, the continued viability of that institution—the ninth largest bank in
the country—was threatened.

Moreover, as mentioned earlier, at this time the First Pennsylvania Bank
was close to failure. The threat to the entire banking system of two big banks in
trouble at the same time was serious indeed, especially given the weakened
financial condition of the banking and corporate sectors at the time.

There were also serious problems if the markets were closed. Then the
brokers and banks would have to call for the immediate repayment of the loans
that were based upon silver collateral. Without additional bank lending the
bankruptcies could indeed be large.

It was decided that the market should stay open on Thursday. Bache liquidated 754 silver futures contracts owned by the Hunts and dumped a large volume
of stock onto the stock market. Silver prices dropped sharply, to a low point of
$10.40 per ounce, and the stock market dropped 32 points. However, an hour
before closing, the market rallied and closed down only two points for the
day. Nonetheless, Wall Street had received quite a scare during "Silver Thursday."

On Friday, March 28th, Bache sold the remaining 3,316 futures contracts
owned by the Hunts. According to Fay:

It was a gamble; it could have been the last straw for the silver market, but it was not; and by the end of trading on Friday, silver was up, settling at $12 an ounce. Bache was able to pay off the $233-million loan, and the worst of the crisis seemed to be over.[23]

However, the contract that the Hunts had made with Engelhard back on January 14th called for them to take delivery of 19 million ounces of silver on March 31st, the following Monday. The Hunts owed Engelhard $665 million for the silver, and Engelhard demanded payment.

The Hunts did not have the cash. The prospect of a default by the Hunts and a crisis loomed once again.

The Hunts appealed to the banks for an additional loan to pay Engelhard. The banks refused. However, a crisis was averted on Monday when Engelhard agreed at the last minute (five o'clock in the morning) to accept some oil properties of the Hunts as payment for their obligation.

A default by the Hunts was still a possibility, however. There still remained the approximately 1 billion dollars that the Hunts owed to the banks, most of which had been negotiated at the very high interest rates that prevailed in the first quarter of 1980. While the Hunts were worth many times that sum, they were still short of cash and unwilling to sell their silver.

The situation was resolved when a consortium of banks agreed to renegotiate the Hunts' loans and stretch them out over a ten-year period. Although the banks were uninterested in silver as collateral, they did agree to accept substantial oil, gas, and other assets of the Placid Oil Company, a Hunt-owned organization.

On May 1, 1980, the loan of $1.1 billion was made between thirteen banks and the Placid Oil Company. The Placid Oil Company, in turn, lent the money to the Hunts.

Criticism of the loan was offered from some members of Congress and other parties, who termed it a bail-out of the wealthy Hunt brothers. The loan agreement, though, did contain a clause stipulating that the Hunt brothers could not use the proceeds of the loan to support any renewed speculative activities. It also specified that the Hunts' remaining silver position be liquidated in an orderly manner.

In view of the threat to the financial system, the Federal Reserve did not object to the loan. Thus the silver crisis of 1980 came to an end.

8

The 1982 Crisis

A financial crisis developed again in 1982. This time it centered around a crisis of confidence in the nation's commercial banks, which were threatened by losses on outstanding loans to U.S. businesses and less developed countries (LDCs). Adding to the financial strains in 1982 were the problems of the thrift institutions and the financial manipulations of a small Wall Street government securities firm.

The events of 1982 in turn were influenced by economic conditions during 1980 and 1981. It is to an understanding of these conditions that we now turn.

Like the recession in 1974–75, the recession in 1980 was very steep. Real GNP declined at an annual rate of over 9 percent in the second quarter. The sharp decline in economic activity led to reduced demands for credit. As a result, interest rates dropped abruptly from the lofty peaks they had attained in March. Corporations used the opportunity of lower long-term rates to lengthen the maturity of their outstanding debt.

However, this "window" of lower long-term rates was quite brief. To the surprise of nearly every forecaster, the trough of the recession was reached in July, and the economy began to recover in the third quarter. Real GNP increased steadily, and by the first quarter of 1981 it was expanding at an 8.7 percent annual rate.

With the increase in economic activity, prices again began to accelerate. The GNP price deflator increased at an annual rate of 10.9 percent in the fourth quarter of 1980 and 10.2 percent in the first quarter of 1981. Apparently inflationary expectations were quick to assert themselves after the brief recession of 1980.

The nonfinancial corporate sector increased its use of external funds in the fourth quarter of 1980, as the financing gap began to widen. Although the rise in stock prices in the second half of 1980 enabled corporations to increase their issuance of equity, they relied primarily upon bank loans. Business loans at commercial banks rose at an annual rate of 18.2 percent in the second half of 1980.

However, the reserves of commercial banks were under strong pressure during this period. The increase in prices and the reemergence of inflationary expectations prompted the Federal Open Market Committee (FOMC) to tighten monetary policy sharply.

Nonborrowed reserves—now the operating target of the FOMC—increased at only a 2 percent annual rate in the last half of 1980. In contrast, nonborrowed reserves had increased by a 35.2 percent annual rate in the second quarter.

The commercial banks attempted to make their meager reserves support more loans by relying on purchased funds, especially negotiable certificates of deposit. They also stepped up their borrowing at the discount window.

The pressure on bank reserves resulted in a sharp increase in the federal funds rate and other short-term rates. Also, on September 25th the Federal Reserve Board raised the discount rate by a full percentage point, to 11 percent. It also approved two additional increases of 1 percent in 1980, on November 14th and December 4th. In slightly over two months, the discount rate had risen by three percentage points. The federal funds rate had risen by over nine percentage points in four months; by December it had reached the unprecedented level of 19 percent. The prime rate passed the 20 percent mark in December.

In addition to raising the discount rate, the Federal Reserve Board on November 14th also imposed a 2 percent surcharge on frequent borrowings at the discount window by depository institutions with $500 million or more in deposits. In December the Board increased this surcharge to 3 percent. (The surcharge imposed in March had been lifted in May, at the same time that the March credit controls began to be phased out. Credit controls were completely removed by July.)

Nonfinancial corporations reduced their need for external funds in the first quarter of 1981, even though investment in plant and equipment increased during this period. Profits of nonfinancial corporations, which usually increase in response to strong economic growth in the early stages of recovery, rose during the first quarter of 1981. Internal funds thus increased, and the financing gap fell. Short-term interest rates fell somewhat in the first quarter, although long-term rates continued to climb.

The increase in profits moderated in the second quarter, however, as the tight monetary policy had its effect on slowing the rate of growth of the economy. Real GNP hardly increased at all in the second quarter; it posted only a 0.6 percent annual rate of increase. For the first six months of 1981, the monetary aggregates, total member bank reserves, and bank credit all slowed their rates of growth in comparison with the last six months of 1980. In July 1981 the economy entered its second recession in two years.

The financing gap continued to increase in the third quarter, though, as capital expenditures hit a peak and internal funds increased only moderately. Both investment in plant and equipment spending and inventory investment posted increases in the third quarter, although they both were probably "involuntary" to some extent. Since contracts and orders for plant and equipment peaked in April 1981, the increase in plant and equipment investment spending in the third quarter most likely contained a significant component of spending that had already been committed. Also, the increase in inventory investment in the third quarter probably represented unintended inventory accumulation due to the declining economy. The inventory-sales ratio increased in both the third and fourth quarters of 1981 before turning down in 1982.

The financing gap in the last half of 1981 was funded primarily by bank loans and other relatively short-term debt. The stock market fell in the last half of 1981, and nonfinancial corporations on balance reduced their net equity outstanding. Both lenders and borrowers continued to avoid the long-term bond market.

Beginning in the fourth quarter of 1981, and especially in 1982, the capital expenditures of nonfinancial corporations declined. Real investment spending for plant and equipment decreased in the first quarter of 1982, and nonfinancial corporations began to liquidate their excess inventory stocks. Since internal funds remained relatively stable, the financing gap started to fall. By the first quarter of 1982 it had fallen to only 6 percent of capital expenditures. It reached a low of ¹17 percent in the fourth quarter of 1982.

A surprising development in the first half of 1982, though, was the continued strength of bank loans to nonfinancial corporations. Business loans by commercial banks increased by a 14.2 percent annual rate in the first two quarters of 1982; in the last two quarters of 1981, they had increased by only 7.5 percent. Moreover, the ratio of bank loans to total funds raised in markets by nonfinancial corporations remained over 50 percent through the first half of 1982. In previous recessions, this ratio had fallen much more quickly.

The Federal Reserve Board attempted to gain some insight into the reason for the continued strength of bank loans in the first half of 1982. In a special supplemental question to its Survey of Bank Lending Practices conducted on August 15, 1982, the Board asked senior loan officers at a sample of sixty banks whether or not they had experienced strong demands for business loans over the past three months even though inventories had run off and plant and equipment spending had weakened.[1]

Of the sixty banks, thirty-three banks reported that they had experienced strong demands for business loans. The demand was primarily at large banks. Of the twenty-seven banks questioned with domestic assets of over $5 billion, twenty-one (78 percent) reported in the affirmative. Of the remaining thirty-three banks, those with domestic assets of less than $5 billion, only twelve (36 percent) reported strong business loan demands.

The thirty-three banks experiencing strong loan demands were asked the reasons for this strength. The vast majority, twenty-eight banks (85 percent), mentioned weakened cash flow on the part of business borrowers. The same number thought that business borrowers were substituting bank loans for other types of financing.

The twenty-eight banks that thought bank loans were being substituted for other types of financing were asked to specify these other forms of financing.

Twenty-seven of the twenty-eight banks, or 93 percent—mentioned long-term financing. Commercial paper borrowing was mentioned by seventeen banks (59 percent), while trade credit was noted by nine.

The sixty banks were also asked if there had been a change over the past three months in the financial condition of customers who had commercial and industrial loans outstanding. Nearly 90 percent, fifty-three banks, reported that there had been; the remaining seven banks reported no change. Of the twenty-seven banks with domestic assets of over $5 billion, twenty-six reported a deterioration in their business customers' financial condition.

Other evidence also demonstrates the poor financial condition of the business sector during the first half of 1982. Profits before tax for nonfinancial corporations had fallen to slightly more than 9 percent of total nonfinancial corporate domestic income—a figure comparable to the low point previously reached in 1974. After-tax profits also declined, but they fared relatively better than before-tax profits due to the substantial decline in corporate income taxes in 1982.

However, because of the back-to-back recessions, profit levels had been generally subpar ever since 1979. This poor overall performance, together with the high interest rates of the 1980–82 period and the sustained short-term borrowing, had brought measures of corporate financial condition to a postwar low.

The liquidity ratio remained depressed, showing no gains from the low point it had attained in 1979. The ratio of nonfinancial corporate total debt outstanding to the market value of equity actually decreased for 1982 as a whole. However, this ratio, reflecting annual data, undoubtedly was influenced by the strong stock market rally in the last half of 1982. Using the more traditional debt-equity ratio based upon historical cost, we find that this ratio, too, reached a new high in 1982. The worsening financial condition of the business sector was reflected in 1982 in a record number of bankruptcies.

It also had an adverse effect on the commercial banking sector. Many banks responded to the inability of some business customers to make timely interest and principal payments on their commercial and industrial loans by restructuring payments, i.e., by extending the maturity of the loan, capping or deferring interest payments, or both. In the Survey of Bank Lending Practices for August 15, 1982 referred to above, 83 percent of the banks reporting a deterioration in the financial condition of their business borrowers resorted to some type of restructuring of payments. In addition, many also increased collateral, if possible, and took other measures, such as a closer monitoring of conditions and increased involvement by senior management.

However, these responses could not prevent the losses on commercial and industrial loans at commercial banks from rising sharply in 1982. Total net charge-offs for all categories of loans jumped sharply in 1982; at the same time charge-offs of commercial and industrial loans increased even more substantially. They grew by 128 percent from 1981 to 1982, and increased from 53 percent of total charge-offs in 1981 to 67 percent in 1982. Net charge-offs of commercial and industrial loans as a percentage of total commercial and industrial loans outstanding also increased dramatically, going from 0.36 percent in 1981 to 0.74 percent in 1982.[2]

Another measure of the quality of bank loans is the amount of nonperforming loans, i.e., those loans on which interest or principal payments are not being made in timely fashion. Data for nonperforming loans are not available by category of loan before 1982, so it is not possible to make specific comparisons for commercial and industrial loans in particular. However, for all loans, data from the largest twenty-five bank holding companies (which control approximately 45 percent of the assets of all U.S. commercial banks) indicate that nonperforming assets increased by 77 percent from 1981 to 1982. In addition, the ratio of nonperforming assets to total loans outstanding increased from 1.9 percent in 1981 to 3.1 percent in 1982.[3]

As would be expected, the deterioration in the quality of the banks' assets had an adverse effect on their income; the income of all insured commercial banks fell continuously from its previous peak in 1979 through 1982.

Although bank liquidity and bank capital ratios improved slightly in 1982, it is clear that banks were under substantial financial pressure. There were thirty-four commercial bank failures in 1982. This total was by far the largest of any previous year since World War II. For every year in this period except for 1975 and 1976 total bank failures amounted to ten or fewer.[4]

Thrift Institutions

The commercial banks were not the only depository institutions in financial trouble in this period. The thrift institutions—savings and loan associations (S&Ls) and mutual savings banks—were also having their difficulties. For the thrifts, however, and particularly the S&Ls, the source of the difficulty had less to do with deteriorating credit quality and more to do with their basic role in financing long-term mortgages in a time of high and rising interest rates.

The previous discussion of the events of 1966 highlighted the problems of the S&Ls in an earlier period of rising interest rates. Then they were threatened with disintermediation. Depositors found that they could obtain a higher return on their money by withdrawing their funds from the S&Ls and investing them directly in various money market instruments. The S&Ls could not prevent this withdrawal of funds because of the existence of legal ceiling rates on the amount of interest they were allowed to pay on deposits. The S&Ls faced serious liquidity problems in 1966, and also in subsequent periods of rising interest rates.

Partly to help the S&Ls and other thrift institutions cope with the problem of disintermediation, a substantial deregulation of interest rates was put into effect in the late 1970s and early 1980s. As was discussed in the previous chapter, retail money market certificates were authorized in 1978. Other accounts were introduced which also allowed the S&Ls to pay a market rate of interest on their deposits.

However, it turned out that in the high interest period of 1980–82, these actions substituted one problem for another. Now the thrifts were no longer threatened with disintermediation. Nevertheless, the unprecedented levels to which short-term interest rates climbed in this period meant that their sources of funds were enormously expensive. At the same time the interest income from their long-term mortgages, which had been issued in a period of much lower interest rates, was grossly inadequate to cover the rising cost of their liabilities.

As a result, the income of thrift institutions was adversely affected. Net income as a percentage of average assets declined sharply in 1980, and it became strongly negative in 1981. The aggregate rates of return for thrift institutions had never before been negative in the entire postwar period.

As the operating losses of the thrifts climbed, their net worth began to deteriorate. The ratio of net worth to total assets for all savings and loan associations insured by the Federal Savings and Loan Insurance Corporation (FSLIC) dropped to 4.23 percent in 1981 and to 3.44 percent in the first nine months of 1982. In previous years this ratio had been well over 5 percent. In addition, as of midyear 1982, approximately 500 savings and loans had ratios of net worth to total assets of less than 2 percent.[5]

Many savings and loans were no longer economically or financially viable. The Federal Home Loan Bank Board (FHLBB) encouraged a policy of mergers of these troubled associations into stronger institutions. Altogether the FHLBB approved 296 mergers in 1981 and 425 mergers in 1982. There were more than 483 associations that ceased to exist in 1982. Of the 425 mergers, 215 were voluntary, 166 were supervisory (i.e., required by the FHLBB to prevent bankruptcy), and 44 received financial assistance from the FSLIC.[6] Advances by the FHLBB to savings and loan associations increased sharply in 1981 and 1982 to approximately 65 million dollars.[7]

No significant runs developed on the deposits of thrift institutions during this period (in contrast to 1984–85). However, by the beginning of 1982 a significant degree of nervousness had developed about the financial viability of the thrifts and also about the adequacy of the insurance funds that stood behind the thrifts' deposits. There was concern particularly about the adequacy of the reserves of the FSLIC, which insures deposits in savings and loan associations. The insurer of the mutual savings banks, the Federal Deposit Insurance Corporation (FDIC), was perceived to have more adequate resources.

To allay these fears, and to help prevent any runs on S&Ls from developing, the Congress, in March 1982, passed a joint resolution in support of the FSLIC. The resolution boosted public confidence in the safety of deposits in S&Ls by stating that the full faith and credit of the government of the United States stood behind the resources of the FSLIC and FDIC.

Another series of measures designed partly to boost confidence in S&Ls

was introduced by the regulatory agencies, the FHLBB and the FSLIC. These measures were essentially accounting innovations designed to boost the reported profitability and net worth position of the S&Ls. They included innovations such as income capital certificates, "contra-assets," "appraised equity capital," "purchase accounting," and "phoenix" mergers.[8] In addition to improving the appearance of the balance sheets of the S&Ls, these accounting techniques gave the regulatory authorities flexibility and added time to respond to the industry's problems.

The most significant development that improved the fortunes of the S&Ls, however, was the drop in interest rates that took place in the second half of 1982. By reducing the thrifts' cost of funds, the decline in interest rates helped to relieve the intense pressure on earnings. It provided real, not cosmetic, relief for thrift institutions. The immediate crisis had passed—although it would return (see Chapter 9).

Steps that attempted to deal with the long-term problems of the thrifts were taken later on in the year with the passage of the Garn-St. Germain Depository Institutions Act of 1982. This law continues the deregulation of the thrifts' liabilities; it authorizes the thrifts (and commercial banks) to issue money market deposit accounts to compete with the highly successful money market mutual funds. However, it also takes steps toward deregulating the assets of the thrifts. It allows the thrifts to increase their proportion of consumer and business loans and removes some constraints on the kinds of investments that thrifts are allowed to make. The law also expands the amount of financial assistance that the FSLIC and FDIC can provide to thrift institutions, and allows troubled thrifts to be merged with institutions in other states and in other industries (e.g., commercial banks) in emergency situations.

The worst problems of the thrifts were overcome without the situation ever reaching the point of destabilizing and sudden depositor runs or disruptions to financial markets. However, the same cannot be said for other events during 1982. Before the year was finished, three crises appeared, more acute than the problem of the thrifts, which threatened the stability of the financial system and created a serious crisis of confidence in the nation's commercial banks. These three crises involved Drysdale Government Securities, Inc., Penn Square National Bank, and international lending by multinational banks.

Drysdale Government Securities, Inc.

The Drysdale incident was the first to make the headlines. On May 17, 1982 it was learned that this small government securities trading firm owed the Chase Manhattan Bank $160 million in interest payments on borrowed government securities and could not meet its obligation. However, to understand the complicated series of events that involved not only Chase, but also several other large banks and securities dealers, it is necessary to understand something about

Drysdale and the type of operations in which it was engaged.

Drysdale Government Securities, Inc., was incorporated on January 29, 1982 with capital of approximately $20 million. Anthony Solomon, the former president of the Federal Reserve Bank of New York, testified at a government hearing called to investigate the Drysdale incident that this capital was not large, but that it was within the normal range of those firms trading in government securities. He indicated, however, that Drysdale's "problems apparently arose because its activities were conducted on a scale out of all proportion to its capital."[9]

Drysdale's capital was at risk when it took a position, i.e., when it bought or promised to deliver securities, but this in itself was not unusual for a dealer in the government securities market. Dealers (as opposed to brokers) trade for their own account, rather than merely arrange transactions between two other parties. Neither was it unusual for a dealer to borrow to finance its position. Even in normal circumstances a dealer's position will exceed its capital base.

The primary way in which dealers borrow to finance their holdings of securities is by means of a "repurchase agreement" (RP). In an RP, the dealer sells some securities to a lender and at the same time agrees to repurchase the securities at some point in the future. RPs are usually done overnight or for several days or weeks. When the dealer repurchases the securities, he pays the lender an additional sum, which represents interest on the amount of money that the lender has advanced to the dealer. Functionally (although not legally) the transaction is equivalent to a collateralized loan, with the government securities serving as collateral.

As a protection to the lender, the money advanced is usually somewhat less than the value of the securities sold. As an additional protection to the lender, the value of the securities is measured exclusive of coupon interest accrued but not yet paid. This practice did not cause any problems as far as RPs were concerned; the trouble began when it was extended to what are called "reverse repurchase agreements."

These transactions are the same as regular RPs except that the party who initiates the transaction wants to borrow securities, not money. For example, a dealer will go to a bank and initiate a reverse RP; the bank will sell securities to the dealer, and the dealer will give the bank money. Although in this case it is still the dealer who is the borrower, the conventions established to protect the lender in the RP transactions were kept intact for the reverse RP. Thus in a reverse RP the value of the securities—including the accrued interest—that the bank sells is greater than the cash it receives.

Drysdale took advantage of this aspect of the reverse RP transactions, and the practice of "blind brokering" (see below), to dramatically expand its operations. Let us examine more closely how this came about.

Dealers wanting to finance their position in government securities would do RPs with a bank, for example Chase Manhattan Bank. Chase would then turn around and do a reverse RP with another dealer such as Drysdale. In the transaction as a whole Chase would be acting in some respects as a broker; in essence it arranged an RP between Drysdale and the other dealers. However, the practice was known as "blind brokering" because the dealers did not know the identity of the party to whom Chase resold their securities. Also, the dealers contended that they were dealing only with Chase, not a third party.

Since the Chase Manhattan Bank was one of the biggest banks in the world, the dealers did not consider that they were taking any risk. They would not have carried on such transactions with Drysdale directly, however. By doing business indirectly and by taking advantage of the accrued interest, Drysdale managed to expand its position enormously. By May 17, 1982 Drysdale was doing $3.2 billion of reverse RPs with Chase.[10]

A numerical example may make it easier to understand the procedure. Suppose the dealer sold $100 million of government securities to Chase for $96 million, agreeing to repurchase them at a later date. Assume further that before the repurchase date the value of the coupon payment that was scheduled to be made was $5 million. As noted above, this future coupon payment was not taken into account in arranging the transaction; it was considered additional security for the lender (Chase in this case). However, when the coupon payment was received by Chase, under the terms of the transaction Chase was required to relay it back to the dealer.

When Drysdale did a reverse RP with Chase, say for $97 million, Chase would sell the securities to Drysdale. Thus Chase made a profit of $1 million and the dealer's securities wound up with Drysdale. Then Drysdale would turn around and sell the securities outright. The key point is that when Drysdale sold the securities it received $100 million plus the value of the accrued interest. If the coupon date were very near, this additional money could amount to, say, $4 million.

Thus Drysdale had $104 million, $7 million more than it had at the beginning. In addition, it had an obligation to resell $100 million of government securities to Chase and to pay Chase $5 million on the date that the coupon was due, even though Drysdale no longer had the securities. (Chase, in turn, had to forward the $5 million to the dealer.)

However, Drysdale considered the $7 million an addition to its working capital. It used the money to add to its risk position. At the same time it speculated that by the time it had to buy the government securities in the market to return them to Chase, the price of the securities would have dropped (the interest rate would have risen) so that it could make a further profit.

However, interest rates went against Drysdale, and by Monday, May 17, 1982, when a coupon payment to Chase was due, its losses were so great that it informed Chase that it could not make the payment. The amount was $160 million. In addition, Drysdale had smaller obligations to two other banks, Manufacturers Hanover and United States Trust Company, that it could not meet.

Chase called the president of the Federal Reserve Bank of New York to inform him of the problem and of the potential disruption to the market. Meetings were hurriedly arranged on the premises of the Federal Reserve Bank of New York among Chase and other firms who were involved in the transactions with Drysdale. Meanwhile, tensions in the market were building:

> Rumors of the situation had spread on Monday afternoon, contributing to a substantial decline in Government securities prices. The market opened on Tuesday in a rather apprehensive and uncertain mood. By mid-morning Tuesday, Chase had confirmed its involvement with Drysdale in a public announcement which referred to $160 million in interest payments which had not been made. As awareness of the problem became widespread, other market participants became unwilling to do business or settle transactions with Drysdale.[11]

As the reaction in the market appeared to worsen on Tuesday, the Federal Reserve indicated that it was ready to intervene in its capacity as lender of last resort:

> By mid-day Tuesday the uncertainty about clearing and financing arrangements seemed to be building. There was concern that investors and traders would draw away from the markets because of uncertainty about the magnitude of the problem, and that major securities firms would be threatened with losses that could jeopardize their ability to function. At an afternoon meeting with the 12 New York Clearing House banks, the Federal Reserve told the banks that it was watching the Drysdale situation closely and stated that the Discount Window stood ready to assist commercial banks in dealing with unusual liquidity problems arising from the situation.[12]

A major sticking point in resolving the situation centered around the role of Chase and the other banks in the Drysdale transactions. Chase maintained that it was merely acting as a broker between Drysdale and the dealers who had done the repurchase agreements with Chase originally. Thus it was Drysdale, not Chase, who was liable to the dealers for the coupon payments on the dealers' securities. On the other hand, the dealers maintained that they had never done any business with Drysdale, and therefore it was Chase and the other banks that had the liability.

This aspect of the situation was resolved on Wednesday when the banks agreed to pay the interest in dispute. Chase still contended that it was not liable, but agreed to pay the interest to avoid further disruption to the market. However, there was still some concern that the Drysdale incident might tie up securities and prevent their orderly flow through the market. Gerald Corrigan, then president of the Federal Reserve Bank of Minneapolis and a major participant in the Drysdale affair (representing Federal Reserve Board Chairman Paul Volcker), indicated that there was concern over the possibility of a "gridlock situation in the market with people failing to deliver securities."[13] To forestall that possibility,

> the Federal Reserve temporarily liberalized its rules regarding the lending of securities from the Federal Reserve's portfolio. . . . Because the Drysdale default threatened a severe disruption to the orderly functioning of the market, the Federal Reserve temporarily allowed firms to borrow securities to make deliveries against short sales and lifted the restrictions on amounts that could be borrowed.[14]

By Wednesday afternoon fears in the market had died down, and it continued to function without further disruption. However, Chase's stock had fallen by $4.75 a share as of the close of trading on Wednesday. Even more damaging to confidence in the banking system was Chase's estimation that it would wind up with a $135 million after-tax loss from the Drysdale affair, a loss that would completely wipe out its earnings in the second quarter.

Penn Square Bank

The Drysdale events had barely quieted down when the nation's banking system received another major jolt: the failure of Penn Square Bank on July 6, 1982. The repercussions from the demise of this small Oklahoma bank were felt by some of the largest banks in the country, and confidence in the banking system weakened further.

Like most banks in 1982, Penn Square had suffered increased loan losses. However, Penn Square's losses were unusually large. Rather than diversify its loan portfolio, it had made most of its loans in the energy industry in Oklahoma. As the recession deepened in the first half of 1982, the oil and gas industries were particularly affected. C. T. Conover, of the Office of the Comptroller of the Currency (OCC), the agency responsible for regulating Penn Square Bank, described the bank's problems as follows:

> The bank had concentrated its loans in the Oklahoma oil and gas production industry. In late 1981 and early 1982, that industry suffered a severe and unexpected decline. Many of Penn Square's major customers began to experience financial difficulties. Rather than reducing its exposure to these firms, Penn Square extended more credit in an effort to "bail out"

its customers. In late 1981 and early 1982, the bank originated an extraordinary volume—over $800 million—in new
loans. The vast majority of those new loans were to energy-
related borrowers.

When the decline in the oil and gas industry continued
to deepen, many of the new loans became non-performing.
Loan losses greatly exceeded the bank's capital, thus, resulting in a book insolvency. Simultaneously, a severe decline in
market confidence in the bank led to a run-off of deposits
and other funding sources, thus causing a liquidity insolvency. Accordingly, the combination of a large volume of poor
quality credits and a severe downturn in economic conditions
directly resulted in the failure of the bank.[15]

As Conover notes, the bank was overzealous in its desire to increase its
loans. In its emphasis on growth, it paid less attention to loan quality. By April
1982, despite warnings from the OCC, the bank had classified assets (i.e.,
problem loans) that were more than 3.5 times its gross capital funds. In addition,
nearly 13 percent of its loans were delinquent in payment, and there were more
than 3,000 credit and collateral exceptions (problems).[16]

The difficulties created by Penn Square's failure extended far beyond this
small Oklahoma bank, however, because it was not only Penn Square that was
frantically expanding its loan portfolio. A number of other banks, including very
large ones such as Continental Illinois, had bought large loan participations from
Penn Square. Under this arrangement, Penn Square would initiate the loan and
then arrange for other banks to come in. John Lytle, who was the manager of
Continental Bank's Mid Continent Oil and Gas Division and responsible for the
oil and gas participation loans with Penn Square, described the growth of Continental's participations as follows:

The dollar amount of Continental participation and other
loans with Penn Square customers increased each year in
1979 and 1980, increased dramatically in 1981 and continued to grow in the first quarter of 1982. These are approxi-
mate numbers. As of 12/31/80, Continental's loans with
Penn Square customers were $250 million; as of 9/31/81,
$550 million; as of 12/31/81, $800 million; and as of
6/30/82, $1.056 million. This growth, in part, reflected the
boom in the Oklahoma oil and gas economy and drilling activity which continued to expand at a rapid rate until approximately May of this year. The growth also reflected the
Continental Bank's aggressive pursuit of this business.[17]

Continental Illinois's loan participations were the largest, but it was not
alone. Altogether forty-three other banks had loan participations from Penn

Square which totaled an additional $1 billion. The most prominent of these were Seattle First National Bank (Seafirst), with $400 million, Chase Manhattan Bank ($212 million), Michigan National Bank ($200 million), and Northern Trust Co. of Chicago ($125 million).[18]

The losses from these loans were significant at all of the banks involved. They contributed to Seafirst's problems, which eventually forced the Seattle bank into a merger with the Bank of America to avoid failure. The losses at Continental Illinois resulted in an unprecedented government bailout in 1984 (the subsequent problems of Seafirst and Continental Illinois are discussed in Chapter 9). During the summer of 1982, Continental Illinois had to pay a premium of as much as a full percentage point to raise funds in the certificates of deposit (CD) market.

However, it was not only Continental and the other banks directly involved that were affected. All banks had difficulty selling their CDs, as a flight to higher quality investments developed. The spread between interest rates on CDs and Treasury bills increased to over 2.5 percentage points in the week following Penn Square's failure. A credit analyst for a major money market fund was reported to have struck all but 35 of the 120 largest banks from his list of approved CD purchases.[19]

A part of the reluctance of investors to buy bank CDs stemmed from the way that the Penn Square Bank was closed. Because of the existence of possible fraud and the difficulty of accurately assessing the eventual total of the Bank's liabilities, a deposit payout was employed at Penn Square rather than the usual procedure of a purchase and assumption (P&A). Only those with insured deposits of $100,000 or less were paid off immediately.

With a P&A, another bank purchases the assets of the failed bank and assumes its liabilities. Thus no depositor loses any money, even though deposits over $100,000 are not insured. Penn Square's failure was the first time in the history of the Federal Deposit Insurance Corporation (FDIC), which was founded in 1933, that a P&A was not used for a major bank failure.

Thus depositors who had CDs over $100,000 with Penn Square were subject to losses. Credit unions were particularly affected. It turned out that there were 435 credit unions that had deposited funds with Penn Square. Of these, 140 had uninsured deposits of over $107 million, for which they obtained receiver's certificates from the FDIC for claims upon the assets eventually recovered from the Penn Square liquidation.[20]

Penn Square was able to obtain such a large amount of money from such a variety of sources because of the practice of brokered deposits. Brokers would scan the rates on CDs for banks across the country and invest their customers' money at the banks with the highest rates. There was little attention paid to possible loss on deposits over $100,000. Thus a bank like Penn Square, by simply paying a high enough rate of interest on its CDs, could obtain large amounts of money very quickly to fund its rapidly growing loan portfolio.

In the wake of the Penn Square failure, with depositors and major banks suffering large losses, the crisis of confidence in the banking system grew. A respected business publication reported that "fears are widespread that further financial shocks could trigger an institutional run on troubled banks, or even on banks rumored to be in trouble."[21]

Indeed, on July 9, 1982, just three days after Penn Square was closed, an article appeared in the *Dallas Morning News* which charged that there were problems with the energy loan portfolio of the Abilene National Bank. Out-of-state investors quickly withdrew $50 million in deposits—12 percent of the total—from the bank.[22] Abilene National denied the charges, and the Federal Reserve, in its role as lender of last resort, lent the bank $31 million. However, the bank was closed on August 9, 1982.

The Federal Reserve Board, concerned about the implication of the events surrounding Penn Square's failure for the health of the financial and banking systems, took several actions. In response to the potential liquidity needs of credit unions and others who faced large losses from Penn Square's failure, the Board announced that their receiver's certificates would be acceptable as collateral for borrowing at the discount window. In addition, at a special telephone meeting on July 15, 1982 the Federal Open Market Committee concluded that, as regards the target ranges for monetary growth,

> it would tolerate for some period of time growth somewhat
> above the target range should unusual precautionary de-
> mands for money and liquidity be evident in the light of cur-
> rent economic uncertainties.[23]

The banking system survived the Penn Square failure without further major disruptions. However, soon afterwards it was hit by what was potentially the most serious crisis of all: the debt repayment problems of the less developed countries (LDCs). In August, Mexico announced that it could no longer make its payments on loans outstanding to over 100 commercial banks.

Mexico

The threat of a default by Mexico posed a very serious problem for banks in the United States. Of the approximately $80 billion in loans that Mexico had outstanding, $24.9 billion, as of June 1982, was owed to U.S. banks.[24] In addition, the nine largest U.S. banks had loans to Mexico totaling $13.4 billion, which represented nearly 50 percent of the nine banks' total capital of $27.1 billion; of the $13.4 billion, $7.6 billion was due within one year.[25]

The adverse economic events of 1982 had affected Mexico in much the same way that they had affected the banks' borrowers in the United States. The deep recession in the United States and in other industrial countries was an important contributing factor. The demand for a broad range of Mexico's exports fell off, particularly from the United States, its main trading partner. Oil, Mexico's major export product, was particularly affected by the recession-induced decline in world demand during 1982.

High interest rates in the United States also increased Mexico's debt burden, since by 1982 a substantial portion of Mexico's debt was short-term and subject to floating interest rates. Thus increases in interest rates were quickly translated into higher interest charges on Mexico's loans.

A study on lending to developing countries by banks concluded that, since mid-1979, commercial banks'

> short-term lending to developing countries has grown rapidly, suggesting that yields on unpublicized short-maturity loans may have become somewhat more attractive. . . .
>
> The interest and participation by U.S. banks in syndicated term loans to developing countries appear to have revived since late 1980, partly because banks now face financially more attractive options to set the floating interest rate on many such loans at some margin above the prime rate in the United States rather than to link it to the interbank rates prevailing in the Eurodollar market.[26]

Furthermore, the fact that its debt was denominated in U.S. dollars put additional pressure on Mexico. By the summer of 1982 the exchange value of the U.S. dollar was in the midst of a sharp rise from its low point in 1980. The Mexican peso, tied to the dollar, was greatly overvalued in real terms. This exchange imbalance further worsened Mexico's competitiveness in world trade, thus adding to Mexico's burgeoning balance of payments deficit.

A devaluation of the peso in February 1982 failed to correct the imbalance in exchange rates. Inflation rates of close to 100 percent during the summer led to continuing massive balance of payments deficits which were covered over only by increased borrowing from multinational banks. A substantial and sustained capital flight developed as the situation worsened.

Investors in Mexico and in foreign countries converted pesos to dollars in large numbers to profit from higher real interest rates overseas. As fears mounted that the Mexican government was unable to control the soaring price level, the capital flight accelerated. Speculators anticipating a second devaluation increased the pressure on the peso.

The run on the peso made another devaluation inevitable. The Mexican government allowed the peso to float to a new trading level on August 5, 1982. However, this action failed to stop the continuing capital flight.

Nervous bankers apparently refused to continue to lend money to Mexico. *The New York Times* reported that, after August 5th, "foreign bankers promptly put away their checkbooks.''²⁷ This decision brought the crisis to a head. In desperation, Mexico imposed temporary exchange controls and appealed to the United States for aid.

On Thursday, August 12, 1982, the Mexican government, in addition to temporarily closing foreign exchange markets, declared that all foreign-currency bank accounts in Mexico would be convertible only to pesos. In addition, the government made it illegal to take U.S. dollars out of Mexico without specific permission.

That weekend, Finance Minister Jesus Silva Herzog flew to Washington to meet with officials from the Federal Reserve Board and the International Monetary Fund. He told officials there that Mexico could no longer pay its debt to foreign banks, that it needed emergency aid, and that at least part of the estimated $40 billion in interest and principal payments due within the next twelve months would have to be postponed.²⁸

Over the weekend of August 14–15 the United States granted Mexico $2 billion in emergency credits. Advance payments were made by the Department of Energy for $1 billion worth of Mexican oil, and the United States Commercial Commodity Corporation granted $1 billion for grain imports from the United States. In addition, a $1.5 billion ''bridge'' loan was arranged from the Bank for International Settlements, an organization made up of central banks from the major industrial countries.

On Friday, August 20, 1982, Mexican officials met at the Federal Reserve Bank of New York with representatives of over 100 banks from around the world to consider a restructuring of Mexico's foreign debt. The agreement that was finally worked out included a postponement for 90 days of $10 billion in debt principal that was coming due, and $1 billion in new credits from American banks guaranteed by the U.S. government. In addition, an announcement was made that $4.5 billion of new credits from the International Monetary Fund were expected by mid-October.²⁹

Before the agreement was arranged, fears were widespread that a default by Mexico would severely damage the banking system. Nervous investors dumped bank certificates of deposit in favor of safer Treasury bills. The spread between interest rates on CDs and Treasury bills went from 117 basis points on Wednesday, August 18th, to over 250 basis points on Friday.

The emergency aid helped to calm fears of a collapse of the banking system, although similar emergency measures had to be arranged later in the year for both Argentina and Brazil. However, by the end of the year the immediate crisis had passed. An article in The Wall Street Journal on December 31, 1982 concluded that most financial authorities agreed with the following statement by Otmar Emminger, former president of the Bundesbank (West Germany's central bank): ''No one believes any longer there will be a crash of the banking system.''³⁰

In addition to the emergency aid, the pressure on the banking system was relieved by the ending of the recession in the United States in 1982 and by lower interest rates in the second half of the year. In response to continuing liquidity pressures, as well as a decline in the domestic demand for credit, the Federal Reserve Board eased monetary policy. Nonborrowed reserves in the second half of the year increased by 13.5 percent. Fiscal policy also helped to move the economy away from crisis. The full employment budget deficit jumped sharply in the last half of 1982; it went over the $100 billion mark by the end of the year.

The Legacy of 1982

The financial crises that erupted during 1982 were managed in such a way that a cumulative debt-deflation process, of the sort that had led to depressions in the past,[1] was avoided. Nonetheless, the problems of 1982 did not disappear. In fact, their subsequent reemergence again threatened the financial system and the economy with financial crisis.

In general, the problems that borrowers and financial intermediaries had during the recession in 1982 continued on into the subsequent economic recovery and expansion. The severity of the 1981–82 recession, and its occurrence so soon after the 1980 recession, significantly impaired the quality of loans of financial intermediaries. The combination of high real interest rates, low inflation, and the strong dollar, which continued into the expansion, put further pressure on borrowers and made the usual cyclical improvement in credit quality more difficult.

In particular, the failure of Penn Square Bank in 1982 played a major role in the effective failures of Seattle First National Bank (Seafirst) in 1983 and Continental Illinois National Bank and Trust Company in 1984. The structural problems of the nation's thrift institutions, which caused serious concern during 1980–82, contributed to two critical outbreaks in the recent period: the run on the deposits of American Savings and Loan Association (a subsidiary of the Financial Corporation of America and the nation's largest thrift), and the crisis of state-insured savings and loan associations in Ohio and Maryland.

In addition, problems in the use of repurchase agreements (RPs), which were involved in the Drysdale incident in 1982, again reappeared. Losses on RP transactions by Home State Savings Bank of Cincinnati played an important role in the Ohio thrift crisis.

The Aftermath of Penn Square

As mentioned in Chapter 8, a number of the nation's largest banks suffered losses as a result of the loans they had purchased from Penn Square. The two banks with the largest losses were Continental Illinois and Seafirst. Although Continental survived until 1984, Seafirst had to be rescued by an emergency merger with the

Bank of America in 1983. Seafirst's demise after its involvement with Penn Square was relatively swift.

Prior to Seafirst's brush with Penn Square, though, it had enjoyed an excellent reputation. As the decade of the 1970s came to a close, the Seafirst Corporation (the parent of Seattle First National Bank), with $7.6 billion in assets, was one of the largest bank holding companies in the country, and had benefited from a steady increase in income and dividend payments.

In 1979, though, energy prices were escalating rapidly, and lending to the energy industry seemed to be a promising avenue for even higher earnings. Seafirst established an energy division in 1979 as it sought to expand its energy portfolio.

However, Seafirst was a relative newcomer to energy lending. As it moved out beyond its home base, the Pacific Northwest, it found that it had to lend to relatively less creditworthy energy borrowers. It also discovered Penn Square in Oklahoma, which was making more loans that it could fund and was looking to sell loans to out-of-state banks.

From the end of 1978 to early 1981, Seafirst's energy loan portfolio grew from $11 million to more than $300 million, $50 million of which came from Penn Square. In the last two months of 1981, Seafirst bought $350 million more in energy loans from Penn Square. Its energy loan total reached $1.3 billion at the end of the first quarter of 1982. At this point, nearly $1 out of every $8 of Seafirst's loans was in energy.

The energy industry's fortunes took a turn for the worse in 1982. As they did, the quality of Seafirst's loans deteriorated. Moreover, Penn Square's failure in July revealed the particularly poor quality of the energy loans that Seafirst had purchased from Penn Square. These loans were affected not only by the general condition of the energy industry; they also suffered from poor credit checks, inadequate or optimistically evaluated collateral, and other problems. As energy prices continued to rise into 1981, Penn Square acted as if there were no such thing as a bad energy loan. Apparently this was also the attitude of the banks that bought loan participations from Penn Square.

Seafirst was forced to set aside $125 million on June 20, 1982 for possible future losses on its energy loans. This provision resulted in a net loss of $56.2 million for the second quarter. It also signaled the beginning of the end for Seafirst. With $400 million of poor quality loans from Penn Square on its books, and an overall energy portfolio that also had weaknesses, it had nowhere to go but down unless the energy industry dramatically improved. Such a turnabout in energy did not materialize.

Seafirst's cost of funds was reported to have risen by one-half a percentage point following the announcement of its second quarter loss, as investors demanded a risk premium for lending to the troubled bank.[2] It also faced a gradual attrition of its large certificates of deposit and other money market funds. Although other large banks had difficulties in the CD market during the summer of 1982 (as discussed in the previous chapter), Seafirst's problems continued throughout the year and into 1983. Large CDs outstanding dropped from $3 billion on March 31, 1982 to $1.3 billion on March 31, 1983, as its losses from Penn Square continued to mount.

By the end of 1982, Seafirst's loan losses had risen to $186.2 million. Of this total, losses of $125.2 million were due to Penn Square and other energy-related loans. Its nonaccrual loans (those problem loans for which the bank had stopped recording the payment of interest) totaled $636.1 million at year-end 1982; $407.8 million of these nonaccrual loans were due to Penn Square and other energy loans.

On January 20, 1983 Seafirst announced a net loss for the year of $91.3 million, including a $61.8 million loss in the fourth quarter alone. It also announced a reduction in its dividend rate, from 36 cents per share to 12 cents per share, effective on its dividend payment scheduled for April 1, 1983.

Seafirst's stock price dropped on the heels of this announcement.[3] Also, Moody's promptly downgraded Seafirst's credit rating, from A-3 to Baa-3 on its long-term debt, and from prime-2 to prime-3 on its commercial paper.[4]

More drastic consequences were perhaps avoided by the simultaneous announcement of a $1.5 billion ''safety net'' put together for Seafirst by a group of approximately a dozen of the nation's largest banks. The group of banks stood ready to lend Seafirst up to $1.5 billion in federal funds if a large run on its deposits developed. According to former Federal Reserve Board Governor Andrew F. Brimmer, the president of the Federal Reserve Bank of New York ''took the lead in organizing'' this assistance for Seafirst from the other banks ''because of fear that an early and dramatic failure of Seafirst would be a shock to the money market both at home and abroad.''[5]

The safety net was not used in January. However, the energy situation worsened during 1983, as energy prices dropped sharply at the beginning of the year. The quality of Seafirst's energy loans continued to deteriorate.

Seafirst did begin to borrow from this group of banks in May. The total of borrowed funds reached approximately $1.0 billion in early June. At this point, Seafirst also began to borrow from the Federal Reserve discount window, at the Federal Reserve Bank of San Francisco.[6]

The situation was resolved by the emergency merger of Seafirst into the Bank of America Corporation. The merger took place on July 1, 1983, after legislation allowing the interstate merger was passed by the State of Washington, and after expedited approval was provided by the Federal Reserve Board.

After Seafirst's merger, the bank again attained access to the money markets. But although troubles were ending for Seafirst, they were continuing for another victim of Penn Square: Continental Illinois National Bank.

Continental Illinois

The story of Continental Illinois is similar to that of Seafirst. Continental also had rapidly expanded its energy lending, and had bought large loan participations from Penn Square. The losses from Penn Square, in the context of the decline of the energy industry and the general credit quality problems of the banking industry, dug a deep hole for Continental from which it was unable to escape.

However, the sheer size of Continental made its situation qualitatively different. With $35 billion in assets on June 30, 1984, Continental Illinois Corporation ranked as the eleventh largest bank holding company in the country, even though its asset total had shrunk considerably since 1982. It was just too big to be merged into another bank. Another solution had to be found. Before discussing that unprecedented solution, let us first briefly examine the history leading up to Continental's difficulties.

In 1976 Continental made a decision to become, by 1981, one of the top three lenders to corporate business in the country. It embarked upon a program of rapid loan growth, especially energy loan growth.

Continental's decision to concentrate on business lending was partly due to bank branching laws in Illinois, which made the development of a large retail banking base difficult. (Continental was restricted to only one deposit-taking branch in Illinois.) At the same time, Continental's commitment to rapid growth meant that it would have to rely heavily on funds purchased in the national money markets such as fed funds and large certificates of deposit. The volatility of these funds eventually contributed to Continental's undoing.

However, Continental's strategy was initially a success. Through 1978 its earnings and asset growth were higher than its peers', and its loan losses were lower.[7] It was also highly regarded by the market. In 1978 it was voted one of the five best-managed companies in America by *Dun's Review*.

As energy prices rose sharply in 1979, Continental stepped up its energy loan growth. From 1979 to 1980 its energy loans grew by nearly 100 percent; from 1980 to 1981 they showed an additional 50 percent growth. Energy loans were one-fifth of Continental's total loans by 1981 and 47 percent of its business loans. As its energy loan growth expanded, it began making loans on properties whose production potential was uncertain.[8]

Continental also began to increase the loans it bought from Penn Square. According to Comptroller of the Currency C. T. Conover, these loans grew from $167 million at year-end 1980 to over $500 million by August 1981, and to $1.1 billion at their peak in the spring of 1982.[9]

These loans resulted in large losses for Continental, and negatively affected its earnings. Continental Illinois Corporation was forced to set aside $262 million in the second quarter of 1982 as a provision for possible loan losses. Its net income for the quarter was a negative $63 million.

Its nonperforming loans grew from $653 million at year-end 1981 to $1,937 million by the end of 1982. Energy-related loans accounted for $900 million of the 1982 total, and loans from Penn Square were responsible for $594.5 million. Nonperforming loans by December 31, 1982 stood at a very high 5.6 percent of total loans.

In 1982 Continental wrote off $393 million in loans, compared with only $71 million during 1981. Net losses on participations purchased from Penn Square Bank accounted for $191 million in 1982. From June 1982 to June 1984 Penn Square loans accounted for 41 percent of Continental's loan losses. Nearly $500 million of the total $1.1 billion in loans from Penn Square were judged to be a total loss as of June 1984.

As a result of its second quarter loss, and the revelation of its connection with Penn Square, Continental had difficulty raising money in the national markets. As noted in Chapter 8, it had to pay a premium of as much as 1 percent on its large CDs during the summer of 1982. Continental faced similar difficulties in the commercial paper and fed funds markets. Its ratings on commercial paper and long-term debt were lowered by the rating agencies.

A decision was made by Continental's management to replace these domestic money market funds with foreign sources. Continental's annual report for 1982 stated the following:

> To meet the changing conditions in domestic markets during
> the second half of 1982, funding sources were shifted sub-
> stantially to offshore markets. Increased borrowing in the
> Eurodollar interbank market compensated for reduced reli-
> ance on commercial paper, Federal funds, and domestic cer-
> tificates of deposits.[10]

Continental managed to survive the second half of 1982, and also 1983, without reporting any further losses in earnings. For each of these six quarters, it charged approximately $100 million against its income as a provision for loan losses.

In the first quarter of 1984, Continental's provision increased to $140 million. It reported a net income of $29.4 million. However, it would have had a $128.1 million loss had it not added $157.5 million to its income from the sale of its $1 billion Town and Country credit card business to Chemical Bank of New York. This maneuver, although it enabled Continental to report a positive net income and to continue to pay its quarterly dividend of 50 cents per share, further undermined investor confidence.

During the week of May 7, 1984 rumors began to circulate overseas that Continental was in imminent danger of failing. A report was carried on a Japanese news wire service that the U.S. Comptroller of the Currency was seeking a merger partner for Continental in Japan. Despite a denial of the rumor by the Comptroller on May 10th, Continental's stock price fell sharply and a major international run on Continental's deposits began.

The foreign deposits which Continental had used to replace its domestic money market funds proved to be just as volatile as the domestic funds. According to William M. Isaac, Chairman of the Federal Deposit Insurance Corporation:

> The bank lost approximately $9 billion in funding and the
> prospect was for the total to reach the $15 to $20 billion
> range in short order. Moreover, the funding problem at Con-
> tinental was beginning to affect financial markets generally.
> Something needed to be done quickly to stabilize the situa-
> tion.[11]

Continental increased its borrowing at the Federal Reserve discount window, from $850 million on May 9th to $4.7 billion on May 16th.[12] In addition, on
May 14th a $4.5 billion line of credit for Continental was announced. The funds
were pledged by a group of sixteen large banks headed by the Morgan Guaranty
Trust Co. of New York.

These efforts failed to stop the run. Thus on May 17th, the three banking
regulators—the Comptroller of the Currency (OCC), Federal Deposit Insurance
Corporation (FDIC), and the Federal Reserve Board (FRB)—announced an unprecedented temporary assistance program designed to enable Continental to
meet its obligations. The program consisted of (1) a capital infusion of $2 billion
in subordinated notes ($1.5 billion from the FDIC and $500 million from a group
of seven large banks), (2) continued access to the Federal Reserve's discount
window, (3) an increase in the line of credit from the banks to $5.5 billion (and an
increase in the number of banks participating to twenty-eight, and (4) a guarantee
by the FDIC that *all* depositors and other general creditors of Continental Illinois
Bank would be "fully protected."

The regulators took this course of action because, according to FDIC
Chairman Isaac, there was not sufficient time to arrange a merger or another
more permanent solution, and the consequences of the failure of Continental were
too threatening to the financial system. Due to the growing interdependence of the
banking system, almost "2,300 small banks had nearly $6 billion at risk in
Continental; 66 of them had more than their capital on the line and another 113
had between 50 and 100 percent."[13]

Comptroller of the Currency C. T. Conover testified that, if Continental
had been liquidated, the 66 banks certainly would have failed, and probably a
good number of the 113 would also have failed. In addition, he indicated that
there would have been a large number of corporate bankruptcies. Conover said
that, in the collective judgment of the directors of the FDIC, the Chairman of the
Federal Reserve Board, the Secretary of the Treasury, and himself, "had Continental failed and been treated in a way in which depositors and creditors were not
made whole, we could very well have seen a national, if not an international
financial crisis the dimensions of which were difficult to imagine."[14]

Despite the assistance program, including the unprecedented guarantee that
no depositor or other general creditor of Continental would lose any money, the
run continued, albeit at a reduced pace. The temporary assistance program had
bought some time, but it soon became clear that depositor confidence was not

going to be easily restored to Continental.

A search for a merger partner was begun. Several large bank holding companies, such as First Chicago Corporation, Chemical New York Corporation, and Citicorp (the nation's largest bank holding company) expressed interest. However, by the middle of June each had announced that it was no longer interested in acquiring Continental. Continental was too big even for Citicorp.

Meanwhile, although the panicky run had moderated, the drain on Continental's deposits was continuing. Despite the FDIC guarantee, corporate money managers apparently were concerned about the possibility of delays in obtaining their money, and the need to explain to skeptical supervisors why they still had money in Continental.[15] Since the costs of withdrawing their money and depositing it in another bank were minimal, there was little incentive to stick with Continental.

At the beginning of July it was reported that Continental had sold nearly $5 billion in assets in the previous sixty days in order to cover the continuing loss of deposits.[16] Also, Continental increased its borrowing from the group of banks to an average of $4.1 billion a day during June, compared with $2.25 billion in mid-May. Its daily borrowings at the beginning of July totaled more than $8 billion a day.[17] On the news of increased borrowing at the Federal Reserve discount window, Continental's stock fell to a new low of $4.125 per share on July 6th.[18]

The possibilities for a solution to the Continental crisis were narrowing: no bank holding company wanted to buy Continental, and it had become clear that Continental could not survive without further aid. Thus a permanent assistance program was fashioned by the government in order to avoid the disruption and crisis that would result from Continental's failure. A key concept in this program was the separation of the "good bank" from the "bad bank." If Continental's poor loans were taken out of the bank, it was anticipated that Continental would be able to survive.

The details of the permanent assistance program were announced on July 26, 1984 by the three bank regulatory agencies. The FDIC purchased loans from Continental with a book value of $4.5 billion; in exchange it agreed to pay $3.5 billion of Continental's borrowings from the Federal Reserve Bank of Chicago. The $1 billion difference represented the amount that Continental was required to charge off on the book value of these "bad" loans.

To replace this $1 billion, the FDIC augmented Continental's capital by a $1 billion purchase of nonvoting preferred stock. This stock, convertible into 160 million shares of common stock, effectively diluted the investment of the holders of the existing 40 million shares of Continental's stock by 80 percent. In addition, if the FDIC sustains losses from the loans it purchased from Continental, it could be compensated by obtaining the remaining 40 million shares and thus completely eliminating private stockholder ownership of the bank. Because of these provisions, many have claimed that Continental was "nationalized."

In addition to the purchase of the bad loans and the capital infusion, the permanent assistance program provided for a change in the top management at Continental. The earlier assistance—the guarantee by the FDIC, discount window support by the Federal Reserve, and the $5.5 billion line of credit from the group of banks—remained in place. Finally, to underscore its commitment to resolving the crisis at Continental, the FDIC pledged the following: "If, for any reason, the permanent financial assistance package proves to be insufficient, the FDIC will commit additional capital or other forms of assistance as may be required."[19]

Although the deposit drain did not stop immediately, the permanent assistance program appeared to establish the conditions under which Continental could continue in existence as a viable, although smaller, banking institution. The immediate crisis of the banking system subsided.

The Continuing Problems of Thrift Institutions

As with the banks, the problems of thrift institutions continued from 1982 into the recent period. A recent survey of the thrift industry came to the following conclusion: "The thrift industry survived the losses of the early 1980s though they left a legacy of problem institutions with which regulatory authorities are still dealing."[20] It was the unsuccessful attempt to avoid this legacy by three savings and loan associations that helped to bring about the recent crisis in the financial system.

As noted in Chapter 8, the large losses of thrift institutions in 1981 and 1982 were due primarily to the difficulties encountered by their traditional portfolio structure in an environment of deregulation and high interest rates. Many of the long-term mortgages on the books of thrifts in the early 1980s had been made in an earlier period of relatively low interest rates. As interest rates rose in 1980–82, the costs of the thrifts' short-term liabilities rose as well. Since deregulation now permitted—and competition required—the thrifts to pay a market rate of interest on their deposits, their expenses increased at a faster rate than the relatively fixed interest income from their mortgage assets. Most thrifts suffered operating losses and an impairment of their net worth.

The decline in interest rates in the second half of 1982 improved the fortunes of the thrifts, although profitability remains far below the levels of the late 1970s. Moreover, as mentioned above, a legacy of problem institutions remains. In the second quarter of 1984, nearly 25 percent of all institutions insured by the Federal Savings and Loan Insurance Corporation (FSLIC) reported losses.[21] Although the percentage is an improvement over the extraordinary 85 percent figure in the second half of 1981, it still indicates an industry with serious problems.

In response to these difficulties, thrifts have developed several strategies that attempt to mitigate their dependency on a portfolio of low-interest mortgage loans. The most important of these strategies include rapid growth, a restructuring of the mortgage portfolio, and an increase in the proportion of nonmortgage loans.[22]

The strategy of rapid growth attempts to dilute the influence of low-interest mortgage loans on earnings by aggressively adding new fixed-rate mortgage loans at the higher interest rates now prevailing. Of course, this strategy depends upon a relatively quick downturn in rates, or at least a stabilization. If interest rates continue to rise after a large volume of fixed-rate mortgages have been added to a thrift portfolio, the original problem is compounded and the institution is likely to suffer increasing losses. In addition, a thrift that attempts to grow rapidly becomes dependent on purchased funds to support such growth, runs the risk of making bad loans, and may have difficulty maintaining its ratio of capital to assets.

The second strategy, restructuring the mortgage portfolio, also maintains the traditional focus of the thrifts on mortgage lending; in this case, though, the form of the mortgage assets held by the thrifts changes. The two most important new types of mortgage assets are adjustable-rate mortgages (ARMs) and mortgage-backed securities.

Adjustable-rate mortgages increase the sensitivity of mortgage assets to changes in interest rates. In 1981, all federally chartered institutions were allowed to issue ARMs, although they were not issued in substantial numbers until 1983, when activity in the mortgage market began to recover from the 1982 recession. By the end of 1983, nearly two out of every three mortgages made by thrifts carried an adjustable-rate provision.[23]

Mortgage-backed securities represent shares in a pool of mortgage loans. Many are guaranteed by the Government National Mortgage Association (GNMA), and nearly all are backed by one-to-four-family, fixed-rate mortgages. During 1982 and 1983, FSLIC-insured institutions increased their net holdings of government-insured, mortgage-backed securities by an average of $29 billion, compared with $7 billion in 1980–81 and $3 billion in 1977–79.[24]

The yields on these securities are roughly comparable (actually, slightly lower) to yields on the underlying fixed-rate mortgages. Thus mortgage-backed securities, unlike ARMs, do not improve the interest sensitivity of thrifts' mortgage assets. However, mortgage-backed securities are more liquid than mortgage loans, and thrifts can use them as collateral for borrowing. They have been important in enabling thrifts to raise funds by means of repurchase agreements.

The third strategy represents an attempt by thrifts to diversify their portfolios away from their traditional reliance on mortgage lending. Under the Depository Institutions Deregulation and Monetary Control Act of 1980, and especially under the Garn-St. Germain Depository Institutions Act of 1982, federally chartered thrift institutions were given the power to considerably expand their nonmortgage lending into consumer, business, and other areas. The purpose was to enable these thrifts to shorten the maturity of their assets and thus mitigate the effects of their long-term, low-interest mortgages. State law had already given state-chartered thrifts many of these same powers.

Although many federally chartered thrifts have been slow to expand into nonmortgage areas, the growth in nonmortgage lending has been more rapid at savings banks and other state-chartered institutions.[25] Indeed, the rapid expansion of some thrifts into these areas has been criticized by Federal Home Loan Bank Board Chairman Edwin Gray. Speaking at a convention of the U.S. League of Savings Institutions, Gray criticized the "go-go thrifts" that have made loans in "windmill farms, fast food restaurants, airlines and oil drilling operations."[26] Recently the Federal Home Loan Bank Board asked Congress to restrict the activities of those federally insured, state-chartered thrifts that have moved too aggressively into nonmortgage lending. Gray contends that some thrifts are making risky loans which are endangering FSLIC, the federal thrift deposit insurance fund.[27]

Although the dangers of nonmortgage lending are perhaps more obvious, there are risks inherent in all three strategies used by thrifts in recent years. In fact, thrifts employing these three strategies played a major role in bringing about financial crises during 1984–85. In each of three different incidents, a thrift employing a different strategy was involved.

The first incident involved the Financial Corporation of America (FCA), the holding company of American Savings and Loan Association, the nation's largest thrift. FCA had embarked upon a strategy of rapid growth. It concentrated on expanding its portfolio of fixed-rate mortgages, and funded them by relying heavily on purchased funds, such as large certificates of deposit, from institutional investors.

As mentioned above, such a strategy, in addition to making thrifts dependent on volatile funding sources, runs the risk of deteriorating credit quality and stretching net worth too thin. Indeed, by mid-1983 FCA's net worth had dropped to 2 percent of liabilities. (FSLIC normally requires that federally insured thrifts maintain net worth equal to 3 percent.) Also, it had been estimated that, of the $9.3 billion in loans FCA had on its books in mid-1983, $1.3 billion had gone bad by September 1984.[28]

Nonetheless, this strategy was mostly successful during the latter part of 1982 and 1983, as interest rates fell from the lofty heights they had reached during 1981. In the first half of 1984, though, interest rates began to increase again, and FCA's strategy began to crumble.

Institutional investors, concerned about FCA's management policy, withdrew $1.4 billion in large certificates of deposit during July. Investor confidence during this period was also weakened by the difficulties of Continental Illinois.

The loss of large CDs was partly replaced by increases in retail deposits, so that the net loss during July was only $582 million. However, on August 15th, FCA was required by the Securities and Exchange Commission (SEC) to restate its second quarter earnings. This restatement changed a $31.1 million gain in net income into a $107.5 million loss, and further jolted investor confidence in FCA.

The SEC claimed that FCA was using improper methods in accounting for reverse repurchase agreements of $2 billion in mortgage-backed securities issued by GNMA. FCA had acquired the securities from dealers between February and May 1984 and financed the acquisition by selling the same securities back to the dealers subject to an agreement to repurchase them.

The point emphasized by the SEC was that FCA never actually took delivery of the securities, i.e., it never obtained an ownership interest. Thus the transaction functionally resembled a forward contract, in which an investor contracts to buy or sell a security at a stated price on a specific date in the future. If the price of the security rises, the investor makes a profit; if it falls, he suffers a loss.

Since interest rates were moving up in the spring of 1983, the price of the securities declined, and FCA should have been experiencing losses. However, by extending the repurchase agreements (and at the same time hoping for lower rates), FCA avoided recognizing the losses—that is, until it was forced to do so by the SEC.[29]

The $107.5 million loss for the second quarter was said to be the largest single-quarter loss ever recorded by an American thrift institution. On the day it was announced, FCA's stock fell by $2.25 a share in heavy trading on the New York Stock Exchange. It closed the day at $5, down from $11 a month earlier.[30]

The run on deposits of American Savings and Loan accelerated. For the third quarter as a whole, deposits fell from $25.0 billion to $18.2 billion—a decline of $6.8 billion.[31] FCA turned to the government for help.

By August 28th FCA's borrowing from the Federal Home Loan Bank Board (FHLBB) had jumped from $600 million in June to $2.7 billion. On that same day Charles Knapp resigned as Chairman and Chief Executive Officer of FCA and was replaced by William J. Popejoy. Apparently the ouster of Knapp, who was responsible for FCA's rapid growth strategy, was demanded by the FHLBB as a condition of the assistance. It was reported that FCA and the FHLBB signed an agreement on August 28th that gave the FHLBB the power to remove any officers or directors it chose, and also gave the regulatory agency "broad control over Financial Corp.'s operations."[32]

Popejoy, upon his installation, promptly instituted a cost-cutting program. He also maintained FCA's regular dividend payment in an attempt to restore confidence. By the end of the third quarter, FCA's borrowings from the FHLBB had reached $3.3 billion. It had also sold $2.3 billion of assets to improve its liquidity, and had borrowed $5.5 billion by means of repurchase agreements of mortgage-backed securities.[33]

These actions apparently boosted depositor confidence, because by October the run on FCA's deposits had stopped. The danger of a financial crisis had diminished, but FCA was not yet out of trouble. Its nonperforming assets increased in the third quarter, and it was forced to post a $512.1 million loss for the fourth quarter. The loss was due in part to an increase in its reserve for possible loan losses of $472.5 million. Its nonperforming assets at the end of December stood at $1.1 billion.

FCA lost money again in the first quarter of 1985—a total of $38.2 million. On May 28, 1985 William Popejoy announced that nonperforming assets had risen to $1.5 billion. Thus FCA's financial condition remained quite precarious after the run on its deposits in the summer of 1984.

Although the threat of a crisis arising from FCA had moderated by the spring of 1985, doubts about the thrift industry (including FCA) continued. Troubles at state-insured thrifts in Ohio and Maryland led to an old-fashioned run by small depositors. For the first time since the Depression, depositors camped out overnight at financial institutions and waited in long lines to withdraw their money.

State-Insured Thrifts

The run on state-insured thrifts in Ohio came about as a result of depositor fears about the adequacy of Ohio's deposit insurance fund. These fears developed during the week of March 4th, 1985, after large losses were announced at Home State Savings Bank in Cincinnati, the largest thrift covered by the fund. Home State's losses, in turn, were due to its dealings with ESM Government Securities Inc., a small securities dealer in Fort Lauderdale, Florida. ESM failed on March 4, 1985.

The complicated transactions between Home State and ESM, which centered around extensive reverse repurchase agreements, have yet to be totally brought to light. There are also uncertainties that involve the extensive financial empire of Marvin L. Warner. Warner, in addition to owning Home State, was allegedly involved with the principals of ESM in a number of business ventures.[34] Although the motivations and details are not completely clear, the general outlines of the story can be recounted.

ESM Government Securities Inc. was founded in 1976. According to ESM's court-appointed receiver, Thomas Tew, ESM began losing money in 1977, and continued losing money until its demise in 1985. However, ESM covered up its losses, estimated at between $250 million and $300 million, by transferring them to its parent holding company, ESM Group Inc. The parent then listed the losses as "accounts receivable" from another affiliate, ESM Financial Group, Inc.[35] Apparently Alexander Grant & Co., the accounting firm that audited the books of ESM Government Securities Inc., was not the auditor for the parent or affiliate.

ESM Government Securities Inc. was involved in both repurchase agreements (RPs) and reverse repurchase agreements. ESM would do the RPs with organizations such as municipalities looking to invest their available cash for a good return. In exchange for the cash, ESM would sell securities to the municipality subject to a promise to repurchase them at a later date.

The reverse RPs were undertaken with thrifts such as Home State. In this case, ESM would purchase the securities and agree to buy them back at a later date. Another thrift that was heavily involved with ESM was American Savings and Loan Association, in Miami, Florida. (There is no connection between this S&L and the Financial Corporation of America subsidiary of the same name. There was, however, a connection between the Miami-based American Savings and Loan and Marvin Warner; Warner had been an owner of American until 1984.)

As it turned out, the parties on both sides of the RP transactions with ESM suffered losses when ESM was shut down. In addition to Home State's estimated loss of $150 million, American Savings and Loan lost $55.3 million. The city of Beaumont, Texas was out $20 million, and Toledo, Ohio lost $19 million. Total losses have been estimated at $315 million.[36]

Apparently ESM had pledged the same collateral to more than one lender.[37] Parties who had been involved in RPs with ESM had not taken actual possession of the securities that ESM had sold them (ESM offered them a higher interest rate if they did not). Thus when ESM failed, they were left with neither money nor securities. Home State's transaction was somewhat more complicated, but underlying it was the same problem: when ESM failed, Home State was unable to obtain the securities that supposedly were protecting its investment.

According to documents filed with the Securities and Exchange Commission, Home State nearly doubled its size during 1983 by engaging in reverse repurchase agreements with ESM. By September 1984 it had purchased $300 million of Government National Mortgage Association certificates and $410 million of U.S. Treasury bills from ESM.[38] Home State put up a part of the purchase price in cash and financed the rest with the repurchase agreements. It sold the securities back to ESM and agreed to repurchase them a year later. Thus Home State pursued the second thrift strategy noted above, the strategy of altering its mortgage portfolio to include mortgage-backed securities. However, it pursued it with such a vengeance that it is perhaps more accurate to say that it distorted this strategy, rather than followed it. Moreover, Home State was also rapidly increasing its assets and making a number of risky, nontraditional loans.[39] Home State was making a profit from the RP deals. The interest it received from the securities it bought from ESM generally exceeded the interest it paid on the loan to ESM.[40] However, Home State was taking quite a risk. The relatively long repurchase period of a year exposed Home State to a loss if the value of the securities fell during that period. Also, the large exposure to such a small firm left Home State vulnerable if the firm should fail, which of course is exactly what happened.

Home State's exposure represented the cash outlay that Home State had put up in order to buy the securities from ESM. Alternatively, it represented the amount by which the value of the securities held by ESM exceeded the amount that Home State had borrowed via the reverse repurchase agreements.

After ESM closed its doors on March 4th, news of potentially large losses by Home State soon became known. A run on Home State's deposits began on March 7th, and by Saturday, March 9th, Home State was ordered closed. Worried depositors had withdrawn more than $90 million (from total deposits of approximately $700 million).

State officials were now estimating that Home State's losses could run as high as $150 million. However, bankers who had examined Home State's books, with a view towards possibly taking over the failed thrift, indicated that the losses could be even greater than $150 million.[41]

The Ohio Deposit Guaranty Fund, which insured seventy thrifts in addition to Home State, had total assets of $136 million. Depositors at these other thrifts began to fear that the losses at Home State could completely wipe out the fund.

Depositors who had, prior to Home State's losses, paid little attention to the details of the insurance on their deposits, began to realize the difference between federal and state deposit insurance. However, even those who had realized that they were covered by state insurance had assumed that the State of Ohio stood behind the Ohio Deposit Guaranty Fund. Despite the official-sounding name, though, the fund was a private organization which could not automatically turn to the treasury of the State of Ohio if its resources were to be depleted.

Thus depositors at other state-insured thrifts began to fear that Home State's $150 million loss had effectively eliminated their insurance. In an effort to restore confidence, the Ohio legislature passed an emergency bill on Wednesday, March 13th, that set up a special deposit insurance fund of $90 million for state-insured thrifts other than Home State. Cleveland Federal Reserve Bank President Karen Horn announced that thrifts facing unusual liquidity pressure would be able to borrow at the discount window.

Despite these efforts, lines began to form at the other state-insured thrifts on Thursday, March 14th. As the apprehension spread, depositors camped out all night Thursday in order to withdraw funds on Friday. A widespread run by small depositors, which had not been seen since the Depression, was developing.

On Friday morning at 7:30 a.m., Ohio Governor Richard Celeste ordered all state-insured thrifts to remain closed. This was the first time since the Banking Holiday of 1933 that such a step had been taken. Investors reacted to the news by a "flight to quality," as Treasury bill rates rose sharply (although there was no dramatic move out of bank certificates of deposit). Overseas, uncertainty about the Ohio situation resulted in a drop in the value of the dollar and a rise in gold.

The state-insured thrifts were told to remain closed until they qualified for federal deposit insurance or until they were merged into other financial institutions. By March 27th, twenty-two thrifts had reopened, and it appeared that Home State was about to be bought by Citicorp. The Ohio savings and loan superintendent, Robert B. McAlister, declared that "the crisis is over."[42]

As it turned out, the plan to have Citicorp purchase Home State fell through. Chemical New York Corporation, the holding company for another

New York money-center bank, expressed interest. Finally, though, it was announced on May 30th that American Financial Corp. of Cincinnati would take over Home State.

Meanwhile, attention had shifted to other developing problems. On Easter Sunday, April 7th, a small New Jersey securities firm, Bevill, Bresler & Schulman Asset Management Corp., declared bankruptcy. Apparently Bevill, Bresler had been engaging in practices similar to those of ESM. When investors, learning from the ESM experience, demanded to take possession of their collateral, the firm was unable to supply the securities and was forced to close. It was reported that regulators feared additional failures of other small securities firms in a similar condition.[43]

The main worry, though, concerned other state-insured deposit insurance funds. Massachusetts, Pennsylvania, Maryland, and North Carolina had state systems similar to the one in Ohio. Customers of state-insured thrifts began to realize that their deposits were not backed by the U.S. government. Would they, too, start a run on deposits?

A second crisis occurred in Maryland. State-insured thrifts had suffered some withdrawals of deposits since the Ohio crisis, but a full-scale run did not begin there until Thursday, May 9th. On that day reports appeared in local newspapers announcing a management change at Baltimore's Old Court Savings and Loan Association. The Maryland Savings-Share Insurance Corp. (MSSIC), the state insurance fund, had ordered Old Court to remove its chief executive, citing serious management difficulties. It marked the first time since MSSIC was founded 24 years earlier that it had used its authority to force a management change at a member thrift institution.

In fact, Old Court was in terrible shape. A letter dated March 22, 1985 from MSSIC President Charles C. Hogg to Jeffrey A. Levitt of Old Court charged the thrift with poor record-keeping, insider loans, and improper and unsecured loans.[44] Examination of Old Court's books revealed that it had lent heavily to finance risky real estate development ventures. Nearly 70 percent of its assets consisted of commercial and land development loans, even though MSSIC guidelines set a limit of 40 percent on such lending.[45]

Old Court had used (in fact abused) the third strategy discussed above—nonmortgage lending—to take unwarranted risks. It financed its risky ventures by paying some of the highest interest rates in the nation. By pulling in money from all over the country, Old Court's assets had grown phenomenally, from $86 million to $839 million in just three years.[46]

Old Court lost $15 million in deposits on Thursday, and the run continued on Friday and Saturday. As in Ohio, the withdrawals were made by small depositors who had waited in long lines to obtain their money. On Monday, May 13th a conservator was appointed for Old Court.

By Monday, though, the run had spread to Merritt Commercial Savings & Loan, another privately insured thrift. It had been announced that Merritt faced possible losses of $2.2 million, approximately 15 percent of its net worth, as a result of dealings with Bevill, Bresler, and Schulman.[47] On Monday, Merritt requested that it also be placed in conservatorship.

Depositors in Maryland began to realize that, despite its official-sounding name, the Maryland Savings-Share Insurance Corp. was a private organization with no attachment to state or federal treasuries. Its fund of $170 million backed deposits of $6.5 billion. On Tuesday the run began to spread to other privately insured thrifts throughout the state.

Maryland's Governor Harry Hughes responded by issuing an emergency executive order at 4:47 p.m. that Tuesday. The order limited withdrawals from deposit accounts at state-insured thrifts to $1,000 a month. The governor also scheduled an emergency meeting of the Maryland General Assembly on Friday.

In a whirlwind fourteen-hour session on Friday, May 17th, the Assembly passed a series of bills designed to enable—and require—Maryland's largest state-insured thrifts to qualify for federal deposit insurance. The previous day the Federal Home Loan Bank Board conditionally approved the application of Chevy Chase Savings and Loan for federal deposit insurance. With $2.2 billion in assets, Chevy Chase ranked first in size of all 102 state-insured thrifts.

These measures seemed to stop the lines, and to limit the run on deposits. As thrifts were approved for federal insurance, they were allowed to resume full service. The panic ended.

Nevertheless, two states had experienced banking crises of the kind that had not been seen since the Depression. Thrifts in other states with private insurance systems began applying for federal insurance. Another crisis could not be ruled out.

Banking and thrift institutions still remained vulnerable to future developments. Moreover, the systematic forces in the economy that had led to financial crises during the past five business cycles were still operative. Thus it is important to abstract the descriptions of specific events in Chapters 4–9 into a model of financial crises that can aid our understanding of how future crises will develop. It is to this task that the next chapter is devoted.

PART III
Understanding the Postwar Experience

10

A Business-Cycle Model of
Financial Crises

A business-cycle model of financial crises attempts to specify the conditions that
develop over the course of the business-cycle expansion that make a financial
crisis likely to occur near the peak.

The model does not assume that financial crises *must* occur at the peak of
the business cycle, nor does it rule out crises at other times. Indeed, a crisis did
not appear in the postwar period before 1966, and Chapter 9 describes crises that
took place before the expansion peak was reached. Explanations for these developments are considered in Chapter 13. Nonetheless, it is asserted that financial
crises do occur as a result of systematic forces that take place near the peak of the
business-cycle expansion, and that the model presented here accurately accounts
for the crises that have appeared at the last five business-cycle peaks.

The model is constructed by beginning with the business-cycle, credit-
market perspective discussed in the Introduction. It is then filled out primarily by
addressing the issues that divide the various theorists. These issues, as noted in
the Introduction, include (1) the reasons for the development of financial difficulties in the business sector, (2) the factors influencing the demand and supply of
credit, and (3) the defining patterns of a financial crisis.

The resolution of these issues, at this point, represents the author's interpretation of how the crises discussed in Part II developed. The model itself is an
attempt to generalize the specific events of Part II into a coherent overall explanation. In the next chapter, an attempt will be made to evaluate the model.

Let us begin then with a statement of the model of how financial crises
develop. As the peak of the business-cycle expansion approaches, the financial
condition of the corporate sector deteriorates. Corporations have more difficulty
in meeting their fixed obligations, especially their payments due to debt. This
difficulty comes about because debt-payment obligations increase at a faster rate
than the ability to meet these payments.

Debt increases in relation to equity, and the maturity of this debt shortens,
thereby causing an increasing proportion to come due for payment. Interest rates
increase, and so a given amount of debt requires a greater repayment obligation

(from either variable rates or refinancing). Also, liquidity and profit rates fall. Thus, corporations have more difficulty meeting debt-payment obligations out of current income or, if necessary, by selling liquid assets.

The first theoretical issue concerns the relative importance of these factors. Minsky's view is that the rise in interest rates plays the key role. Profits do not necessarily fall, in his view, and thus a fall in profits cannot be an important systematic factor in the corporations' financial difficulties. In contrast, the model asserts that all of the above-mentioned factors play a role; moreover, the fall in profits is the main contributing factor.

In addition to debt payments, corporations also have other nondiscretionary costs near the expansion peak which require payment. These include fixed overhead costs and involuntary inventory accumulation due to declining sales (usually after the recession begins). Also, there is "involuntary" investment in plant and equipment, i.e., present investment expenditures that had been committed at an earlier date, and whose abandonment would cause significant financial loss. In addition, a certain portion of plant and equipment investment spending may be involuntary from the point of view of the individual corporation, in the sense that its absence would threaten an irreparable loss of market share.

Corporations that are having difficulties meeting debt obligations and other fixed payment requirements increase their borrowing, even though it is partly expanded debt levels that have aggravated their financial difficulties in the first place. In addition, they attempt to reduce discretionary costs, including spending for new investment in plant and equipment. Fewer new projects are undertaken.

Thus the model of financial crises includes a corporate demand for credit near the expansion peak that is to a large degree "necessitous." Wojnilower's view, that this demand is primarily to fuel the needs of an expanding economy, seems to miss the effect that corporate financial difficulties have on the demand for credit.

The distinction is important for a model of financial crises. If demands for credit are indeed necessitous, then an inability to obtain the needed funds would be expected to result in defaults on debt obligations, the collapse of the debt structure that had been built up during the expansion, and a cumulative downward spiral characteristic of financial crises. On the other hand, a cutoff of borrowing for "voluntary" investment spending would result in a "credit crunch" and perhaps also a recession. However, a decline in discretionary expenditures could conceivably be accomplished without debt repudiations, defaults, or a financial crisis.

Thus, assuming that there is a necessitous demand for credit, it becomes important to understand the reactions of the suppliers of credit. For the corporate business sector there are a number of sources of credit, including, for large corporations in particular, the commercial paper market. However, near the peak of the business-cycle expansion, the corporations come to rely increasingly on their traditional lender, the commercial banks. It is the role of the banks that has received the most attention from financial-crisis theorists.

An important aspect of the business-cycle model of financial crises is the effect that the financial difficulties of the corporate sector have on the banks. Since the corporations have increasing problems in making timely interest and principal payments on their debts, the banks have increasing problems in receiving the income that they expect from their loans. Defaults on loans increase.

In addition, the reserves of the banks are under increased pressure from the central bank. As inflationary pressures increase towards the end of the expansion, the Federal Reserve Board usually tightens monetary policy. Thus the banks typically find themselves faced with a large demand for funds from less credit-worthy borrowers at the same time that their reserves are experiencing slower growth.

At this point an important theoretical issue concerns the attitude of the banks toward the further extension of credit. Veblen, Mitchell, and Minsky stress the limitation of credit due to the decreased creditworthiness of business borrowers. Wojnilower, on the other hand, is of the opinion that the banks try to accommodate the increased demand. The business-cycle model contends that the banks do both: they restrict loans to new or nonestablished borrowers; at the same time the big banks try to meet the needs of their established customers.

To do so, the banks alter the composition of both their assets and liabilities. As concerns their assets, they alter the growth rates of the components of bank credit. Investments in securities decline in relation to loans, and nonbusiness loans decline in relation to business loans. Within the category of business loans, the banks tighten their terms of lending for new borrowers in order to make funds available for their established customers.

The growth of loan commitments is indicative of the banks' response to loan demands in a period of monetary restraint. It indeed indicates their willingness to try to meet funding requests from their long-standing business borrowers, especially the large corporations.

To meet these loan commitments, the banks use liability management, i.e., they alter the composition of their liabilities. Near the expansion peak they rely increasingly on purchased funds, particularly large negotiable certificates of deposit. Other purchased funds include Eurodollar borrowings, federal funds and repurchase agreements, and commercial paper issued by bank holding companies.

Because these purchased funds generally have lower reserve requirements than core demand and savings deposits, the banks thus can support a larger volume of lending per dollar of reserves. However, as funds become increasingly scarce, the market rate of interest that the banks must pay to obtain these funds increases.

In addition to being expensive, purchased funds are quite volatile. Large institutional investors can shift millions of dollars overnight if alternative investments offer a higher interest rate or appear more attractive for other reasons. An important consideration is the financial condition of the bank, because purchased funds are also uninsured, i.e., they are not covered by the insurance protection of the Federal Deposit Insurance Corporation in the event of failure of the bank. This lack of insurance adds to their volatility.

In summary, the business-cycle model asserts that the following situation typically exists in the corporate and banking sectors of the economy near the peak of the expansion phase of the business cycle. The corporations are having increased difficulty in meeting their debt payment requirements and other fixed commitments, and are attempting to borrow from the banks and in the commercial paper market in order to do so. The banks are experiencing increased loan-quality problems and a slower growth of reserves; they are tightening their terms of lending and are cutting back on the growth of investments and nonbusiness loans, but are responding to the loan demand of their best customers by relying on expensive, volatile, and uninsured purchased funds.

In this rather fragile and delicately poised situation, an unexpected event can cause a disruption. Indeed, *once the financial system has become vulnerable* a surprise event can occur which is capable of initiating a financial crisis.

In the financial crises of the postwar period in the United States, these surprise events were of two particular kinds. One was the sudden application of an institutional constraint, which took the form of government regulations whose purpose was to limit the continued expansion of credit by the banks. The second caused lenders to fear for the safety of their funds. In the financial crises considered above, this event was an unexpected failure of a large corporation or bank, or a threatened default on outstanding loan obligations.

This surprise event disrupts the situation summarized above by cutting off normal financing patterns and interrupting the supply of credit. Either it disrupts the corporate borrowing from the banks or from the commercial paper market, or it disrupts the banks' reliance on purchased funds. In either case, the disturbance to the rather strained situation leads to a financial crisis.

The surprise event is capable of initiating a crisis only because the financial system is fragile and therefore vulnerable. At the same time, the fragility of the system makes the appearance of such a surprise event likely. Although the precise timing of the surprise event is of course unpredictable, the existence of such an event should best be understood as itself an endogenous reaction to the pressures building in the financial system as the expansion proceeds.

In the later postwar period, actions by the authorities to control excessive credit creation near the peak of the business-cycle expansion—even over and above tight monetary and fiscal policy—have often become necessary. Because the banking system has been relatively successful in continuing the expansion of credit despite tight monetary policy, such policy responses have become fairly predictable reactions to the given conditions. Likewise, the sudden bankruptcies and defaults that have been discussed above have occurred primarily because the financial system at that point in the business cycle had become exceedingly fragile. The primary question has been which will occur first—the institutional constraint or the surprise default—to interrupt the supply of credit and initiate the financial crisis.

The conditions for a financial crisis are created when the inability of profits to continue to keep pace with the rapid increase in debt threatens the further expansion of the debt structure. The crisis itself occurs because those forms of credit that serve as money or near-money during normal times no longer do so when the supply of credit is interrupted and normal financing patterns are disrupted. The corporations that are unable to continue to obtain credit from the commercial paper market or from the banks desperately scramble for the cash they need to meet their obligations. The banks that are suddenly limited in their ability to obtain purchased funds must seek other sources of liquidity in order to meet their commitments. Nervous investors, apprehensive—and sometimes panicky—about the ability of their borrowers to repay, no longer extend credit and demand cash instead.

The entire interlocking structure of credit that has developed during the expansion, and that has helped the expansion to continue, rests on the foundation of confidence. If that confidence is threatened, or if the continued growth of credit is interrupted because of an institutional constraint, the whole structure can unravel. When it does, credit disappears and only money—hard cash—will suffice.

The desperate scramble for money is associated with a number of other events that are observed during financial crises: the forced sale of securities and other assets, the disruption of financial markets, a denial of funds to creditworthy borrowers, an increase in bankruptcies and uncertainty, a rise in risk premiums incorporated in interest rates, etc. Nonetheless, all of these are a result of the intense search for money that comes about when a surprise event suddenly disrupts a vulnerable system and interrupts the supply of credit. Thus a financial crisis can be defined simply as a sudden, intense demand for money. The money that is sought is cash, as opposed to those forms of credit that had previously served as money.

This definition of financial crises can be further developed by specifying the groups in the financial system who demanded money during financial crises, and the reasons for which money was so urgently demanded. Based on the financial crises that occurred in the postwar U.S. economy, there appear to be three, often related, situations.

In the first situation, the intense demand for money came from corporations in a liquidity bind who needed money to meet debt payment requirements and other fixed commitments. The urgency of their demand came from the disruption of normal financing channels—from either the banks or the commercial paper market—by the kind of surprise events discussed above. In the second situation, it was the banks whose reliance on purchased funds was suddenly interrupted. In the third situation, the urgent demand for money came from investors who feared for the safety of their funds. Their fears were provoked by a surprise event such as a bankruptcy which led them to reevaluate the likelihood of loss.

In each situation, the frantic efforts to obtain money led to disruptions of financial markets and threatened chain reactions leading to bankruptcies and further market disruptions. In the case of panicky investors, their withdrawal from the markets in which they usually lent funds disrupted those markets. In addition, the retrenchment on the part of lenders often fed back and affected the ability of the corporations to pay their debts. It either did so directly, via the disrupted commercial paper market, or indirectly, by limiting the flow of purchased funds to the banks.

The banks' attempts to obtain cash by the forced sale of securities disrupted the market into which the securities were sold. The corporations, with their normal channels for borrowing disrupted, either had to find other sources of financing, pressure others who owed them money to pay up, sell liquid or not-so-liquid assets, or file for bankruptcy. Their efforts often aggravated the financial situation by forcing other corporations closer into bankruptcy, or by disrupting the financial markets into which the illiquid assets were sold.

From the above, the answers to the questions raised in the Introduction about the nature and definition of financial crises become apparent. A financial crisis does involve a liquidation of credit, but this process is abrupt, not gradual, and it includes an intense demand for money. Moreover, it often involves an element of panic. There are regularities in the form that the crisis takes, but no one form occurs to the exclusion of others. A crisis involves the forced sale of assets, intensified efforts to borrow, a disruption of financial markets, and all of the other consequences discussed above.

These consequences come about from the intense search for money. The crises reviewed above were resolved when this intense demand was relieved. For the most part, this was accomplished by the actions of the Federal Reserve Board acting as a lender of last resort. By supplying the cash so urgently sought, the intense phase of the crisis was relieved.

Although these actions resolved the immediate crisis, they did not address the underlying vulnerability of the economy that had led to the crisis in the first place. In the postwar experience, this problem was often alleviated by stimulative monetary and fiscal policy. By providing the conditions under which corporate profitability could recover and the growth of credit could resume, these policies moved the economy—temporarily—away from the dangers of further financial crises.

Since the focus of the model is on the development and immediate resolution of financial crises, the effects of monetary and fiscal policies are not specifically included. However, we will return to this subject in Chapter 13, when an attempt is made to assess the longer-term impact of financial crises and their resolution.

The next step is to evaluate the model of financial crises, which will be done in the next chapter. For convenience in doing so, the model is summarized in the nine points below:

1. Because of increased reliance on debt during the expansion phase of the business cycle, the corporations' financial condition increasingly deteriorated.

2. As profits declined, the corporations experienced increasing difficulty in meeting debt payment requirements and other fixed commitments such as those due to involuntary investment.

3. Corporations borrowed to try to obtain the funds they needed to meet debt payment requirements and involuntary investment commitments; they relied primarily upon bank loans, and, for large corporations, also on commercial paper borrowing.

4. The banks suffered losses on their business loans, which adversely affected their own financial condition, and were restricted by tight monetary policy; they tightened their lending policies, but at the same time attempted to meet the necessitous loan demands from their long-standing customers.

5. They did so by decreasing the growth rate of investments in relation to loans and by decreasing the growth rate of nonbusiness loans in relation to business loans, by restricting the business loans they extended to new customers (as opposed to established customers), and by relying on purchased funds, particularly large negotiable certificates of deposit.

6. A surprise event—either the sudden imposition of an institutional constraint or an unexpected bankruptcy (or the threat of one)—disrupted these financing patterns.

7. The disruption of financing patterns initiated a financial crisis—a sudden, intense demand for money.

8. The urgent demand for money came either from corporations or banks whose sources of funds were disrupted, or from investors who feared the loss of their funds.

9. The immediate crisis was resolved by lender-of-last-resort operations of the central bank, the Federal Reserve Board.

11

Evaluating the Business-Cycle Model

This chapter will evaluate the accuracy of the business-cycle model of financial crises discussed in Chapter 10. The financial crises and related business-cycle developments during the postwar period will be examined to see if they are generally consistent with the main features of the model.

In approaching this investigation, an obvious exception presents itself. This exception consists of the crises that have occurred since the most recent recession in 1982 (those described in Chapter 9). Since these crises appeared before the peak of the business-cycle expansion, they apparently fall outside the purview of the business-cycle model.

In Chapter 9 it was suggested that these crises were a "legacy of 1982." They were partly a delayed result of the failure of Penn Square Bank in 1982, and partly a continuation of the troubles that banks and thrifts had suffered in 1982. The secular and institutional changes responsible for these troubles will be touched upon in Chapter 13, but the point at issue here is the significance of these crises for the validity of the business-cycle model of financial crises.

If the model is taken to be an all-inclusive explanation of the necessary and sufficient conditions for financial crises, then the recent crises clearly are evidence against the model. However, the model should not be interpreted as implying either that financial crises *must* occur at the peak of the business-cycle expansion, or that financial crises *cannot* occur at other times. Rather the model specifies those conditions that develop during the expansion that make financial crises *likely* at the peak. A more complete understanding of financial crises, and their significance for the functioning of the economy and the financial system, requires an integration of the impact of cyclical forces, secular trends, and institutional change. Some tentative ideas about this complex analysis are sketched in Chapter 13.

The more modest task attempted in this chapter is to examine the consisten-

Table 11.1

Dates of Financial Crises

Date of business cycle peak	Date of financial crisis	Number of months by which crisis follows peak
June 1966	August 1966	2
December 1969	June 1970	6
November 1973	May 1974	6
January 1980	March 1980	2
July 1981	June–August 1982	11–13

Source: Dates of business cycle peaks are the National Bureau of Economic Research dates as published in U.S., Department of Commerce, Bureau of Economic Analysis, *Business Conditions Digest*, January 1985, p. 103. Date of growth cycle peak in 1966 is from Geoffrey Moore, *Business Cycles, Inflation, and Forecasting* (Cambridge, Massachusetts: Ballinger Press for the National Bureau of Economic Research, 1980), p. 444.

cy of the business-cycle model of financial crises with developments at the five most recent business-cycle peaks (including the peak preceding the growth recession of 1966). The business-cycle experience in the postwar period before 1961 and after 1982 will not be considered. The reasons for the different nature of events in these two periods will become more evident in Chapter 13.

In carrying out this evaluation, it is useful to recognize that the business-cycle model encompasses two different but interrelated phases. In the first phase, the conditions develop that make the economic system vulnerable to the outbreak of a financial crisis. In the second phase, the crisis itself unfolds. In the summary of the model given at the end of the previous chapter, the first phase is represented by the first five points; the second phase, by the next four.

It is asserted that the first phase is an integral part of the dynamics of the financial developments that occur toward the end of the expansion phase of the business cycle. Therefore, in comparing one cycle with another, one should find similar patterns. Of course, the financial crises themselves also display general features, but the particular events that touch off the crisis may vary from one crisis to another, as do the sectors in which the crisis develops.

Thus the accuracy of the model will be checked in two steps. The first step will consider the period 1961–82 as a whole, and investigate whether or not the first five points are an accurate summary of the relevant business-cycle developments. The second step will focus on the financial crises one by one to see if the particular events of each crisis are of the general form summarized in Chapter 10 by points 6 through 9. (Here it will be relevant to consider the crises after 1982.)

First, though, it would be well to place the financial crises in the context of the stages of the business cycle. Table 11.1 gives the dates of the five financial crises reviewed, and the dates of the corresponding peaks of the expansion phase

Figure 11.1

Debt-Equity Ratio

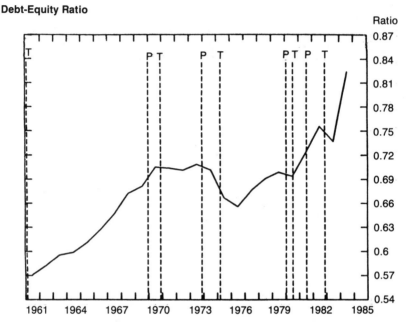

Source: Board of Governors of the Federal Reserve System, ''Balance Sheets for the U.S. Economy, 1945–84,'' table 705.

Note: Nonfinancial corporations. Debt is total credit market borrowing; equity is net worth at historical cost. Calculated from annual levels.
P = Peak of business-cycle expansions, T = trough of recessions, as defined by the National Bureau of Economic Research.

of the business cycle (as defined by the National Bureau of Economic Research). It can be observed that nearly all of the financial crises considered here have occurred very soon after the peak dates. The only exception is the 1982 crisis, which followed the July 1981 peak by approximately a year. Two of the other crises occurred within two months of the previous peak, while the other two appeared six months after the peak. All of the crises fell within the recession dates defined by the National Bureau (including the growth cycle recession which took place from June 1966 through October 1967).

Thus it is appropriate to investigate conditions in the corporate and banking sectors prior to, and immediately following, the cyclical peaks. Point 1 states that the financial condition of the corporations deteriorated during this period of time. Three corporate balance sheet ratios will be used to investigate this proposition: the debt-equity ratio, the debt-maturity ratio, and the liquidity ratio.

Figure 11.1 plots the debt-equity ratio for the nonfinancial corporate business sector. This series is limited because of the availability of the data on an

Figure 11.2

Debt Maturity Ratio

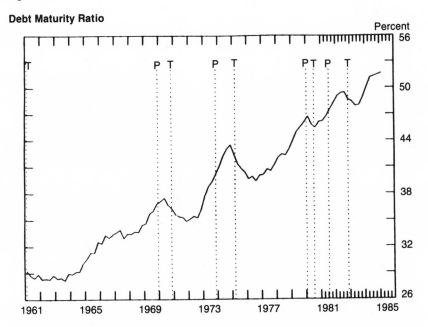

Source: Board of Governors of the Federal Reserve System, Flow of Funds
Section.

Note: Loans and short-term paper as a percentage of total credit market borrowing. Nonfinancial corporations. Quarterly levels, not seasonally adjusted.

annual, as opposed to a quarterly, basis. Nonetheless, the ratio has consistently
increased as the cyclical peaks are approached.[1] A point to note is that the debt-
equity ratio was much lower in 1966 than it was during the other periods of
financial crisis.

The movements of the debt maturity ratio and the liquidity ratio can be
followed more closely than the debt-equity ratio, because the data for these two
ratios are available on a quarterly basis. Figure 11.2 plots the ratio of loans and
short-term paper to total credit market debt outstanding, for the nonfinancial
corporate business sector. Although technically a debt maturity ratio should use
short-term debt, i.e., with maturity of one year or less, in the numerator, this
breakdown is not available in the flow of funds data. The outstanding bank loans,
although not long-term debt, nevertheless include a significant portion of term
loans of intermediate maturity.

However, the inclusion of total bank loans in the numerator may in some
respects be an advantage. The major reason to look at a debt maturity ratio is to
analyze the amount of debt that may have to be refinanced at higher interest rates.
Although bank term loans do not have to be immediately refinanced, for the most

Figure 11.3

Liquidity Ratio

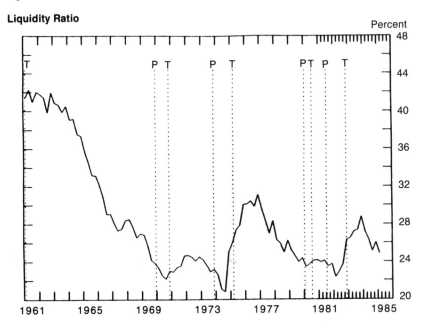

Source: Board of Governors of the Federal Reserve System, Flow of Funds
Section.
Note: Liquid assets as a percentage of total short-term liabilities. Nonfinan-
cial corporations. Quarterly levels, not seasonally adjusted.

part they are made with variable interest rates. Thus higher interest rates are soon
transmitted back to the borrower via the variable-rate provision of the bank loans.
In some respects, then, the loans and short-term paper ratio is a more accurate
indicator of the financial stress that higher interest rates can cause borrowers.

Figure 11.2 indicates that this ratio, without exception, increased as the
peak of the expansion approached, and reached its maximum during the recession
itself. It then started to decline, but increased again as the expansion developed. A
slight exception to this last statement occurred during 1966. The debt maturity
ratio increased prior to 1966, but the decline in 1967 was very mild (corresponding to the very mild growth recession in 1966–67).

Figure 11.3 gives very similar results for the liquidity ratio, the ratio of
liquid assets to total short-term liabilities outstanding, of the nonfinancial corporate business sector. As the expansion developed, the liquidity ratio declined. It
reached its low point during the recession, and then began to improve. It continued to improve during the first phase of the expansion, until it fell again.

Thus all three ratios of corporate financial strength deteriorated as the
expansion developed, as stated in point 1. Point 2 asserts that, as profits declined,

Figure 11.4

Interest Coverage Ratio

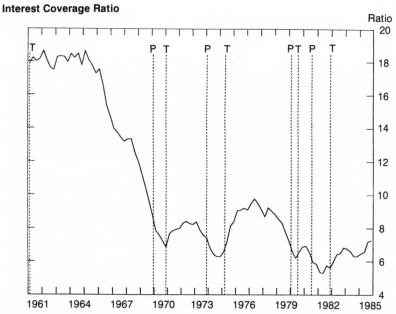

Source: Board of Governors of the Federal Reserve System, Flow of Funds
Section; net interest data from U.S., Department of Commerce, Bureau of
Economic Analysis, *Survey of Current Business*, National Income and Prod-
uct Accounts, table 1.13.

Note: Ratio of profits before tax plus depreciation plus net interest to net interest. Nonfinancial corporations. Seasonally adjusted quarterly flows at annual rates.

the corporations experienced increasing difficulty in meeting debt payment requirements and other fixed commitments.

A basic indicator of the ability of corporations to meet debt payment
requirements is the interest coverage ratio. It measures the amount of times that
interest payments are "covered" by capital income, i.e., the total of gross profits
before tax plus interest payments. As Figure 11.4 indicates, this ratio improved
in the initial phases of the expansion, but then began to decline as the expansion
progressed. It reached a minimum value during the recession itself.

It is instructive to compare the three ratios for which we have quarterly
data—the debt maturity ratio, the liquidity ratio, and the interest coverage ratio—
with the dates of the five financial crises. Table 11.2 indicates how close the
extreme values of these three ratios are to the financial crisis dates. The results are
quite remarkable. In almost every case the financial ratios reached their extreme
points—indicating maximum financial pressure on the corporations—in the
same, or almost the same, quarters as the financial crisis itself.

Table 11.2

Turning Points of Financial Ratios

Date of financial crisis	Peak of maturity ratio	Trough of liquidity ratio	Trough of interest coverage ratio
66Q$_3$	67Q$_2$	67Q$_2$	N.A.*
	(+3)	(+3)	
70Q$_2$	70Q$_2$	70Q$_3$	70Q$_4$
	(0)	(+1)	(+2)
74Q$_2$	74Q$_4$	74Q$_3$	74Q$_4$
	(+2)	(+1)	(+2)
80Q$_1$	80Q$_1$	80Q$_1$	80Q$_2$
	(0)	(0)	(+1)
82Q$_3$	82Q$_3$	82Q$_1$	82Q$_2$
	(0)	(−2)	(−1)

Source: Figures 11.2–11.4.
Note: Figures in parentheses indicate the number of quarters by which the particular ratio leads (−) or lags (+) the financial crisis.
*N.A. = not applicable; no trough observed.

The exception, again, is 1966, in which the ratios hit their extreme points three quarters after the crisis appeared. For the other four crises, however, the extreme point of a ratio occurred in the same quarter as the crisis four times, and followed it by only one quarter three times. In the other five instances, the difference between the peak of a ratio and the crisis was at most two quarters; three times a ratio followed the crisis, and only twice did it precede the crisis. Thus the general picture obtained from Table 11.2 is that the financial crises occurred when the financial condition of the corporations was deteriorating, and when it was close to reaching its low point.

Let us return to the interest coverage ratio; as noted above, it is a basic measure of the ability of the corporations to meet their interest payments. Although it does not indicate the magnitude of the principal payments that corporations are required to make, no available data does (the data on most corporate debt are collected on a net, not gross, basis). Thus the interest coverage ratio will have to serve as the standard by which the ability of the corporations to meet debt payment requirements is measured.

Point 2 contends that it was a decline in profits that led to the corporations' debt payment difficulties. To examine this assertion, it is useful to analyze the variables that affect the point at which the interest coverage ratio declined.[2] This ratio would tend to decline with (1) an increase in the use of debt by the corporations, (2) an increase in interest rates, (3) an increase in the proportion of debt outstanding that becomes subject to these higher interest rates (due to either

Table 11.3

Turning Points of Determinants of the Interest Coverage Ratio

Debt-GNP ratio (T)	Debt maturity ratio (T)	Commercial paper rate (T)	Bank prime rate (T)	Corporate bond rate (T)	Interest coverage ratio (P)	Profits ratio (P)	Memo: liquidity ratio (P)
64Q1 (−4)	63Q3 (−6)	61Q2 (−15)	63Q2 (−7)	63Q1 (−8)	65Q1	65Q2 (+1)	61Q2 (−15)
66Q4	67Q3	67Q2	67Q3	67Q1	N.A.*	N.A.*	68Q1
71Q4 (−5)	71Q4 (−5)	72Q1 (−4)	72Q1 (−4)	72Q4 (−3)	73Q1	73Q1 (0)	72Q1 (−4)
75Q2 (−8)	76Q3 (−3)	77Q1 (−1)	77Q1 (−1)	77Q3 (+1)	77Q2	77Q3 (+1)	76Q4 (−2)
80Q2 (−3)	80Q3 (−2)	80Q3 (−2)	80Q3 (−2)	80Q2 (−3)	81Q1	81Q3 (+2)	81Q1 (0)

Source: Figures 11.2–11.7 and 11.16.

Note: Figures in parentheses indicate the number of quarters by which the particular variable leads (−) or lags (+) the interest coverage ratio. Peak = P, trough = T.

*N.A. = not applicable; no peak observed.

Figure 11.5

Bank Prime and Commercial Paper Rates

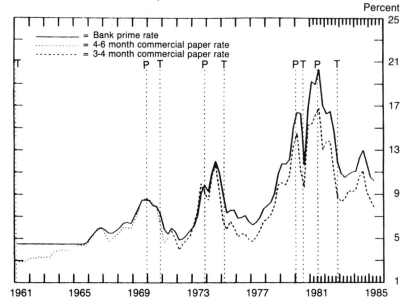

Source: Board of Governors of the Federal Reserve System, *Federal Reserve Bulletin*, tables 1.33, 1.35.

Note: Monthly data, not seasonally adjusted.

variable interest rates or the refinancing of short-term debt), and (4) a decline in profits.

Table 11.3 indicates the turning points of these four variables in relation to the turning point of the interest coverage ratio. It provides some evidence of the influence that increases in debt and interest rates, increases in the amount of debt subject to higher interest rates, and declines in profits have had on declines in the interest coverage ratio. Figures 11.5 and 11.6 graph for convenience the relevant rates for corporate borrowing for the period 1961–82 as a whole; and Figure 11.7 plots the corporate profit rate.[3]

As can be seen from Table 11.3, corporations began to increase their debt three to eight quarters before the interest coverage ratio began to decline; their reliance on short-term and floating-rate debt began to increase from two to six quarters earlier. On the other hand, the relationship between the decline of the profit rate and the corporations' interest payment problems is much closer: in one instance they occurred simultaneously, and in the other three the profit rate turned down either one or two quarters later.

The evidence from the 1974, 1980, and 1982 crisis periods indicates that interest rates generally have had to increase from one to four quarters

Figure 11.6

Corporate Bond Interest Rates

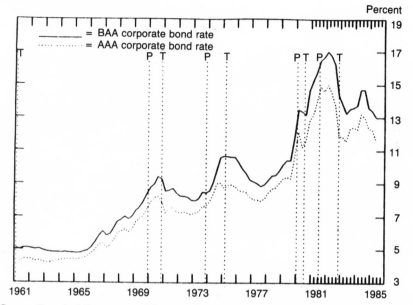

Source: Board of Governors of the Federal Reserve System, *Federal Reserve Bulletin*, table 1.35.

Note: Rated by Moody's Investors Service. Monthly data, not seasonally adjusted.

before the interest coverage ratio started to decline. In the period before the 1966 crisis, the lead time was much longer (due to the fact that the increases in interest-rates were much more gradual).

In the period after the 1966 crisis and before the 1970 crisis, there were no observable peaks in either the interest coverage or profit ratios; they both decreased steadily from 1965 onward. Thus no specific lead time or lag dates can be computed for this period. However, the lack of a peak for both the interest coverage and profit ratios indicates the close relationship between these two variables.

For the period 1961–82 as a whole, the data suggest that corporations can increase their debt and their proportion of short-term and floating-rate debt for quite some time without running into problems in meeting their debt obligations. They can even weather an increase in interest rates for up to a year without encountering problems. However, they cannot have their profits fall without encountering problems immediately.

It is for this reason that point 2 associates the debt repayment problems of the corporations with the decline in profits. However, the other variables clearly

Figure 11.7

Profit Rate

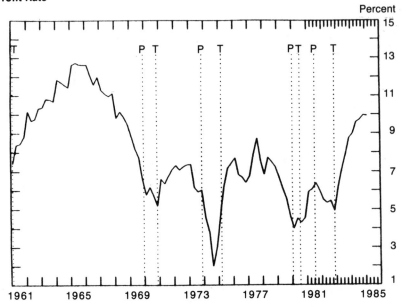

Source: U.S., Department of Commerce, Bureau of Economic Analysis, *Survey of Current Business*, table 1.13.

Note: Profits as a percentage of domestic income. Nonfinancial corporations. Profits are after tax with inventory valuation and capital consumption adjustments. Seasonally adjusted quarterly flows at annual rates.

are important also. Interest rates in particular seemed to exert a significant influence in the last two periods. Also, a decline in liquidity can decrease the ability of corporations to repay their debts without resorting to borrowing. Although it does not affect the interest coverage ratio, the liquidity ratio data is given in Table 11.3 for reference. It too (except for the 1982 period) shows a tendency to lead the interest coverage ratio by a considerable margin.

The economic meaning behind Table 11.3 is that corporations can use debt to exploit profitable investment opportunities, and these actions can increase interest rates (and also draw down liquidity) without necessarily creating debt repayment problems for them. It is only when the means to repay the debt—profits—can no longer keep up with the spiraling debt charges that the trouble begins.

Let us now examine the second part of point 2, that the corporations had difficulty in meeting involuntary investment commitments as the crisis approached, and that these difficulties, too, were associated with the decline in profit rates.

Figure 11.8

Financing Gap

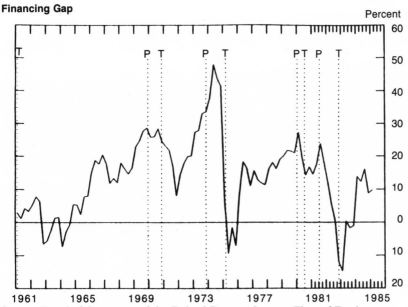

Source: Board of Governors of the Federal Reserve System, Flow of Funds
Section.

Note: Financing gap as a percentage of capital expenditures. Financing gap =
capital expenditures − internal funds. Nonfinancial corporations. Seasonally
adjusted quarterly flows at annual rates.

The first point to note is that the financing gap, which measures the amount
by which internal funds fall short of investment spending, peaked very close to
the dates of the financial crises (the financing gap as a percentage of capital
expenditures is plotted as Figure 11.8). Table 11.4 indicates that the financing
gap peaked in the same quarter as the financial crisis in two instances; in two
others, it peaked one quarter later. Only during the 1982 crisis period did this
relationship fail to hold. In that case the financing gap peaked a year before the
crisis occurred.

As can be seen from Figure 11.8, however, in all five periods the financing
gap increased as the peak of the expansion approached. In addition, in four of the
five periods this gap was at, or nearly at, its maximum during the quarter in which
the financial crisis occurred.

An important question is whether or not this need for funds was due to
voluntary or involuntary investment spending. If it was due to voluntary spending, i.e., the desire to increase inventory to meet anticipated future sales or to
take advantage of profitable opportunities to increase plant and equipment, then
presumably it could be cut back if necessary without serious financial repercus-

Table 11.4

Turning Points of Profit and Investment Variables

Peak of profit ratio	Peak of stock market index	Peak of investment orders	Peak of investment	Date of crisis	Peak of financing gap	Trough of investment orders
$65Q_2$ (−5)	$66Q_1$ (−2)	$66Q_3$ (0)	$66Q_3$ (0)	$66Q_3$	$66Q_4$ (+1)	$67Q_1$ (+2)
N.A.*	$68Q_4$ (−6)	$69Q_2$ (−4)	$69Q_3$ (−3)	$70Q_2$	$70Q_3$ (+1)	$70Q_4$ (+2)
$73Q_1$ (−5)	$73Q_1$ (−5)	$73Q_4$ (−2)	$74Q_1$ (−1)	$74Q_2$	$74Q_2$ (0)	$75Q_1$ (+3)
$77Q_3$ (−10)	N.A.*	$79Q_1$ (−4)	$80Q_1$ (0)	$80Q_1$	$80Q_1$ (0)	$80Q_2$ (+1)
$81Q_3$ (−4)	$80Q_4$ (−7)	$81Q_2$ (−5)	$81Q_4$ (−3)	$82Q_3$	$81Q_3$ (−4)	$82Q_3$ (0)

Source: Figures 11.7–11.11.
Note: Figures in parentheses indicate the number of quarters by which the particular variable leads (−) or lags (+) the quarter in which the financial crisis occurred.
*N.A. = not applicable; no peak observed.

Figure 11.9

Investment Contracts and Orders

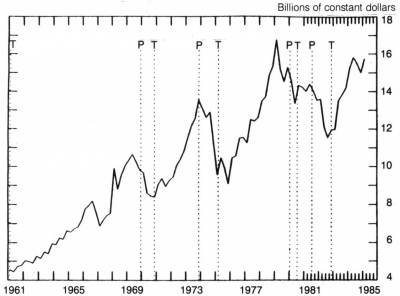

Billions of constant dollars

Source: U.S., Department of Commerce, Bureau of Economic Analysis,
Business Conditions Digest, cyclical indicator #20.

Note: Contracts and orders for plant and equipment. In constant (1972) dollars. Quarterly averages of monthly data. Seasonally adjusted.

sions. On the other hand, if the spending was involuntary, i.e., due to unanticipated inventory accumulation because of a failure of sales to meet expectations, or due to plant and equipment spending that was contracted for in an earlier period, then the implications are quite different. Involuntary investment spending takes the form of a fixed payment commitment, in some respects similar to debt requirements, which must be paid. Failure to do so could result in significant financial loss.

How is it possible to determine whether investment is voluntary or involuntary? Although such distinctions cannot be made with precision, some insight can be gained by examining Table 11.4. There certain relationships are evident which are remarkable for their consistency.

In every crisis period, a particular timing relationship has—with only one exception—occurred. Peaks have been reached in profit and investment variables for the nonfinancial corporate sector, in relation to the financial crisis, in the following order: (1) the profit rate, (2) new contracts and orders for plant and equipment (in constant dollars), (3) investment in plant and equipment (in constant dollars), (4) the financial crisis, and (5) the financing gap. In every instance

Figure 11.10

Plant and Equipment Investment

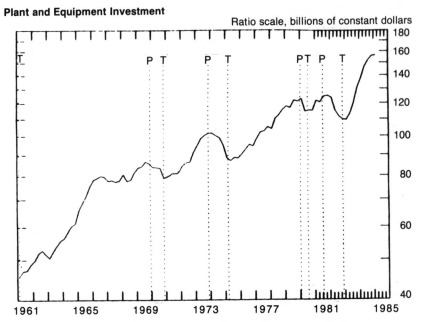

Ratio scale, billions of constant dollars

Source: Board of Governors of the Federal Reserve System, Flow of Funds
Section; implicit price deflator data for nonresidential fixed investment from
U.S., Department of Commerce, Bureau of Economic Analysis, *Survey of
Current Business*, National Income and Product Accounts, table 7.1.

Note: In constant (1972) dollars. Nonfinancial corporations. Seasonally adjusted quarterly flows at annual rates.

the trough of the series on new contracts and orders (COPE) has followed the
peak of the financing gap. In addition, the stock market has peaked, in every
instance except for the period preceding the 1980 crisis, before the COPE series.
(The COPE, investment, and stock market data are plotted in Figures 11.9 to
11.11.)

It seems reasonable to assume that an increase in new contracts and orders
for plant and equipment represents an attempt on the part of corporations to take
advantage of profitable investment opportunities. On the other hand, a decrease
in these orders would represent an attempt to scale back the scope of their
investment operations. Thus a significant portion of investment spending during
times in which new contracts and orders are declining represents investment that
had previously been undertaken but, because of the long gestation period of
investment projects, was still ongoing.

Therefore it will be assumed that during the periods of time in which the
COPE series was declining, there was substantial involuntary investment in plant
and equipment. The fact that the profit ratio declined in almost every instance

Figure 11.11

Stock Market Price Index

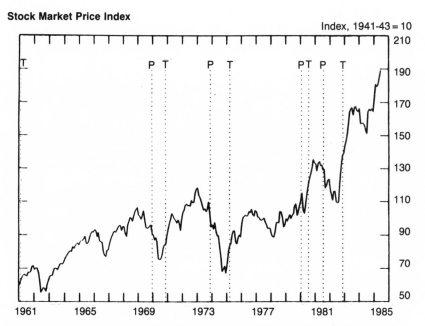

Index, 1941-43 = 10

Source: Board of Governors of the Federal Reserve System, *Federal Reserve Bulletin*, table 1.36.

Note: Standard & Poor's index of 500 stocks. Monthly data.

before the COPE series (except for the 1982 crisis period, in which COPE peaked one quarter before the profits ratio) lends credence to this interpretation. New investment is more likely to be undertaken when the discounted present value of future profits, which is influenced by the present level of profits, is high and rising.

In addition, except for the period preceding the 1980 crisis, the stock market index peaked before the COPE series. If it is indeed the case that stock prices directly reflect investors' views of the discounted present value of future profits, then the interpretation given above would appear even more likely.

The one exception to the timing relationship referred to above occurred in 1966. Then the COPE series peaked in the same quarter as the financial crisis (actually, one month later—September as opposed to August 1966). Thus it is less likely that the funds needed for investment spending immediately preceding the 1966 crisis were due to involuntary investment in plant and equipment. For the other crisis periods, though, the concept of involuntary investment appears to be quite relevant.

Although investment in plant and equipment has constituted most of the capital expenditures for the nonfinancial corporate business sector, inventory

Figure 11.12

Inventory Investment

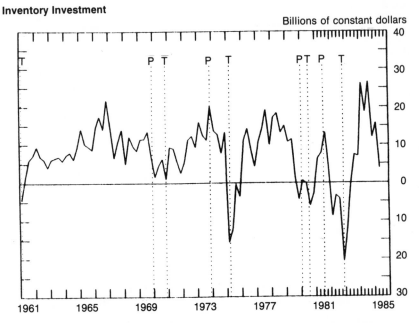

Billions of constant dollars

Source: U.S., Department of Commerce, Bureau of Economic Analysis, *Survey of Current Business*, National Income and Product Accounts, table 1.1.

Note: In constant (1972) dollars. Nonfarm business sector. Seasonally adjusted quarterly flows at annual rates.

investment is also a significant portion of the total. Thus it would be useful to try to determine if involuntary inventory accumulation has played a part in increasing the financing gap.

Figure 11.12 will be of some help in this regard. It plots the increase in inventory investment (in constant dollars) for the nonfarm business sector. Now involuntary inventory accumulation is likely to occur close to the peak of the expansion phase of the business cycle, when the growth of the economy has slowed down, sales have fallen off, and corporations are left with stocks of goods that are relatively high in relation to their ability to sell them. Thus, it would be likely that involuntary inventory investment is taking place when inventory spending is high at the same time that the inventory-sales ratio (Figure 11.13) is high and rising. Thus by comparing Figure 11.12 with Figure 11.13, some idea of the presence of involuntary inventory investment can be estimated.

Inventory investment increased in the second quarter of 1966. Although the inventory-sales ratio rose then, it was still relatively low. It seems clear, though, that the large peak in inventory investment in the fourth quarter of 1966 was involuntary, as the inventory-sales ratio also rose sharply then. However, by the

Figure 11.13

Inventory-Sales Ratio

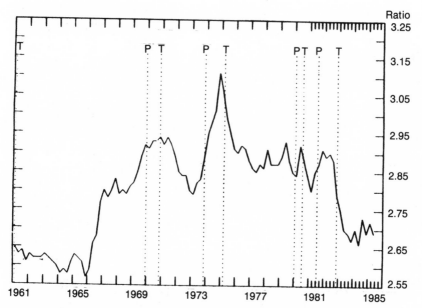

Source: U.S., Department of Commerce, Bureau of Economic Analysis, *Survey of Current Business*, National Income and Product Accounts, table 5.11.

Note: Ratio of inventories to final sales. Nonfarm business sector. Calculated from constant dollar (1972) quarterly data, seasonally adjusted at annual rates.

fourth quarter of 1966 the financial crisis had already passed.

This relationship was reversed in the 1970 crisis period, however. Then the relatively high level of inventory investment in the third quarter of 1969, combined with a rising inventory-sales ratio, indicated involuntary inventory accumulation prior to the financial crisis. During 1970, the year in which the crisis occurred, the increase in inventories fell off sharply.

In 1974 the high level of inventory investment and the sharply rising inventory-sales ratio appear to indicate that involuntary inventory accumulation was taking place. Although this did occur to a certain degree, a portion of the unusually large increase in inventories in this period was due to the stockpiling of inventories in anticipation of future price increases. In both 1980 and 1982, the increase in inventories was very low or negative, although involuntary inventory accumulation appeared to have taken place in the third quarter of 1981.

Thus, to sum up, it appears that involuntary inventory accumulation did not play a major role during the quarters in which the financial crisis appeared, even though in several instances it did increase the need for funds prior to the financial

Figure 11.14

Capital Expenditures and Internal Funds

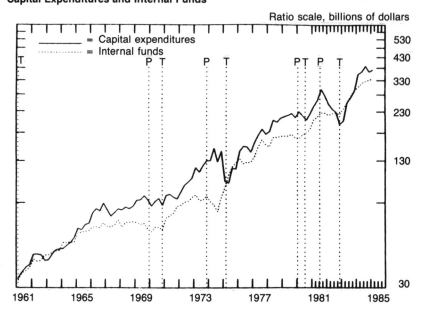

Ratio scale, billions of dollars

_____ = Capital expenditures
.... = Internal funds

Source: Board of Governors of the Federal Reserve System, Flow of Funds
Section.

Note: Nonfinancial corporations. Seasonally adjusted quarterly flows at annual rates.

crisis. In spending for plant and equipment, however, involuntary investment
played a major role in the period up to and including the financial crisis in every
instance except for 1966.

As can be seen from Figure 11.14, the financing gap increased in the
periods immediately preceding financial crises not only because investment
spending increased, but also because internal funds declined. The failure of
internal funds to maintain their rate of growth, in fact their tendency to decline,
resulted in an increasing financing gap. This relationship held for every period
except for 1981, in which the financing gap increased in the third quarter despite
an increase in internal funds.

As a general proposition, however, the financing gap widened as internal
funds declined. As can be seen from Figure 11.15, a decline in profits occurring
near the peak of the expansion generally has been responsible for this decrease in
internal funds. Thus, as point 2 contends, it was the decline in profits that resulted
in corporations having difficulty meeting their fixed payment commitments—due
to involuntary plant and equipment investment as well as debt.

Figure 11.15

Internal Funds and Components

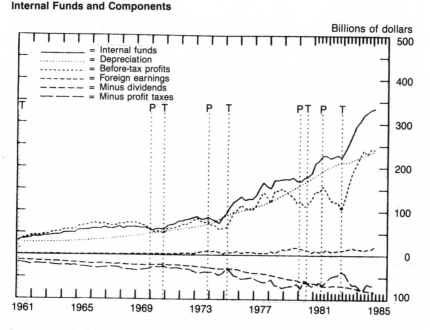

Billions of dollars

_____ = Internal funds
.... = Depreciation
-·-·-·-·-·- = Before-tax profits
- - - - - - - = Foreign earnings
— — — — — = Minus dividends
— — — — = Minus profit taxes

Source: Board of Governors of the Federal Reserve System, Flow of Funds Section.

Note: Nonfinancial corporations. Seasonally adjusted quarterly flows at annual rates.

Point 3 states that corporations relied on borrowing, particularly bank loans, to meet these fixed payment commitments. With the aid of Figure 11.16, which plots total credit market borrowing as a percentage of GNP for the nonfinancial corporate business sector, it is possible to investigate the first part of this assertion. In general, this ratio rose in the second part of the expansion, declined somewhat before the peak was reached, and then jumped up again as the financial crisis approached.

As Figure 11.16 indicates, this ratio reached a peak (for the 1966 crisis period) in the second quarter of 1966, the quarter immediately preceding the crisis. It fell off in the third quarter, but this result was due, in fact, to the event that touched off the crisis itself: the difficulty banks had in meeting the corporate loan demand by selling certificates of deposits.

Preceding the 1970 crisis, the ratio of borrowing to GNP fell from the peak it had attained in the fourth quarter of 1968, but then jumped up again to a new peak in the second quarter of 1970, the quarter in which the crisis occurred. This pattern was again repeated prior to the 1974 crisis. In the second quarter of 1974,

Figure 11.16

Nonfinancial Corporate Debt

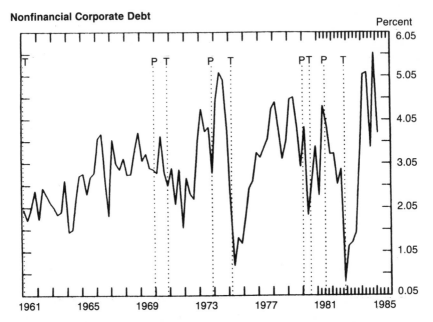

Source: Board of Governors of the Federal Reserve System, Flow of Funds Section; GNP data from U.S., Department of Commerce, Bureau of Economic Analysis, *Survey of Current Business*, National Income and Product Accounts, table 1.1.

Note: Credit market borrowing as a percentage of gross national product (GNP). Nonfinancial corporations. Calculated from seasonally adjusted quarterly data.

when the crisis occurred, the ratio of credit market borrowing to GNP reached a peak for the entire 1961–82 period. In the period preceding the 1980 crisis, this ratio, as in 1970, declined from its previous peak, but then jumped up again during the first quarter of 1980, in which the crisis appeared. Only in 1982 did the ratio of credit market borrowing to GNP fail to increase significantly in the quarter of the financial crisis. It can be seen from Figure 11.8 or Table 11.4 that it was also only in the 1982 period that the financing gap failed to reach its maximum at approximately the same time as the financial crisis occurred.

How much of this total debt took the form of bank loans? The answer to this question can be obtained by examining Figure 11.17, which plots bank loans to nonfinancial corporations as a percent of their total credit market borrowing. Here the general pattern is for bank loans to decline somewhat from the peaks they had obtained prior to the beginning of the recession, but to remain quite high during the quarter of the financial crisis. After the crisis, bank loans as a percentage of total borrowing dropped off sharply.

Figure 11.17

Nonfinancial Corporate Bank Loans

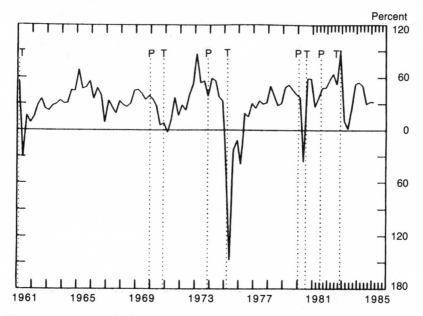

Source: Board of Governors of the Federal Reserve System, Flow of Funds Section.

Note: Bank loans as a percentage of total credit market debt. Nonfinancial corporations. Calculated from seasonally adjusted quarterly flows at annual rates.

In four of the five quarters in which a financial crisis occurred, bank loans were close to 40 percent or more of total nonfinancial corporate borrowing: in the third quarter of 1966, 40.1 percent; in the second quarter of 1974, 56.3 percent; in the first quarter of 1980, 38.4 percent; and in the third quarter of 1982, 49.8 percent. In the second quarter of 1970, bank loans were 27.2 percent of total nonfinancial corporate borrowing. As was observed earlier, however, it was during the second quarter of 1970 that corporate commercial paper outstanding reached its cyclical peak.

Let us investigate how the developments in the corporate sector discussed above were affecting the banks. As point 4 states, the banks suffered losses on their business loans as the financial condition of the corporate sector deteriorated. Figure 11.18 plots loan losses (i.e., those loans charged off by the banks) as a percentage of average total loans. The data plotted are on an annual rather than a quarterly basis, there are discontinuities, and data are not available for the entire period for particular categories of loans (such as business loans, loans to individ-

Figure 11.18

Bank Loan Losses

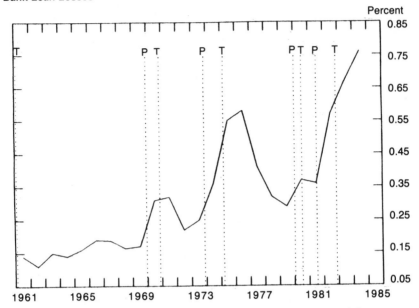

Source: Reports of Condition and Income filed by all insured commercial banks.

Note: Net charge-offs as a percentage of average total loans. All insured commercial banks. Annual data.

uals, etc.). Nonetheless, the figure does show a tendency for loan losses to rise sharply in the year in which a financial crisis occurred. In addition, loan losses generally stayed high or increased in the following year, indicating a probable substantial deterioration in the quality of loans in the crisis year. Borrowers who are having difficulties making debt payments are usually given a certain period of time before their loans are charged off.

Here again, 1966 was somewhat of an exception. The percentage of charge-offs to average total loans did increase in 1966, but the increase was very moderate, and the ratio then declined slightly in 1967. Moreover, its level was lower than it was in subsequent periods, although the data for 1968 and earlier is not strictly comparable to later periods.

Since 1978, data for different loan categories are available. It can be seen from Table 11.5 that business (commercial and industrial—C & I) loan charge-offs, as a percentage of C&I loans outstanding, increased sharply in the years of the recent financial crises considered here, 1980 and 1982. (In fact, they have been on an upward trend from 1979 through 1985, which probably indicates that more than cyclical forces are involved. See Chapter 13 for discussion.)

Table 11.5

Net Charge-offs of Commercial and Industrial Loans

Millions of Dollars	1978	1979	1980	1981	1982
Net charge-offs of commercial and industrial loans	619	730	1,069	1,324	3,024
As a percentage of C&I loans outstanding	.25	.23	.34	.36	.74
As a percentage of total net charge-offs	36	37	44	53	67

Source: Report of Condition and Income filed with regulatory agencies by all insured commercial banks.
Note: Data are for those large banks with assets over $300 million, for domestic and foreign activities.

Figure 11.19

Business Loan Demand

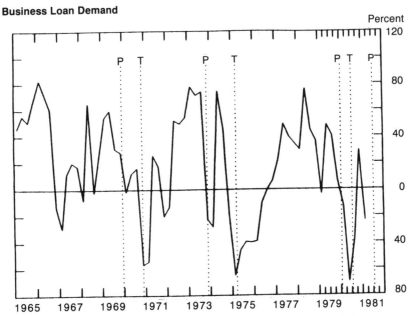

Source: Board of Governors of the Federal Reserve System, *Federal Reserve Bulletin*, "Changes in Bank Lending Practices," for 1967–81; Banking Section, for 1965–66.

Note: Change in strength of business loan demand at commercial banks. 122 banks participating in Survey of Bank Lending Practices. Net percentage of banks reporting stronger loan demand compared with 3 months earlier. Quarterly data.

The increased losses on business loans, due to the general deterioration in the financial condition of the corporate sector, adversely affected bank incentives to expand business lending. Also, the pressures that the Federal Reserve Board was putting on bank reserves, as it tightened monetary policy towards the end of the postwar cyclical expansions, made the banks less able to continue lending.

At the same time that these forces were operating to decrease the supply of bank loans, the demand for business loans was increasing, putting more pressure on banks to expand their lending. The banks resolved these opposing forces, as point 4 contends, by restricting their lending overall, but by attempting to meet the necessitous loan demands from their long-standing corporate customers. Let us look at the evidence for these assertions.

Figure 11.19 gives an indication of the strength of the demand for business loans at large commercial banks. It is taken from the Federal Reserve Board's quarterly Surveys of Bank Lending Practices. The surveys asked 120 banks (sometimes up to 125, and before 1967, 81) to rate the strength of demand for commercial and industrial loans compared with three months earlier. Figure 11.19 plots the net percentage of banks that reported a stronger loan demand, i.e., the percentage of banks reporting increases minus those reporting decreases.

Two different types of conclusions can be drawn from the data on this graph. First, one can identify those quarters during which business loan demand showed the greatest increase over its level three months earlier. These quarters are those in which the graph reaches its highest points. For example, loan demand increased the most during the first quarters of 1966 and 1973, and the second quarters of 1974 and 1978.

However, for our purposes the more interesting statistic gives those quarters in which business loan demand reached its highest levels. For example, in the first quarter of 1966, business loan demand increased at 82.7 percent of the banks surveyed. It increased at 71.6 percent in the second quarter and 60.5 percent in the third, before falling to –13.6 percent (i.e., 13.6 percent of the banks reported weaker demand) in the fourth.

The first quarter of 1966 showed the largest single increase, but, assuming bankers' judgments are consistent, it was the third quarter in which loan demand was the greatest. Loan demand presumably becomes greater as the number of quarters in which it increases continues. Using this criterion, it turns out that loan demand was at its peak in the third quarters of 1966, 1970, and 1973, and the fourth quarter of 1979. Except for 1974, these quarters either coincide with the financial crisis (1966), follow it by one quarter (1970), or precede it by one quarter (1980). Since the question of the strength of loan demand was discontinued from the survey in 1981, a comparison with the 1982 crisis cannot be made.

Preceding the 1974 crisis, business loan demand fell from its peak in the third quarter of 1973. It weakened at 22.4 percent (net) of the banks in the fourth quarter, and at 28.2 percent in the first quarter of 1974. However, loan demand increased at 74.2 percent of the banks surveyed in the second quarter (the actual survey date was May 15th), so it is safe to assume that loan demand was not far from the peak it had reached in 1973.

Of course, the data reviewed above record subjective opinions and may be somewhat imprecise. Nonetheless, it does seem that, at least as a first approximation, for each of the financial crisis periods covered by the survey data, business loan demand was at, or close to, its maximum.

Figure 11.20 gives some insight into how banks reconciled this increased loan demand with the pressures on them to restrict lending referred to earlier (increased loan losses and tighter monetary policy). This figure again relies upon data drawn from the Survey of Bank Lending Practices. It plots the answers to a question asking how banks' practices had changed (compared with three months earlier) regarding review of credit lines or loan applications for nonfinancial business (although beginning in 1978 this question no longer specifically referred to nonfinancial business loans).

As can be seen from the figure, near the peaks of the cyclical expansions,

Figure 11.20

Bank Lending Practices

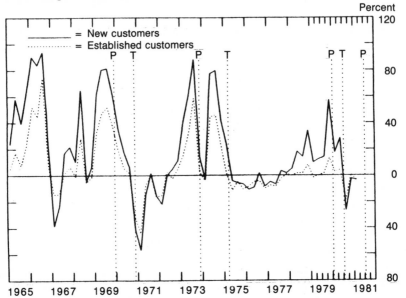

Percent

```
_____ = New customers
············ = Established customers
```

Source: Board of Governors of the Federal Reserve System, *Federal Reserve Bulletin*, "Changes in Bank Lending Practices," for 1967–81; Banking Section, for 1965–66.

Note: Changes in bank lending practices. 122 banks participating in Survey of Bank Lending Practices. Net percentage of banks reporting firmer lending policy compared with 3 months earlier. Quarterly data.

banks tightened their nonprice lending policies. (They also increased interest rates, as can be seen from Figure 11.5.) However, their degree of tightness differed between their new and their established customers. Banks responded to the pressures on them to restrict lending by consistently cutting back their new customers more than their long-standing ones. The gap between the two curves, for new customers and for established customers, widened whenever the degree of tightness increased. On the other hand, when banks were easing credit, a greater number of banks eased credit for their new customers than for their established ones (which probably reflected the degree to which new customers had been shut out during previous periods of restraint).

There is one exception to the general conclusion that, during periods in which credit tightened near the peaks of the business cycle expansions, banks forced their new customers to bear a disproportionate share of the restraint. This exception is a significant one, and it occurred in the third quarter of 1966. In that quarter 93.8 percent of the banks surveyed indicated that they had tightened the terms of credit for their new customers, the highest percentage for the entire period surveyed. However, 74.1 percent of the banks reported that they had also tightened credit terms for their established customers, also the highest percentage for the period surveyed. Thus only 19.7 percent of the banks tightened credit for their new customers but not for their established customers. This was the lowest differential by far for any period of time during which at least half of the surveyed banks tightened credit for their new customers.

As discussed above, in the third quarter of 1966 banks were unable to issue new certificates of deposit because of Regulation Q ceilings on CD interest rates. Thus they were forced to cut back on lending even to their established customers. Nonetheless, this exception, as well as the general conclusion—that banks restricted new customers far more severely than established customers during periods in which they tightened credit—is consistent with point 4 above. There it was stated that banks did tighten their lending practices, but at the same time attempted to meet the necessitous loan demands from their long-standing customers.

Although in 1966 the banks were prevented from meeting the loan demand of their established customers, evidence of their desire to do so is provided by their reaction to the 1966 events. In general, they attempted to devise new lending practices and sources of funds so that, in the future, they would not be forced to restrict lending so drastically to their established customers.

One innovation was the introduction of formal loan commitments. The banks apparently felt that they could not be pressured into discontinuing their business lending if they had formal, legally binding, commitments to lend. The Federal Reserve Board, it will be remembered, in its letter to the banks on September 1, 1966, made the slowing down of business lending a precondition for discount window assistance to banks facing a runoff of their certificates of deposit. As Figure 11.21 indicates, the rapid growth of business loan commitments since 1975 (when statistics were first collected) testifies to the banks' desire to meet the loan demands of their established customers.

After 1966 the banks also developed new financing methods, in the event that their main source of purchased funds, large negotiable certificates of deposit, was again restricted by Regulation Q interest-rate ceilings. In the late 1960s there was a surge in the growth of bank holding companies; they could issue commercial paper and then transfer the funds obtained to their affiliate banks by buying the banks' loans. In addition, the banks developed more fully another source of purchased money—Eurodollar borrowing from their foreign affiliates. In 1969, when Regulation Q forced an even more drastic runoff of CDs, banks were able to maintain their lending by replacing CDs with Eurodollar borrowing.

Figure 11.22 shows how money borrowed from the banks' European affiliates, and other purchased funds, evened out the drastic drop in funds caused by the runoff of CDs. The figure plots large time deposits (mostly CDs), and total purchased funds—large time deposits, Eurodollar borrowing, commercial paper,

Figure 11.21

Loan Commitments

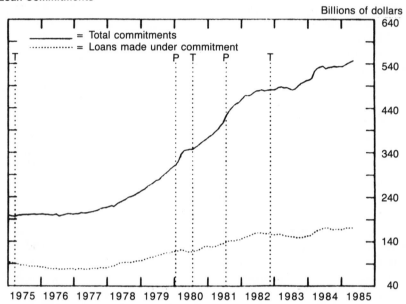

Billions of dollars

Source: Board of Governors of the Federal Reserve System, "Commercial and Industrial Loan Commitments at Selected Large Commercial Banks," Statistical Release G.21.

Note: Commercial and industrial loan commitments. Large commercial banks.

and federal funds and security repurchase agreements—as a percentage of total bank liabilities outstanding. As can be seen from the figure, large time deposits as a percentage of total liabilities dropped drastically in 1969, but total purchased funds showed a much more moderate decline.

Two other points can be noted from Figure 11.22. First, large time deposits are the largest component of purchased funds, although their relative share has declined somewhat in recent years. Second, purchased funds as a percentage of total liabilities have shown sharp increases as the business cycle expansions have approached. This data is consistent with the contention in point 5 which states that an important way that banks funded the necessitous business loan demand near the expansion peaks was by relying on purchased funds, particularly large negotiable CDs.

Point 5 also states that banks altered the composition of their loans and investments in order to meet this loan demand. The accuracy of this statement can be checked with the aid of Table 11.6 which gives the rates of growth of the

Figure 11.22

Bank Purchased Funds

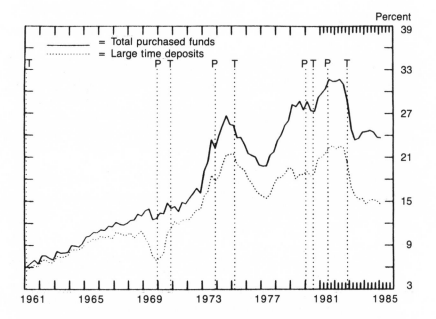

Source: Board of Governors of the Federal Reserve System, Flow of Funds
Section.

Note: Commercial bank purchased funds as a percentage of total outstanding
bank liabilities. Calculated from seasonally adjusted quarterly levels.

components of bank credit in the periods immediately preceding the financial
crises.

As Table 11.6 demonstrates, in these periods of time, in every instance but
one, banks increased the rate of growth of their loans faster than their investments. In addition, in every instance banks favored the growth of business loans
over all other loans.

The only exception occurred during the period from December 1969
to May 1970, when banks increased their total loans by 3.4 percent,
their business loans by 7.4 percent, and their investments by 11.5 percent.
Part of the explanation for this period may have to do with the degree of
tightness of monetary policy. The policy of the Federal Reserve Board
and the Federal Open Market Committee was extremely restrictive in 1969.
Banks were forced to liquidate their investments at a 9.9 percent annual rate
during the last six months of the year. U.S. Treasury securities held by commercial banks fell at a 20.4 percent annual rate, and other securities posted a 1.7

Table 11.6

Changes in Components of Bank Credit Prior to Financial Crises

	June 66–Aug. 66	Dec. 69–May 70	Feb. 74–April 74	Dec. 79–Mar. 80	Dec. 81–June 82
Bank Credit	2.5	5.8	16.5	10.6	8.0
Total loans	4.9	3.4	22.5	11.6	8.9
Business loans	15.1	7.4	38.3	15.7	14.2
Other loans	−0.9	0.7	13.8	9.5	5.8
Total investments	−2.3	11.5	1.6	7.4	5.4
U.S. Treasury securities	−1.1	13.6	−20.7	3.4	8.6
Other securities	−3.7	10.1	11.3	9.4	3.9

Source: Board of Governors of the Federal Reserve System, Banking Section, Division of Research and Statistics.
Note: Data are for annual percentage rates of growth between the given dates. Bank credit is equal to total loans and investments for all insured commercial banks. Business loans include loans sold to bank affiliates.

percent decline (their first decline since 1966).

Monetary policy during the first half of 1970, as the economy moved into recession, eased somewhat from the quite restrictive stance of 1969, although it still remained relatively tight. The pressure on banks' sources of funds was not relieved until the Federal Reserve Board suspended Regulation Q interest-rate ceilings on large CDs following the Penn Central bankruptcy in 1970. However, the slight easing, combined with the use of the commercial paper market by the corporations during this period, may have been responsible for the increase in bank investments during the first half of 1970.

Now that the evidence for the first five points of the model of financial crises has been examined, it appears that this first part of the model generally corresponds to the observed financial patterns in the business cycle expansions in the 1961–82 period. In addition, the comparison of the model with the data for the period 1961–82 as a whole has clarified the model somewhat. It was found that involuntary inventory accumulation did play a role in increasing the corporations' need for funds, but that the involuntary investment generally did not take place in the periods of time immediately preceding the financial crises. Involuntary investment in plant and equipment was more relevant in those times.

Although the model generally summarized the postwar patterns, the events leading up to the 1966 crisis consistently differed from the overall results. First, the financial vulnerability of the corporate sector was less at the time of the 1966 crisis than it was during other crisis periods. Although measures of corporate balance sheet strength—the debt-equity, debt maturity, and liquidity ratios— showed the same cyclical pattern as they did preceding other crisis periods, the magnitude of the cyclical movements was much diminished. Also, as was observed in Table 11.2, the turning points of these ratios lagged the 1966 crisis by three quarters. For other crisis periods, the cyclical deterioration in the financial ratios was greatest at approximately the same time that the crisis occurred. The absolute magnitudes of the financial ratios were also less in 1966 than at other crisis periods.

Second, it seemed that corporations experienced less difficulty in meeting fixed payment commitments in 1966 than they did during other crisis periods. Again, the interest coverage ratio was at a higher absolute level in 1966, and it reached its trough (which was more like a temporary level than a trough) a year after the crisis occurred. Also, the series on new contracts and orders for plant and equipment peaked a month after the financial crises. The implication of this timing pattern is that the corporations were attempting to finance new investment rather than investment commitments made at an earlier period.

Thus the sudden cutoff of funding from the banks would not have been as likely to cause financial distress among the corporations. Indeed, bank loan losses were smaller in 1966 than during other crisis periods (although bankruptcies per 10,000 concerns were higher than they were in every subsequent year until 1981).

On the other hand, the behavior of the banks during 1966 was no different than during other crises. They restricted investments and nonbusiness loans, sharply cut back their lending to new customers, and relied on CDs in order to meet the loan demand from their established customers. The main difference was that the purpose of the bank loans appeared to be to finance new plant and equipment investment rather than to meet debt payment requirements and other fixed commitments.

However, the significance of the difference between the events prior to the financial crisis in 1966 and prior to other crises is not that the patterns of cyclical financial developments discussed for the period 1961–82 did not operate in 1966, or were contradicted in 1966. A more plausible explanation is that the sudden cutoff of bank CDs because of Regulation Q ceilings initiated a financial crisis before the cyclical developments (and, probably, the secular trends) had reached the point where a more "typical" financial crisis would have taken place.

Before concluding the discussion of points 1 through 5, another difference in the general pattern should be mentioned. It was noted in the discussion of Table 11.4 that the financing gap of nonfinancial corporations peaked in the third quarter of 1981, close to a full year before the financial crisis of 1982 occurred. As Figure 11.8 indicates, the financing gap dropped to relatively low levels in 1982. Thus corporations apparently were not in need of funds to meet involuntary investment commitments in 1982.

However, it is relatively clear that the corporations were in financial distress in 1982. The debt-equity and debt maturity ratios had reached their highest point for the entire 1961–82 period, and the liquidity and interest coverage ratios were at or near record lows. The after-tax profit ratio did not reach a record low (it did for before-tax profits), but, on the other hand, profits had been relatively depressed since 1979 and the cumulative effect had resulted in a record number of bankruptcies. Thus, although corporations did not experience increasing difficulty in meeting debt payment requirements *and* other fixed commitments, as point 3 states, they did experience difficulty—probably the most of the entire 1961–82 period—in meeting debt payment requirements (as respondents in the Survey of Bank Lending Practices reported). Moreover, they did borrow heavily from the banks during 1982, as stated in point 3.

Thus, overall, the first part of the model of financial crises, points 1 through 5, is a fairly accurate summary of the relevant developments that took place in the economic and financial system prior to the five financial crises of the 1961–82 period. Let us now investigate how well points 6 through 9 explain the financial crises themselves.

In this part we will examine each crisis separately, rather than the five crisis periods as a whole. Was there a surprise event that disrupted financing patterns and initiated an intense demand for money according to the scenario described in points 6 through 9 of the model?

In 1966 Regulation Q interest rate ceilings caused a runoff of bank certificates of deposit. Since the banks were relying on CDs to fund the strong corporate loan demand, the imposition of Regulation Q ceilings disrupted this financing relationship. The imposition of ceiling rates, or more accurately, the failure to increase ceiling rates when open market rates rose up through the ceilings in June and July, constituted the surprise event mentioned in point 6: it took the form of an institutional constraint.

The cutoff of funds from CDs caused the banks to seek funds urgently by selling municipal securities. These actions thoroughly "disorganized" the thin municipal securities market and required lender-of-last-resort operations by the Federal Reserve Board. The Board sent a letter to all commercial banks on September 1, 1966 advising them that the discount window would be open to those banks that exercised restraint in their expansion of business loans and that refrained from further liquidation of municipal securities.

In 1970, the surprise bankruptcy of the Penn Central Transportation Company, and its default on its commercial paper, disrupted the commercial paper market and cut off many corporations from this source of funding. Nervous investors were unwilling to roll over outstanding corporate commercial paper because they feared loss. The Federal Reserve Board, in its capacity as lender of last resort, made funds available to the banks. The banks, in turn, lent the money to the corporations to replace their commercial paper borrowings. Thus in this case the urgent demand for money came from both sectors: corporations that needed funds to meet payment commitments, and nervous investors who withdrew from the commercial paper market.

In 1974, the surprise event was again a bankruptcy. This time it was the announcement of the financial difficulties of the Franklin National Bank in May 1974 that initiated the financial crisis. Investors in the markets in which Franklin had borrowed, particularly the domestic market for certificates of deposit and the Eurodollar interbank market, feared the loss of their funds, not only from Franklin but from other bank borrowers as well. A tiering developed, and all but the very largest banks had difficulty in obtaining funds.

Again lender-of-last-resort operations were required by the Federal Reserve Board. The Board's discount-window lending to Franklin from May through October 1974 reached a peak of $1.7 billion. The purpose apparently was to prevent Franklin from defaulting on its liabilities and to keep it alive until a purchase and assumption merger with another bank could be arranged by the Federal Deposit Insurance Corporation. In that way investors' fears were assuaged, and the crisis did not escalate out of control. Nonetheless, corporate bankruptcies did escalate rapidly toward the end of the year.

A "mini-crisis" also appeared in the period prior to the Franklin crisis. It involved the real estate investment trusts (REITs), and, again, it followed the general pattern indicated in the model.

The unfolding of the crisis was very similar to the situation in 1970. The REITs had borrowed heavily in the commercial paper market when real estate was booming. However, in late 1973 and early 1974, the fortunes of the real estate industry took a turn for the worse and the financial condition of the REITs deteriorated. The bankruptcy of a prominent developer who had been financed by twenty REITs put the financial problems of the REITs into the spotlight. Nervous investors refused to continue to buy the REITs' commercial paper. After their source of credit was disrupted, many REITs were saved from bankruptcy only by massive bank loans.

Again, a bankruptcy had disrupted the financing of a group of corporations having financial difficulties. The urgent demand for money came from nervous investors, and their withdrawal from the commercial paper market put the REITs into a position in which they were desperate for funds to meet payment commitments. Money to meet this intense need came from the banks. Although lender-of-last-resort operations apparently were not explicitly employed by the Federal Reserve Board, their encouragement of the banks' lending served essentially the same purpose.

In 1980 it was not the financial difficulties of the nonfinancial corporate sector that set off the financial crisis. It came instead from another group of business borrowers, the Hunt brothers of Texas. Nonetheless, the series of events leading to the financial crisis paralleled those in the corporate sector.

The Hunts began to have increasing difficulty in meeting their debt payment requirements (margin calls) toward the end of January 1980, when the price of silver started to fall from its extraordinary peak of over $50 an ounce. They borrowed heavily from the banks. As noted above, approximately 13 percent of *total* business loans in February and March 1980 went to the Hunts, although a substantial portion of this total was borrowed indirectly from the banks via securities dealers such as Bache Halsey Stuart Shields.

A surprise event—the imposition of credit controls by the Federal Reserve Board—disrupted this financing pattern. Banks were prohibited from lending to finance speculative activities, and an overall limit on bank business lending was imposed. The Hunts' brokers (who were responsible for paying the Hunts' margin calls), particularly Bache, were in urgent need of money. Bache responded by dumping the Hunts' silver futures contracts and stock holdings onto the markets.

Again, explicit lender-of-last-resort operations were not employed by the Federal Reserve Board. However, the Board was concerned about disruptions to the financial system as a result of the crisis. They followed the situation very closely and did not object to a $1 billion loan that was renegotiated by the Hunts from the banks.

In 1982 three separate surprise events occurred: the default of the Drysdale Government Securities Company on interest payment obligations, the failure of Penn Square National Bank, and the threatened default of Mexico on its loans to multinational banks. All three involved a bankruptcy or default, and all three sparked fears among uninsured holders of bank CDs about the safety of their funds. In addition, all three prompted lender-of-last-resort activities by the Federal Reserve Board.

Thus the events of 1982, taken together, conform to points 6 through 9 of the scenario. At the same time, each incident had its own particular circumstances.

The Drysdale incident did not conform to the earlier scenario (points 1 through 5) in the sense that Drysdale was not a corporation having financial difficulties because of systematic financial developments taking place near the peak of the expansion phase of the business cycle. It got into trouble because it engaged in some questionable practices and suffered heavy losses on speculative activity.

The importance of speculation in the Drysdale situation (as in the Hunt brothers' activities) warrants a further discussion of its role in financial crises. Speculation "pure and simple" has not received much attention in the business-cycle model because a primary objective of the model has been to identify those systematic forces that develop over the course of each business-cycle expansion and that make financial crises likely. The appearance of speculative activities is far less regular. However, it should be recognized that speculation is often financed with debt, and that the collapse of speculative activities usually involves the kind of intense demand for money associated with financial crises. The international speculation in foreign exchange of the 1960s and early 1970s could be cited as an example.

At the same time, it is true that the financial developments taking place in the corporate and banking sectors of the economy during the course of the business cycle involve an element of speculation. Corporations speculate when they borrow to finance investment projects that are expected to generate sufficient future profits to repay the debt incurred. Banks speculate when they loan the corporations money to undertake these projects. Speculation is an inherent part of the financial developments summarized in the business-cycle model.

Nonetheless, Drysdale's activities involved the "pure and simple" type of speculation, so its role in the 1982 financial crisis should be considered somewhat of an exception to the general model.

The other two events were more consistent, however. Penn Square failed due to huge losses on oil and gas industry loans. Although it is true that Penn Square failed to adequately diversify its loan portfolio, and that Continental Illinois and other banks were rather reckless in their acceptance of Penn Square loan participations, the basic difficulty still was due to the profitability problems that all corporations were experiencing during the 1982 recession.

Mexico's difficulties in meeting its debt payment requirements can be traced also to the severe recession that occurred in 1982. Just as domestic corporations were having trouble paying their debts as their profits declined during the recession, Mexico's inability to market its exports, particularly its oil, in the recessionary environment of 1982, increased its balance of payments difficulties and also made it difficult to repay its debts.

Two other aspects of the Mexican situation should be pointed out. First, the event that triggered Mexico's potential default was apparently the decision in early August 1982 by multinational banks to discontinue further lending to Mexico. This particular turn of events was not by itself different from what had happened in earlier financial crises. After all, Penn Central probably could have avoided bankruptcy and default on its commercial paper had bankers not decided in June 1970 that no further loans would be extended. The difference between Penn Central and Mexico, though, is the following: Penn Central's default triggered a financial crisis not only because of the money that investors lost directly to Penn Central, but also because of the fears of further losses in the commercial paper market; although Mexico's potential default provoked fears of other less-developed-country defaults, the size of Mexico's outstanding loan obligations was so huge that even the threat of a default by Mexico could initiate a financial crisis all by itself.

The second aspect of the Mexican situation worth noting is that, as an international problem, it required international lender-of-last-resort operations. Loans from both the Bank for International Settlements and the International Monetary Fund were crucial in resolving the crisis. With the growing interdependence of the world's economic and financial systems, such international lender-of-last-resort actions may again be necessary in the future.

The most recent crises had aspects that were similar to previous crises; they also had some novel aspects. The crises involving Seafirst and Continental Illinois were similar to those at Penn Square and Franklin National. In each case, investors began withdrawing large blocks of purchased funds when they became aware of serious difficulties at the bank. Unlike the other three, Continental was able to survive the initial run for nearly two years, but a rumor in May of 1984 of its impending collapse sparked a run by investors of such massive proportions that it, too, was forced to succumb.

Both Seafirst and Continental Illinois borrowed at the discount window until a permanent solution could be arranged. For Seafirst, this was a merger with BankAmerica Corporation. For Continental Illinois, it was the unprecedented bailout arranged in July 1984.

Thus the general form of these crises corresponds to the model: the threat of failure, a disruption of the banks' financing patterns, an intense demand for money by nervous investors (and, as a result, by the banks), and Federal Reserve actions as a lender of last resort. Two novel aspects of the Continental situation were the guarantee by the FDIC that *all* depositors and other general creditors would be fully insured against loss, and the failure of this policy to stop the run on the bank. Although this guarantee and the lender-of-last-resort actions by the Federal Reserve did not stop the run, they did slow it down enough to enable a more permanent solution to be found.

The state-insured thrift crisis started off in much the same way as the Drysdale events in 1982: the sudden failure of a small securities dealer resulted in losses for a financial institution and caused investors to fear the loss of their funds. However, in Ohio and Maryland the "investors" were not large institutional investors; they were small depositors. The difference, of course, was due to the lack of confidence in the state insurance systems.

Despite the difference, the events of the state-insured thrift crisis discussed thus far follow the scenario sketched by the model. However, the resolution of the crisis was somewhat different. Although the Federal Reserve did use the discount window to aid troubled thrifts in Ohio and Maryland, the run was stopped by the temporary closing of the state-insured thrifts in Ohio and the limitation of withdrawals of deposits in Maryland.

The purpose of a lender of last resort is to provide the money that is being so urgently sought during a financial crisis. The idea is that when people see that money is being made readily available, they will stop demanding it. However, in Ohio the opposite strategy was employed. Money was not made readily available; it was restricted. (This was the strategy recommended by Milton Friedman and Anna Schwartz in their discussion of bank runs during the Depression.)

The restriction on withdrawals in Ohio and Maryland did not result in business failures and a widening crisis, as it had in earlier crises before the existence of a lender of last resort. Although some depositors had to delay the settlement of house purchases, and some businesses had difficulties meeting their payrolls, the crisis was sufficiently small, temporary, and localized, so that there were not widespread dislocations. Moreover, the crisis did not spread to other financial institutions (that were federally insured) because the state-insured thrifts were seen as a special case.

Despite some minor differences, then, the business-cycle model appears to summarize accurately the way that financial crises have developed in the postwar period. The major exception that was noted was the timing of the recent crises. This exception will be discussed more thoroughly in the last chapter. First, though, we turn back to the theories of financial crises. After having reviewed the postwar experience, we are in a better position to understand and evaluate these theories.

12

Evaluating the Theories
of Financial Crises

In this chapter we turn our attention back to those authors whose theories of financial crises were reviewed in Part I. Those that were considered in the context of the general business-cycle, credit-market perspective will be discussed first. The detailed examination of postwar crises, and their generalization in the business-cycle model, should be helpful in further understanding and evaluating the contributions of these theorists. We will consider the earlier theorists as well as the more contemporary ones; since Milton Friedman's theory does not fit within the business-cycle context, it will be evaluated independently.

Earlier Theorists

Before discussing these earlier theorists, it would be well to recognize the problems inherent in such an undertaking. These writers based their theories upon the experience of the nineteenth and early twentieth centuries; the business-cycle model of financial crises is based upon the last twenty years. How closely should we expect these theories to correspond to the modern experience?

Actually, these earlier theorists were specifically included because it was felt that at least some features of financial crises are due to the basic workings of an industrialized capitalist economy. Indeed, the business-cycle model of financial crises is a mixture of these features; in addition, some parts are more dependent upon the specific institutional structure of the postwar U.S. economy. To evaluate more properly the earlier theorists, it would be well to identify these institutional aspects of the model.

The institutional differences are fairly apparent. The model discusses the monetary policy and lender-of-last-resort activities of the Federal Reserve Board, which was not created until 1913. It also mentions the use of commercial paper by large corporations. Although commercial paper is not new, its widespread use by large corporations as an alternative to bank credit is a relatively recent phenomenon. Finally, the model discusses liability management by the banks, which is a product of the last twenty-five years.

Some of these institutional changes have not affected the analysis of financial crises in a major way. The use of the commercial paper market has changed the form that a crisis might take (for example, in 1970), but not the nature of financial crises. The gold standard in earlier times produced approximately the same result, as the peak of the expansion approached, as tight monetary policy has in recent years. The ability of the Federal Reserve to act as a lender of last resort has certainly reduced the severity of financial crises (as has the existence of federal deposit insurance and the use of monetary and fiscal policy to counteract recessions). However, it has not changed the causes of financial crises, nor the way in which they develop.

For the analysis of financial crises, the most significant institutional change has been the use of liability management. It has allowed the banks to bid for funds long past the point at which they previously would have been forced to restrict their lending. Thus some corporations having trouble meeting payment commitments have been able to continue to borrow, until a surprise event disrupts their supply of credit. This development has changed the way financial crises have developed, and it has also reinforced the postwar secular trend of increased reliance on debt (see Chapter 13).

With this background, let us examine the theories of the earlier writers.

Thorstein Veblen

Veblen analyzed several important features of financial crises. First, he focused on the key role that the increase in debt plays in business-cycle expansions. Second, he assigned a primary role to movements in the rate of profit in affecting economic and financial behavior. Third, he understood that extensions of credit are affected by profits.

As was discussed in Chapter 2, Veblen focused on two kinds of debt: trade credit and loans. His view was that, as profits increased in the business-cycle expansion, both of these types of debt would increase. Although the business-cycle model of financial crises emphasizes the increased use of debt during the business-cycle expansion, it does not specifically focus on trade debt. However, trade debt (as a percentage of sales) has generally increased as the business-cycle expansions progressed.

Veblen also theorized that a decline in profits would bring about a liquidation of this debt. In fact, trade debt has declined along with profits in the postwar recessions, even though, as the end of the expansion approached, there has been a substantial lag between the peak of the profits rate and the subsequent peak in trade credit.

Overall, Veblen identifies the financial crisis with the liquidation of outstanding debt. His theory does not include a period of increased attempts to borrow after profits have fallen, nor the importance of sudden, surprise events in disrupting the supply of credit. This omission is partly due to the different institutional conditions of his day, as noted above. On the other hand, Wesley Clair Mitchell has a similar view to Veblen's on the liquidation of credit, and he does incorporate these events to some extent into his theory.

In many respects Mitchell's theory is a more developed and more sophisticated version of Veblen's. It is considered next.

Wesley Clair Mitchell

Mitchell went far beyond Veblen in developing an understanding of the dynamics of the business cycle. From the viewpoint of analyzing financial crises, his descriptions of the financial aspects of business-cycle developments are still remarkably helpful and accurate, even though his analysis was written in 1913.

Particularly noteworthy is his emphasis on movements in the rate of profit. He also stressed the increased use of short-term debt as the peak of the expansion approached, and he recognized the existence of involuntary investment. His view was that high interest rates and the increasing costs of construction combine to reduce contracts for new investment, but that the work on old contracts usually did not decline until after the financial crisis had passed.

Mitchell, like Veblen, focused primarily on the implications of a decline in profits on the liquidation of credit. He did not stress the importance of the decline in profits for directly limiting the ability of businesses to repay debt, and for bringing about a necessitous loan demand.

Mitchell did see corporations coming under financial pressure, and as having a necessitous loan demand, but he saw this primarily as an indirect consequence of the liquidation of credit rather than the deterioration of balance sheets and the decline in profits over the course of the business-cycle expansion. He said that the financial readjustments brought about by the liquidation of credit caused the corporations to subordinate the goal of making profits on current transactions to the much more urgent one of maintaining solvency.

This difference in emphasis may be due to the different institutional conditions in Mitchell's day. If the profits of a business are falling and it is under pressure to meet payment commitments, *but* it is able for a period of time to refinance its obligations, then it is clear that the declining profits are the source of the financial pressure (which, for the time being, is being relieved). On the other hand, if it is *unable* to refinance, because its creditors want to liquidate its outstanding credit, then it is understandable why some authors like Mitchell (and Veblen) focused on the liquidation of credit itself as playing a more important role in explaining the source of the pressure on the corporation.

Mitchell was rather vague in his book about the exact identity of these "creditors." Apparently he had in mind other corporations that had extended trade credit to a particular corporation, and banks at which the corporation had outstanding obligations. Presumably the corporation, feeling pressure from the creditors, applies to other banks that might possibly lend additional money.

However, Mitchell stressed that the banks are particularly loath to grant the corporations new loans at this point. As noted above, the banks in Mitchell's day could not use liability management to expand their supply of funds. In addition, Mitchell observes, like the business-cycle model of financial crises, bank incentives to make new corporate loans are reduced by the financial situation of the corporations and the rising default rate on corporate loans. As a result, banks tighten their lending policies. (Moreover, point 3 of the model states that corporations that are able to borrow do so to meet fixed payment commitments; it implicitly assumes that the corporations' demand for new plant and equipment investment, and the banks' desire to fund such investment, are much reduced.)

Also, the banks' ability to lend is restricted because of a reduction in their reserves. Mitchell noted this condition when he observed that the banks lost reserves because a good portion of their available cash was required for day-to-day transactions due to the increased level of trade. As noted above, this result of the automatic workings of the gold standard in Mitchell's day (before the establishment of a central bank in 1913) is now achieved by the Federal Reserve Board as a matter of conscious policy (to combat inflation, and at times to strengthen the dollar) towards the peak of the business-cycle expansion.

Let us now turn to the events of the financial crisis itself, as summarized in points 6 through 9 of the model. Here Mitchell's analysis is particularly noteworthy for recognizing the important role that surprise events can play in initiating financial crises. However, Mitchell spoke of both a financial crisis and a financial panic. He identified the financial crisis with the liquidation of credit; therefore, it was a financial panic that was touched off by the surprise event, which Mitchell considered would be a bankruptcy of an important enterprise.

In accord with point 7 of the model, Mitchell saw the crisis itself as an intense demand for money. This demand comes from the corporations' creditors who fear for the loss of their funds and, as a result, also from the corporations themselves. The panic, in Mitchell's terminology, differs from the crisis only in that it involves an even more intense demand for money.

Thus Mitchell's analysis of the financial crisis itself is close to the summary given by points 6 through 9 of the model. There are, however, two differences which arise from the different institutional conditions discussed earlier. First, the identity of the "investors" who feared the loss of their funds (mentioned in point 8) is different. In the model, the term "investor" refers primarily to large institutional investors who lend money in the commercial paper market or who buy bank certificates of deposit and similar obligations; for Mitchell, these "investors" represented (in addition to businesses that had extended trade credit) small depositors. Since there was no insurance of deposits in Mitchell's time, a shock to confidence would cause depositors to start a run on a bank (or banks). This was, of course, a major aspect of financial crises before the introduction of federal insurance of deposits in 1933. However, even though federal deposit insurance changed the form of financial crises—and also their intensity—it did not represent a major change in analysis. (The recent crises in Ohio and Maryland serve to underscore the accuracy of Mitchell's analysis.)

The second difference concerns point 9 of the model, which states that the immediate crisis was resolved by lender-of-last-resort operations by the central bank, the Federal Reserve Board. As mentioned earlier, when Mitchell was writing, there was no central bank. However, the major banks at times acted in Mitchell's day as the "functional equivalent" of a central bank. In those financial crises (or, in Mitchell's terminology, panics) that were promptly controlled, the big banks did what the Federal Reserve Board does today in its capacity as lender of last resort. They made it clear that they were prepared to provide money to all who were so urgently seeking it: to the corporations that were again requesting loans, and to the small depositors who were lined up outside the banks to withdraw their savings. Such actions often quickly calmed the panic.

Often the banks did not act with such unity, however, and with such concern for the financial stability of the banking system as a whole. Indeed, Mitchell commented that the panics in the United States were frequently much more severe than those in Europe because of the absence of a central bank in the United States. Thus, the analysis of how to resolve a financial crisis was clearly understood by Mitchell, but the different institutional setting of his time meant that crises often were not, in fact, promptly resolved without serious damage to the financial system.

Karl Marx

As opposed to Veblen and Mitchell, Marx placed more emphasis on a key element in financial crises: the difficulty corporations have in meeting fixed payment commitments when profits decline. However, due to Marx's fragmentary and incomplete analysis of the business cycle and financial crises, it is difficult to compare his theory in detail with the model. Thus this review of his theory will focus on some key points.

One of the key points in his theory concerns the role of credit in the business-cycle expansion. As discussed in Chapter 2, Marx saw credit as essential and necessary to this expansion. He saw credit as being capable of extending production to its absolute limits. This view is, of course, in accordance with the extensive use of debt in the postwar business-cycle expansions in the United States.

Second, as did Veblen and Mitchell, Marx recognized the importance of the rate of profit in affecting economic and financial behavior over the course of the business cycle. In addition, as mentioned above, a key element of his theory is the difficulties that businesses have in meeting fixed payment commitments as profits fall towards the end of the business-cycle expansion.

Third, Marx contended that firms would seek to borrow to meet these fixed commitments. His view was that during times of financial crises, the demand for what he called loan capital, or the money to pay back outstanding debts, is at its maximum. At the same time the demand for industrial capital, to be used for productive investment in plant and equipment, is at its minimum.

Fourth, Marx identified the financial crisis as a tremendous rush for means of payment because it is only money (means of payment), as opposed to other assets, that is capable of meeting payment commitments denominated in the money unit. This definition is essentially the same as the one given in point 7 of the model.

In attempting to further compare Marx's theory with the scenario of financial crises, an issue of interpretation arises: did he consider what we have called involuntary investment to be part of the fixed payment commitments for which businesses so desperately need money? On the one hand, though it is perhaps involuntary, it still represents an investment in plant and equipment. The demand for this kind of investment Marx felt would be at its minimum. Also, the only fixed charges that Marx explicitly mentioned were interest and rent.

On the other hand, the reason involuntary investment was linked with debt payment requirements in the model is precisely because both represent fixed charges in the sense that both represent obligations that were arranged in the past and are required to be paid in the present. In resulting in an inelastic demand for money, or a necessitous loan demand, both play a similar role. Moreover, a need for funds for involuntary investment is, in fact, consistent with the demand for investment in plant and equipment being at its minimum. Involuntary investment does not represent new investment. It is only that part of investment previously committed which cannot be avoided in the present.

Turning to the analysis of the crisis itself, we find that surprise events were not emphasized by Marx. Neither did he stress the point that an intense demand for money can arise from those who had lent, as opposed to borrowed: creditors, investors, and depositors. However, the essence of these two points is captured in Marx's statement that a financial crisis occurs because "credit suddenly ceases."

Points 6 through 8 of the model indicate that the surprise events initiated a financial crisis—a sudden, intense demand for money—either because they disrupted the corporations' or banks' sources of funds, caused investors (and creditors) to fear the loss of their funds, or both. The result in either case is that "credit suddenly ceases." Corporations have an intense desire for *money* precisely because their sources of *credit* have been cut off. Likewise, the sudden jolt to investor and creditor confidence caused by the surprise event leads them to press for repayment of their funds. In both instances the driving force leading to the financial crisis is the sudden cessation of credit.

One final point should be made concerning point 9 of the scenario, which states that the immediate crisis was resolved by lender-of-last-resort operations by the central bank. It is clear from the example of the Bank of England during the Panic of 1847, discussed in Chapter 2, that Marx appreciated how a central bank was capable of alleviating a financial crisis by making money available to those who were so urgently demanding it.

Contemporary Theorists

Hyman P. Minsky

Hyman P. Minsky has probably written more about the general topic of financial instability, and what he calls "financial fragility," than any other modern author. Indeed, as noted earlier, he was writing about these topics even before the first financial crisis of the postwar period appeared in 1966. He is clearly one of the leading theorists of financial crises today, and his views have influenced the thinking of many people. It is thus with particular interest that we approach the task of comparing his theory with the model of financial crises.

Minsky's theory is clearly in accord with point 1 of the model, which states that the financial condition of the corporations deteriorated as their reliance on debt increased during the expansion phase of the business cycle. In fact, Minsky has devoted a major share of his attention to demonstrating how this deterioration takes place and why it is an endogenous part of the business-cycle expansion. His characterization of hedge, speculative and Ponzi finance, and his view that the increased use of debt, and especially short-term debt, moves the financial spectrum closer to Ponzi finance, is a particularly dramatic way of expressing the content of point 1.

Minsky's views also coincide with the statement in point 2 that corporations experience increasing difficulty meeting debt payment requirements and other fixed commitments such as involuntary investment. He says that the existence of speculative and especially Ponzi financing—that increasingly develop as the expansion proceeds—results in an interest-inelastic demand for funds. Also contributing to this interest-inelastic demand is what Minsky terms sequential as opposed to prior financing.

With sequential financing, all the funds required for an investment project are not raised at the beginning of the project. Thus as projects continue into the present, funds must be obtained to meet these fixed commitments either from the revenues of the corporation or from borrowing. Minsky's discussion of sequential financing is similar to the use of the term "involuntary investment" in the model of financial crises.

However, a major difference in presentation between Minsky's theory and the model—probably the major difference—is that Minsky sees the corporations having difficulty in meeting these fixed payment commitments only because of higher interest rates—not because of lower profits. Higher interest rates certainly contributed to a deterioration in the interest-coverage ratio, but so did profits;

Table 11.3 suggests, in fact, that profits had the major influence.

Minsky contends that interest rates and debt payments accelerate rapidly as the peak of the expansion approaches, whereas profits grow only at a steady (full employment) rate. Technically, though, in Minsky's system, the narrow concept of corporate profits could be falling while the broader concept (quasi-rents) is growing at a steady rate. His analysis, however, differs from the empirical record for the postwar period: both the growth rate of profits, and corporate profit rates—using either concept—fell near the expansion peaks.

Moreover, in focusing on interest rates and de-emphasizing movements in the rate of profit, Minsky relies primarily on developments within the financial system to explain financial crises. His theory pays less attention to developments within the system of production. Changes in the level of investment can lead to a decline in profits, in his view, but these changes are also determined by financial variables in his system. This reliance on financial variables seems to overlook the important role that independent movements in the system of production (leading to a decline in profits) can play in creating the conditions for financial crises.

Let us move on to points 3 through 5 of the model. In a sense, Minsky's views conform to this aspect of the model. Since Minsky's speculative and Ponzi units by definition have to borrow to meet payment commitments, Minsky does see corporations borrowing to try to meet fixed payment commitments. Also, Minsky is certainly aware that banks suffer loan losses, are restricted by tight monetary policy, and use asset and liability management to meet loan demand.

The important question about liability management, however, is not whether it occurs, but when. It is to what degree it is used to accommodate a necessitous loan demand from the corporations just prior to the financial crisis that is important, i.e., to what degree does it take place after the corporations experience difficulty meeting payment commitments?

It is not clear to what degree Minsky sees the banks accommodating this necessitous loan demand. One interpretation of his theory, however, is that not much of this sort of loan accommodation takes place. The reason is that Minsky expresses the opinion that a rise in interest rates, by causing cash payment commitments to fall short of cash receipts, causes rather quick revaluations of the desirable and acceptable amounts of financing that banks and other creditors undertake. (His view on this point seems similar to the one expressed by Veblen and Mitchell.)

In comparing Minsky's views on how a financial crisis unfolds to points 6 through 9 of the model, which are concerned with the financial crisis itself, we again have a difficulty. His main interest is in the endogenous evolution of the financial system over the course of the business-cycle expansion, and how that system becomes increasingly fragile. He has paid less attention to the specifics of how a financial crisis comes about, and has not constructed a standard scenario himself.

However, he has stated that a financial crisis starts when a unit cannot refinance its position through normal channels and must sell illiquid assets or resort to other unconventional financing techniques to raise money. This statement captures the essence of the disruption of financing patterns and the intense demand for money mentioned in point 7 of the model.

Minsky is also aware of the effect that surprise events can have on the financial system, and the tendency of large institutional investors to withdraw their funds if trouble is suspected. The main difficulty, though, is that these observations remain only insights to be searched for in Minsky's writings, rather than a systematic scenario of how and why events unfold during a financial crisis.

However, Minsky has been very clear on how the financial crises of the postwar period have been arrested by lender-of-last-resort operations by the Federal Reserve Board. Moreover, he has pointed out how government deficits have played a role in increasing profits and in helping to avoid the harsh depressions that have followed some of the financial crises of the past. Overall, his theory captures much of the essence of the experience of financial crises in the postwar U.S. economy.

Albert M. Wojnilower

Wojnilower's articles are a fascinating account of the postwar financial crises by someone who is obviously very familiar with the inside operations of U.S. financial markets. So it should be particularly instructive to compare his theory to the model of financial crises developed in Chapter 10.

Wojnilower sees an interest-inelastic demand for credit developing near the peaks of the postwar business-cycle expansions. Moreover, he contends that the banks attempt to meet this loan demand by using liability management and other measures. However, he does not think that this demand is necessitous in the sense of attempting to meet fixed payment commitments, nor does he incorporate the financial difficulties of the corporations into his theory. He makes no mention of how the corporations' reliance on debt has systematically affected their financial condition.

Likewise, he pays little attention to movements in the rate of profit, and the effect of these movements on the ability of the corporations to meet fixed payment commitments. He also does not make a distinction between involuntary and voluntary investment. For Wojnilower, it is the general propensity to spend that is inelastic near the business-cycle peaks. Presumably this propensity to spend is for new investment as well as for already-committed investment.

Wojnilower gives an informed account of how the banks used liability management in order to accommodate the corporate loan demand. However, he does not note any significant bank disincentives to lend, and he does not mention any tightening of their lending policies to new customers (prior to the "crunch," as discussed below).

Wojnilower does not incorporate into his theory how loan losses affected the banks. Moreover, he conveys the opinion that liability management by the banks was capable of surmounting (again, until the crunch) the restrictions placed on bank lending by the tight monetary policy of the Federal Reserve Board. The effect of the tight monetary policy was to force the banks to pay more for their purchased funds, and therefore to charge their customers higher rates. Since the corporate loan demand is interest-inelastic, monetary policy, in his opinion, did not affect the amount of funds going to the corporate sector.

Essentially, Wojnilower sees the financial system as out of control near the peak of the business-cycle expansion. Corporations have nearly unbounded demands for funds to finance real spending, whereas banks have nearly unlimited incentive—and ability—to accommodate this demand. The main point of his article is that it has required crunches of various sorts—which affected the availability, rather than the cost, of credit—to stop this go-go expansion.

The model of financial crises, on the other hand, contends that it is only the necessitous loan demand of the banks' established customers that is accommodated. It is true that this necessitous loan demand is interest-inelastic, but the system is not out of control; this necessitous loan demand is limited in both amount and duration.

The surprise events discussed in point 6 of the model play a crucial role in Wojnilower's theory. They are significant for him, though, not because they initiate a financial crisis; their importance is in bringing the out-of-control expansion to an end.

To understand this difference, it is appropriate to examine the difference between the two terms, "financial crisis" and "credit crunch." A financial crisis is a sudden, intense demand for money, as discussed in the model; a credit crunch, on the other hand, is either a slow or abrupt restriction of credit. Although it is an abrupt cessation of credit due to a surprise event that brings about the financial crisis, the meaning of the two terms is definitely different.

Wojnilower considers the surprise events discussed in the model to be one form of credit crunch, and he sees the credit crunches as the only way to stop the expansion of credit. This approach caused difficulty for Wojnilower, however, in those times when the financial crisis occurred after there had already been a significant restriction of credit, as in 1969–70. The use of debt by nonfinancial corporations (Figure 11.16), and bank loans as a percent of debt (Figure 11.17), both declined in 1969, as did investment in plant and equipment (Figure 11.10). Because Wojnilower's theory does not countenance a restriction of lending and a slowdown in investment without a credit crunch, he had to demonstrate that there had been, in fact, a credit crunch in 1969 which restricted the availability of credit.

His explanation—that Congressional outcry over a full percentage-point increase in the prime rate in the summer of 1969 caused the banks to limit further increases in the prime and further lending—was considered in Chapter 5. It was found to be less than fully satisfactory. Moreover, he then had to recognize that a second crunch, the Penn Central default, occurred in 1970, even though the economy was not expanding as strongly in 1970 as it had been in 1969.

However, Wojnilower's theory appears to explain the events of 1966 better than does the model. As was noted earlier, the 1966 crisis remained somewhat of an exception to the model. Moreover, the ways in which the 1966 events differed from the model are precisely the ways in which Wojnilower's theory differs from it. As will be recalled, the financial condition of the corporations was less vulnerable in 1966; they seemed to be having fewer difficulties meeting fixed payment commitments, and their demand for funds seemed to be primarily for investment in new plant and equipment. Their expansion was abruptly stopped when Regulation Q interest-rate ceilings prevented the banks from marketing their large negotiable certificates of deposit.

Nonetheless, subsequent crisis periods have conformed less well with his theory. Even so, his articles should be studied carefully by anyone wanting to understand the financial crises of the postwar period. His views on the evolutionary changes that have taken place in the financial system as a response to the crisis periods are important. They have not been considered yet in this study (but see Chapter 13), although they are a major—if not *the* major—focus of his article.

Allen Sinai

In many respects, Allen Sinai's theoretical perspective is the opposite, or the complement, of Albert Wojnilower's. Wojnilower, as we saw, emphasizes the expansion of the economy and the inability, as he sees it, of traditional policies to slow it. Sinai, on the other hand, emphasizes the pressures on the economy which have resulted in a slowing of its growth. Wojnilower feels that banks have been successful (at least before the crunch) in funding corporate loan demand and have not needed to restrict their lending policies. In contrast, Sinai sees the pressures on them which contribute to a tightening of lending and a restriction in the amount of funds made available. Wojnilower focuses on the abrupt events which he feels are the only way that the credit expansion can be halted. Sinai ignores these abrupt events and emphasizes the steady squeeze on liquidity throughout the economy which, he feels, gradually slows down the creation of credit as pressures mount in a Crunch Period.

How can two knowledgeable economists looking at the same phenomena come to such opposite conclusions? The answer appears to be that each is looking at only part of the total picture. According to the model of financial crises, both an expansion and a contraction of credit are going on at the same time. By focusing only on the expansion, Wojnilower misses the contraction. Likewise, Sinai sees the contraction but not the expansion. By combining the strengths of both Wojnilower's and Sinai's theories, one gets a more balanced picture of financial and economic developments near the peak of the business-cycle expansion.

To appreciate both the strengths and weaknesses of Sinai's views, let us compare them with the specific points of the model of financial crises. Sinai's approach to point 1 of the model is that the overall financial condition of the corporate sector does indeed decline, but that these developments are not particularly crucial to his theory. He does focus on the liquidity condition of the corporations, though, and liquidity, broadly defined, plays a central role in his definition of a credit crunch. It will be recalled from Chapter 2 that he defines a credit crunch as a credit crisis resulting from the inability of the financial system to provide enough liquidity for the needs of an expanding economy.

Sinai does not mention a decline in profits directly, but he does take note of a decreased corporate cashflow during Crunch Periods. His conclusion, though, is not so much that corporations have increasing difficulty in meeting fixed payment commitments, as point 2 states. It is rather that the decreased cashflow results in an increased demand for funds to carry out all desired expenditures, in the same way that decreased personal saving leads to an increased demand for funds by the household sector. He makes no distinction between fixed payment commitments and other spending, or between voluntary and involuntary investment.

Sinai notes that commercial and industrial loan growth slowed down late in each Crunch Period. However, from this fact alone one cannot say for sure whether loan demand slowed, whether banks became more unwilling to continue lending, whether they became less able to lend, or some combination of the three. Yet it is over precisely these questions that important theoretical differences exist, as we saw above, and it is the answer to these questions that is crucial for an understanding of the events leading to a financial crisis.

Sinai apparently feels that the slowdown in loans does reflect an easing in loan demand, but his main conclusion is that the banks were finally and gradually forced to restrict lending because of slow deposit growth and pressures on their reserves. Wojnilower, on the other hand, feels that banks were not affected by the pressures to which Sinai refers, and that corporate loan growth slowed only when it was disrupted by a surprise event. The way to reconcile these conflicting perceptions is to realize that loans to fund new investment spending do fall off as the crisis approaches, whereas loans to meet fixed payment commitments increase. Thus it is possible to observe both forces at work simultaneously. This dual perspective is also evident in point 4 of the scenario, which states that the banks tightened their lending policies, but at the same time attempted to meet the necessitous loan demands from their long-standing corporate customers.

It is the tightening which Sinai emphasizes, while at the same time downplaying the significance of the mostly successful attempts by the banks to fund a part of the total loan demand. Although Sinai does not focus on the increased loan losses suffered by the banks and the resulting disincentives for continued lending, he does stress the tight monetary policy of the Federal Reserve Board. He mentions this policy explicitly as a cause of the credit crunch and it plays a crucial role in the developments he analyzes.

Let us now consider the financial crisis itself, as summarized in points 6 through 9 of the model. It can be seen that Sinai's views do not conform at all to this part of the model. Sinai does not see surprise events initiating a financial crisis, nor does he see the crisis associated with any specific events at all. He does not mention lender-of-last-resort activities by the Federal Reserve Board in connection with the credit crises he discusses.

Although Sinai is quite specific about the dates of the postwar Crunch Periods, he is vague about the dates of the crisis itself. As a matter of fact, he does not really define what a financial crisis is. As we saw in Chapter 2, Sinai defines a credit crunch as a credit crisis, but he does not define the credit crisis itself. He only points to some of the things that happen during a credit crisis: liquidity positions are depressed; interest rates rise sharply, as do yield differentials; and many borrowers are unable to obtain funds at any price.

In some respects, Sinai's views are similar to Veblen's and Mitchell's. They both saw the financial crisis as the effects of a restriction, or liquidation, of credit. Mitchell, though, also went on to define the category of financial panic, which came about as a reaction to a surprise event such as the unexpected bankruptcy of a major concern.

Veblen and Mitchell saw the liquidation of credit to be caused by a decline in profits, which reduced the value of the collateral backing outstanding loans. Lenders, as a result, were no longer *willing* to continue to extend credit. Sinai, on the other hand, sees the financial crisis (or money or credit crisis, as he refers to it) as coming about because of the *inability* of lenders, particularly banks, to continue to extend credit.

In turn, he sees this inability to be a result of slowed deposit inflows and, especially, the pressure on bank reserves from tight monetary policy. In fact, the Federal Reserve Board has tightened monetary policy toward the end of each postwar expansion. This fact may therefore explain why Sinai alone, of all the theorists writing about postwar financial crises, believes that credit crises occurred during the 1950s.

Milton Friedman's Theory of Financial Crises

As will be recalled from Chapter 2, Friedman considers the basic cause of financial crises to be erratic control of the money supply by the Federal Reserve Board. Erratic is interpreted to be a rapid increase followed by a sharp decline. According to Friedman, the sharp drop in the money supply after a previous increase puts pressure on the commercial banks. It forces them to dump assets, primarily bonds, onto the market in a desperate effort to obtain the reserves they need. The sharp drop in price and rise in interest rates which these actions cause are characteristic of financial crises.

Thus the procedure that will be followed to evaluate Friedman's theory of financial crises will be to first identify those periods of time during which the money supply showed erratic growth. Then we will investigate how the erratic growth in the money supply affected the rate of growth of bank investments (primarily U.S. government and state and local securities). Whenever the timing relationship between the growth of the money supply and the growth of bank investments is observed, his theory will be considered to be confirmed (even though such an observation may not conform with the dates of the financial crises discussed in Part II).

Identifying this timing relationship, though, involves the existence and the length of lags. It will be recalled from Chapter 2 that Friedman said the money supply grew too rapidly prior to April 1966. In April 1966 the Federal Reserve Board tightened monetary policy, in his opinion, too abruptly and too much. Friedman then concluded that this erratic control of the money supply produced a money crunch in the fall of 1966.

For a crunch to be produced in the fall of 1966 from a tightening of monetary policy in April requires at least one of two lags to be operating. In the first situation, there may have been a lag between Federal Reserve Board actions to tighten in April and the resulting effect on the money supply. In other words, the erratic growth of the money supply may have appeared with a lag after the tightening actions. In the second situation, Federal Reserve actions to tighten may have produced an immediate decline in the money supply, but this drop may not have affected bank investments until the fall, i.e., with a lag. We will attempt to take both of these lags into account in testing Friedman's theory.

Let us examine the relevant data. Figure 12.1 gives the monthly growth rates of the basic money supply, M_1. It indicates by what percentage (expressed at an annual rate) the money supply increased over its level a month earlier. It can be easily seen from the figure that, if one is looking for erratic growth of the money supply, one can surely find it.

It is possible to look at quarterly or semi-annual growth rates, too. A quarterly growth rate, for example, would show by what percentage the money supply had increased over its average level in the previous quarter. However, a quarterly growth rate may miss erratic changes during the quarter that cancel themselves out. A semi-annual growth rate would have this drawback even more.

To avoid overlooking instances of erratic growth of the money supply, and therefore opportunities for confirming Friedman's theory, the monthly growth rate was chosen. It is true that a weekly growth rate would exhibit even more erratic behavior. However, week-to-week changes in the money supply are too subject to noise and statistical aberrations to be meaningful and reliable.

From Figure 12.1 those instances were identified in which the growth rate in a particular month was less than the rate in the previous month by 10 percentage points or more. This criterion would seem to identify accurately those instances in which the money supply exhibited erratic growth in the downward direction. There were twenty instances in which this criterion was satisfied between January 1961 and May 1985 (see Table 12.1).

Figure 12.1

Monthly Growth Rate of M₁

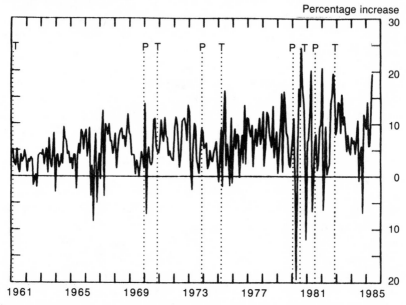

Source: Board of Governors of the Federal Reserve System, *Federal Reserve Bulletin*, table 1.21.

Note: Simple percentage increase from previous month, at annual rates. Calculated from seasonally adjusted monthly data.

Let us consider Friedman's theory using the first lag assumption, which is that Federal Reserve Board actions to tighten monetary policy affected the growth of the money supply only after a lag (although the subsequent decline in the money supply is assumed to affect bank investments in the same period).

For the empirical results in this situation, it does not matter when the Federal Reserve Board decided to tighten. In Friedman's example, the Board tightened in April, but we assume that its tightening action did not affect the money supply and bank investments until the fall (October, say). Thus, assuming the length of the lag is consistent, to check the validity of Friedman's relationship between the money supply and bank investments, we need only to look at their behavior in October.

In doing so, we find that Friedman's predictions are confirmed in this instance. The growth rate of the money supply dropped by 13.2 percentage points in October 1966. We find also that bank investments in October decreased by 21.3 percent from their level in September.

Friedman's theory also receives confirmation in two other instances in 1966. In May the growth rate of the money supply dropped by 12.9 percentage

Table 12.1

Selected Monthly Growth Rates of M₁ and Bank Investments

Date	Decrease in M₁ growth rate	Change in bank investments	Change in bank investments after	
			3 mos.	6 mos.
Dec. 63	11.2	10.0	0.0	5.0
May 66	12.9	−2.4	−1.2	− 3.6
July 66	10.6	−3.5	−21.3	20.8
Oct. 66	13.2	−21.3	20.8	10.6
Apr. 67	16.3	10.6	24.9	12.9
Feb. 70	21.0	6.9	16.8	23.7
Feb. 73	10.2	−15.7	0.9	1.8
Apr. 75	10.8	22.3	21.5	14.0
July 75	14.3	21.5	14.0	8.9
Dec. 75	12.4	11.3	8.6	4.6
Nov. 76	11.2	11.7	5.8	8.6
Feb. 78	10.5	4.6	0.9	2.7
May 79	15.1	1.6	4.6	4.2
Mar. 80	12.6	7.0	17.3	10.3
Apr. 80	17.9	1.2	22.2	13.8
Dec. 80	18.5	10.6	6.1	5.8
May 81	26.8	7.0	1.3	1.2
Feb. 82	27.0	6.0	−0.6	7.9
July 84	11.6	7.7	−4.2	7.2
Oct. 84	12.7	−4.2	7.2	− 13.1

All figures are annual percentage rates of increase.
Source: Basic data available from Board of Governors of the Federal Reserve System, Banking Section, Division of Research and Statistics. Percentages calculated by the author.

points and bank investments declined by 2.4 percent; in July the comparable figures were −10.6 and −3.5.

When we look at the rest of the data, however, this association rapidly disappears. In only two other instances in the entire 1961–85 period was a sharp money supply decline followed by a decrease in bank investments. These occurred in February 1973 and October 1984.

However, some problems exist even for the 1966 period. Since we do know in fact that Friedman traced the source of the erratic change in the money supply to Federal Reserve Board tightening in April, some other assumptions have to be made to explain the May and July data. If the six-month lag between Federal Reserve Board tightening and its effect on the money supply is maintained and, again, is assumed to be consistent, then the Board would have had to tighten also in November 1965 and January 1966. In fact, as also mentioned in Chapter 2, Friedman is of the opinion that the Federal Reserve Board did tighten in January 1966. However, he also states that this tightening caused banks to unload investments and produce the symptoms of a financial crisis in February. The implication of this statement is that Federal Reserve Board tightening in January affected the money supply and bank investments in February and also in July. Thus we not only have a lag that vaiies from one instance of tightening to the next; the lag takes on two different values at the same time.

Instead of assuming that the May and July drops in the money supply were due to two separate additional actions to tighten monetary policy in November 1965 and January 1966, it would be possible to assume that they were due to the single action in April. This assumption only compounds the problem, however, for it now produces three different lags instead of two.

Another alternative is to change the original assumption concerning the lag structure. In other words, instead of assuming that the lag is between the tightening action and the money supply, one could assume that it is between the change in the money supply and the resulting influence on bank investments. Thus, to return to Friedman's original example, the tightening in April is assumed to result in an immediate drop in the money supply, which then influences bank investments in the fall (October) six months later.

This possibility is also considered in Table 12.1 where data are given for the change in bank investments six months after the decline in the money supply. One immediate problem can be noted about this assumption: the money supply did not show a decline in April. (In fact it increased by 3.2 percent.)

The growth of the money supply did slow in May 1966, however. Also, it can be seen from the table that, six months after this decline, bank investments fell by 3.6 percent. So, using this lag assumption, Friedman's theory is confirmed for this instance. However, even more trouble arises for this lag assumption than for the initial one as other periods of time are examined. It turns out that in only one other instance (October 1984) was the decline in the money supply followed six months later by a decline in bank investments.

One final lag assumption will be examined, which will attempt to use the two different possible lags simultaneously. Let us begin with Friedman's view that the Federal Reserve Board tightened monetary policy in April, and with the realization that the money supply fell in May, not April. From Chapter 4 we also know that the banks dumped municipal securities into the market in August. Perhaps the lag structure is as follows: the tightening in April was followed by a decline in the money supply with a one-month lag (May), which then influenced bank investments with a three-month lag in August.

Thus, to examine whether or not this lag structure is capable of confirming Friedman's theory, we need to see in how many instances a decline in the money supply (following a previous increase) was followed three months later by a decline in bank investments. Aside from the May example, this series of events occurred only two other times in the 1961–85 period, one of which was July 1966.

Although one could experiment with different lag assumptions indefinitely, the overall conclusion must be that Friedman's theory is not confirmed, although it is supported to a certain extent by developments in 1966. However, we also found that Albert M. Wojnilower's theory can explain the 1966 events. Moreover, an approach using the general business-cycle and credit-market framework provides much better results for the rest of the period considered. One is therefore led to believe that the simple device of an erratic money supply is not sufficient to explain the interrelated and multifaceted phenomena known as financial crises.

13

Changes in Financial Crises: The Role of Long-Term Trends and Institutional Change

The events after 1982 make it clear that more than cyclical forces are needed to explain at least the timing of financial crises. Although these recent events were to a large degree a continuation of the problems that existed in 1982, these problems themselves were partly due to noncyclical changes affecting banking and thrift institutions which need to be explained.

In fact, if we take a broader look at the history of financial crises in the United States, we find other significant changes in financial crises. For example, in the late nineteenth and early twentieth centuries (through the Great Depression), financial crises were much more severe than those since 1966. The liquidation of credit was more widespread, financial markets were more severely affected, and failures of businesses and financial institutions were more extensive. In contrast, during the early postwar period (from 1946 to 1965), financial crises seemed to disappear.

What can explain such disparate behavior? Is the business-cycle model relevant only to the 1966–82 period, with separate explanations necessary for other periods (including the events since 1982)?

It is asserted (not proven here) that the cyclical forces described in the business-cycle model (with the exception of those institutional differences discussed in Chapter 12) are a part of the basic workings of a modern industrialized capitalist economy. Nonetheless, to understand financial crises in different historical periods it is necessary to integrate an understanding of these cyclical forces with two other developments affecting the economic and financial system: long-term (secular) trends and institutional change.

This chapter explores some hypotheses about how secular trends and institutional change have affected financial crises and have produced the different characteristics discussed above. Starting with the financial crises from 1966 to

1982 (described by the business-cycle model), an attempt is made to explain the differences between these crises and those taking place in the early twentieth century, the early postwar period, and the recent period since 1982.

The approach is exploratory, not definitive. The hypotheses mentioned are not proven. The purpose of the discussion is to suggest some possible explanations and hopefully to help stimulate further research in this field. An understanding of how the interaction of cyclical forces, secular trends, and institutional change affect financial crises is an important goal, and one that is necessary to comprehend the future evolution of the financial system in the United States; it is in the spirit of helping to contribute to the development of that understanding that the following is put forward.

1966–82 vs. the Early Twentieth Century

The financial crises that occurred in the later postwar period were, as noted above, less severe than those during the late nineteenth and early twentieth centuries. Three institutional changes that took place since the Depression may have been responsible for the difference. These were federal deposit insurance, an active role for the Federal Reserve as a lender of last resort, and anti-Depression government policy.

1. *Federal Deposit Insurance*. In the aftermath of the banking crises of the early 1930s, the federal insurance of deposits was instituted. By assuring small depositors that the resources of the federal government stood behind their deposits, this institutional change did much to eliminate the banking runs that had previously played a prominent role in financial crises.

The recent events in Ohio and Maryland serve to underscore this point. At the same time that runs took place on the deposits of privately insured thrifts, federally insured institutions were largely unaffected.

Federal deposit insurance also minimized the severity of financial crises by limiting the cumulative liquidation of credit that was typical of earlier crises. It enabled the banks to avoid the restriction of lending that had previously followed from the loss of deposits.

2. *Lender of Last Resort*. The Federal Reserve System was created in 1913 mainly to help eliminate financial crises like the Panic of 1907. However, Friedman and Schwartz's examination of the banking crises of the 1930s concluded that the lender-of-last-resort powers of the central bank were applied very timidly during the Depression.

In contrast, it was clear from an examination of the postwar crises since 1966 that the Federal Reserve Board intervened very actively as a lender of last resort. By making it clear to all concerned that it was prepared to provide the money necessary to meet urgent demands, the Federal Reserve did much to calm the developing feeling of panic and limit the financial crises.

3. *Anti-Depression Government Policy*. After the Great Depression, an

important objective of government policy was to avoid the recurrence of such a catastrophe. A Full Employment Act was passed in 1946. Although full employment has not been achieved, the resources of the government were used to mitigate the severity of the postwar recessions, including the disruptions to the financial and economic systems that had previously followed in the wake of earlier financial crises.

Both monetary and fiscal policy were consciously used in the postwar period to bolster aggregate demand and thus prevent postwar financial crises from leading to the cumulative debt-deflation process characteristic of earlier crises. Minsky in particular stresses the role that government deficits have played in the postwar recessions. His view is that, by boosting corporate profits and providing financial markets with default-free liabilities, government deficits have limited the worst effects of financial crises.[1]

Another series of institutional changes that should be included in the general category of anti-depression government policy are the social insurance programs initiated in the 1930s. These "automatic stabilizers" have also increased the government deficit during recessions; by providing funds through unemployment insurance, for instance, the government has acted to stabilize aggregate demand and smooth out the downside of the business cycle.

1966–82 vs. the Early Postwar Period

Financial crises were less severe after 1966 than they had been in the early part of the century. Yet from 1946 to 1965 it seemed that financial crises had disappeared. What explains the absence of crises in this period and their subsequent reappearance in 1966?

Certainly the federal insurance of deposits played a role in explaining the disappearance of crises. Yet it did not prevent the reappearance of crises in 1966. Moreover, anti-depression policy was less consciously employed in the early postwar period, and there was not a need for a lender of last resort until 1966.

There were, though, certain features of the early postwar period that made it relatively unique in U.S. financial history. Coming on the heels of the worst depression and the most extensive war effort in U.S. history, the financial system in the early postwar period was remarkably robust: debt levels were unusually low, and liquidity unusually high. There are three likely reasons for this situation.

1. *Debt Reduction During the Depression.* The sharp financial crises during the Depression, and the length of time during which the economy was depressed, reduced outstanding debt levels. As Wesley Clair Mitchell pointed out, the financial crisis involves an intense liquidation of credit, and the subsequent recession/depression is a less intense, but longer, period of continued liquidation. Thus by the beginning of World War II debt levels had been much reduced.

2. *World War II Financing.* During the war, financial markets were domi-

nated by the financing needs of the federal government. The sharp rise in the federal budget deficit during the war rapidly expanded the government's outstanding debt. Opportunities for private debt creation were limited. In addition, all sectors of the financial system wound up holding a large stock of high-quality, highly liquid assets: U.S. Treasury securities.

    3. *Depression-induced Financial Conservatism.* The trauma of the Depression was fresh in people's minds as the postwar period began. The dangers of too-rapid debt creation were taken as constraints upon the expansion rate of the financial system. Although this legacy of the Depression gradually faded, it most likely limited the use of debt during the early postwar period.

    The remarkably low levels of debt and highly liquid condition of financial sectors in the early postwar period help to explain the absence of financial crises. Although Sinai's article makes it clear that the same cyclical forces were present in the early postwar period as in the later period,[2] apparently the overall levels of debt and liquidity were such as to eliminate financial disturbances. Even though there were cyclical deteriorations in financial strength, the financial condition of businesses and financial institutions was still sufficiently strong. Minsky expresses the situation as follows:

> There is no way that a financial crisis could develop in an economy in which bank protected assets, mainly U.S. Government debt, were 60 percent of total liabilities. Similarly household and business balance sheets and liability-income relations were such that business could readily fulfill its payment commitments.[3]

    Minsky also has an explanation for why the financial structure changed over the course of the early postwar period, so that the economy once again became vulnerable to financial crises. He views the early postwar period as a "long-swing" expansion, or a period of time in which business-cycle recessions were very mild. Over the course of this prolonged expansion, the financial structure evolves to make financial crises likely:

> During the expansion phase of a long swing, or alternatively over a period in which only mild recessions occur, systemic changes in the financial structure occur. . . .
>   . . . The financial panic is made possible by the changes in the financial structure that take place during the long-swing expansion.[4]

    Over the prolonged expansion, the willingness to take on debt increases, and the perceived need for liquid assets declines. The financial system becomes, as Minsky notes, increasingly fragile.

Another possible explanation for the transition from a robust to a fragile financial system emphasizes developments during the recessions of the early postwar period, rather than the expansions. Over the course of a series of mild recessions, certain financial developments do not occur that do occur in a more severe recession. As was noted earlier, the level of outstanding debt was much reduced during the Depression. Also, inefficient firms went out of business, asset values fell, and liquidity improved. During the mild recessions of the early postwar years, these developments did not occur to a significant extent, and the financial system progressively deteriorated.[5]

If it is indeed the case that the financial system changed from robust to fragile from the early postwar period to the later period, then the mid-1960s would be an appropriate transition point. This perspective puts the 1966 crisis in an interesting light. It will be recalled that the 1966 experience was somewhat of an exception to the business-cycle model. The corporate sector was financially less vulnerable, and had less difficulty meeting payment commitments in 1966 than during other crisis periods. If 1966 marks the transition between a robust and fragile financial system, then this different behavior in 1966 is exactly what one would expect.

The following figures document the dramatic difference in the financial system before and after the mid-1960s. (Here annual data are used to highlight the secular trends rather than the cyclical movements.)

Figure 13.1 illustrates the higher levels of debt for the nonfinancial corporate business sector.[6] Figure 13.2 shows that the maturity of that debt became increasingly shorter after the mid-1960s; it also portrays the secular decline in liquidity. Figure 13.3 indicates the decline in liquid assets for the banking sector. It is interesting to note that the debt maturity ratio shows a relatively stable trend through the mid-1960s followed by a progressive deterioration in the later postwar years, whereas the deterioration in the liquidity ratios took place primarily in the early postwar years. (The decline in liquid assets in the banking sector through the mid-60s led to the increased use by banks of purchased funds to meet liquidity needs.)

1966–82 vs. the Post-1982 Period

If 1966 is a transition point between two different financial structures, then perhaps 1982 is as well. Although the events in 1982 generally conformed to the business-cycle model, it is interesting to note that there were three separate crises in 1982, and crises have followed at a rapid pace in the period since 1982.

In addition to being more frequent, and appearing before the peak of the business-cycle expansion, have crises also become more severe and difficult to manage? Continental Illinois was of course the largest bank ever to fail in the history of the United States, and the dimensions of its rescue were unprecedented.

Figure 13.1

Debt-Equity Ratio

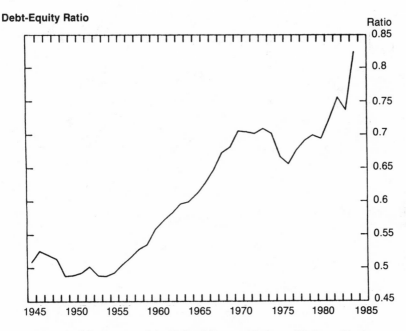

Source: Board of Governors of the Federal Reserve System, "Balance Sheets for the U.S. Economy, 1945–84," table 705.

Note: Nonfinancial corporations. Debt is total credit market borrowing; equity is net worth at historical cost. Calculated from annual levels.

Also, it was noted in Chapter 9 that even the guarantee by the FDIC that *all* of Continental's depositors and other general creditors would be fully protected failed to stop the run on Continental's deposits.

The period after 1982 has also seen the first bank run by holders of *small* deposits since the Depression. It is true, of course, that the situation of the privately insured thrifts is a special case, and that federally insured thrifts were relatively unaffected. At the same time, though, the private insurance systems had existed for many years without troubles of this sort.

The 1980s

Several important changes have taken place in the 1980s that have made the economy more vulnerable to financial crises. Most of these are temporary or unique developments that will not necessarily continue. However, they have affected present conditions.

They are primarily developments that have affected the financial condition

Figure 13.2

Debt Maturity and Liquidity Ratios

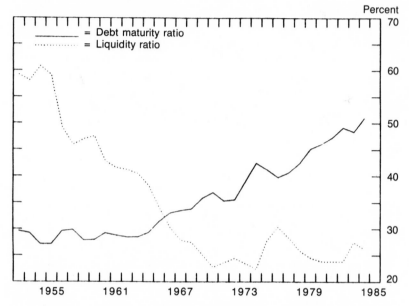

Source: Board of Governors of the Federal Reserve System, Flow of Funds
Section.

Note: Debt maturity ratio is loans and short-term paper as a percentage of total credit market borrowing; liquidity ratio is liquid assets as a percentage of
total short-term liabilities. Nonfinancial corporations. Annual levels.

the corporate sector and thus the quality of loans held by the banks and other
lenders. In part they are responsible for the problems that borrowers and financial
intermediaries had during 1982 (the "legacy of 1982"). They consist of the
following:

1. *Back-to-Back Recessions.* The recession of 1980 was sharp, but relatively brief. However, the subsequent expansion was equally brief. By July of
1981 the economy was heading into its second recession in two years. Before the
loan problems from the 1980 recession had been resolved, additional problems
were developing.

2. *The Severity of the 1981–82 Recession.* This recession was by far the
worst since the Depression. Unemployment in 1982 surpassed even the level of
the 1974–75 recession. Also, business bankruptcies rose to a record number for
the postwar period, in both absolute numbers and as a percentage of existing
firms. The financial distress that borrowers were under as a result of the recession
clearly influenced their ability to meet loan repayment commitments.

3. *The Transition from High to Low Inflation.* The inflation rate since 1981

Figure 13.3

Bank Asset Liquidity Ratio

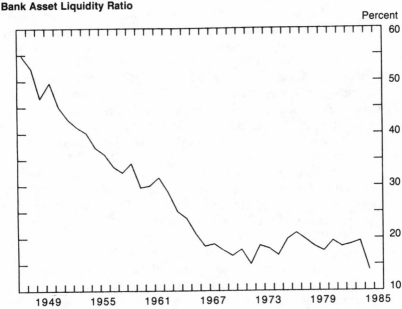

Source: Reports of Condition and Income filed by all insured commercial
banks.

Note: Cash and balances due from depository institutions (less cash items in
process of collection, vault cash, and reserves at Federal Reserve banks) plus
U.S. government securities, as a percentage of total assets. All insured commercial banks.

has been substantially lower than it was in 1981 and earlier. Lower rates of
inflation have clearly benefited many sectors of the economy that previously had
suffered from the distortions and uncertainty caused by the inflationary 1970s.
However, the *transition* has been a difficult one for many borrowers and their
banks.

Debt that had been incurred on the expectation of a continuing inflationary
environment caused difficulties for borrowers. The expected appreciation of
collateral did not materialize, and real debt burdens became more onerous for
borrowers who had expected to repay their debts in dollars of lower value. The
rising tide of inflation had lifted the boats of quite a few borrowers, who were left
grounded when the inflationary tide receded. These developments, of course,
contributed to an increasing number of defaults on bank loans.

4. *High Real Interest Rates.* The condition of borrowers would have been
better if interest rates had fallen along with prices. However, interest rates have
remained remarkably high. Despite a decline from the record levels of 1981,
interest rates in the 1980s remain higher, relative to inflation, than at any other

time in the postwar period. Thus even refinancing brings little improvement to borrowers with high real debt burdens.

5. *Volatile Interest Rates*. In addition to being high, interest rates during the 1980s (especially during 1980–1982) were much more variable than they had been in the past. This volatility was due in part to the new operating procedures introduced by the Federal Open Market Committee in October 1979, but perhaps more fundamentally to the uncertainty and instability in financial markets.

The volatility of interest rates made financial planning more difficult for most corporations and financial institutions. In addition, it opened the door to speculation by those individuals and companies that thought they could outguess the market. The unsuccessful speculation by Drysdale and ESM Government Securities, Inc., helped to initiate financial crises in 1982 and 1985.

6. *High Value of the Dollar*. Although it has declined somewhat in 1985, the exchange value of the dollar rose during the 1980s to unprecedented levels, as can be seen from Figure 13.4. This rise in the dollar has exacerbated the debt repayment problems of the less developed countries (LDCs), whose debt is denominated in dollars. Although the problems of the LDCs have not reached the crisis stage since the resolution of the Mexican situation in 1982, the problems still exist. They could erupt in more intense form if not handled correctly, and if the dollar shows any further significant appreciation.

It is true that the strong dollar contributed to lower prices in the United States, as domestic prices had to compete with the lower cost of imported products. At the same time, though, domestic markets have been penetrated by these low-priced imports, and U.S. exporters have had a difficult time selling U.S. products abroad. The agricultural sector has been particularly hard-hit by the decline in exports.

7. *The Decline of the Agricultural and Energy Sectors*. In addition to the strong dollar, the agricultural sector has been affected by the transition to low inflation and the associated collapse of farm land values. Farmers who had borrowed heavily with the expectation of rising prices of agricultural products and land now find themselves with inadequate collateral and unable to meet debt payment requirements.

Many banks whose loan portfolios are heavily concentrated in agriculture face severe difficulties, and many have failed. These banks are primarily small, with assets of less than $100 million. Their failure has not thus far posed a risk to the financial system as a whole.

The decline of the energy industry has likewise resulted in losses for banks that have been heavy energy lenders. The major difference is that the banks affected by the energy industry have been much larger. As was discussed earlier, the troubles at Penn Square, Seafirst, and Continental Illinois were attributable to energy. In addition, some large Texas banks have suffered large losses due to energy lending. Here the price of oil is a critical barometer of the ability of these large banks to weather the energy storm successfully.

Figure 13.4

Exchange Value of U.S. Dollar

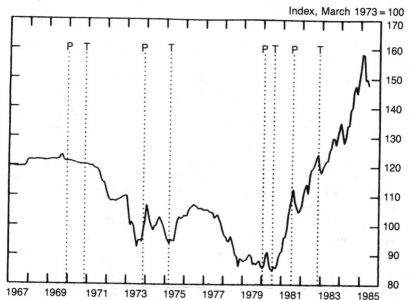

Index, March 1973 = 100

Source: Board of Governors of the Federal Reserve System, *Federal Reserve Bulletin*, Table 3.28.

Note: Index of weighted-average exchange value of U.S. dollar against currencies of other G–10 countries plus Switzerland. Monthly data.

The above problems have already contributed to a record number of bank failures. As noted in Chapter 8, there were 34 commercial bank failures in 1982. That total was, at the time, far above the number of bank failures in any year since the Depression. Yet 45 commercial banks failed in 1983, 78 in 1984, and 118 in 1985.

In response to the deteriorating financial condition of the banking system, bank regulators have progressively raised bank capital requirements. The component of bank capital that consists of stockholders' equity (which is the overwhelming majority) protects a bank against failure. Bank capital also provides a buffer in the event of failure for uninsured depositors and the FDIC.

At the same time, bank capital requirements can restrain the growth of bank lending. If a rapid increase in a bank's loans were to reduce its capital-asset ratio below the minimum, then the bank may have to forego the additional lending.

This development could affect the ability of large banks to use liability management to continue to fund loan growth during periods of tight money. If so, it could alter the dynamics of how financial crises occur in the future. As noted in Chapter 12, the use of liability management in the later postwar period represented an important change from the early twentieth century in the way that financial crises developed.

Long-Term Changes

Whether or not a change will occur along these lines is difficult to predict. Also, it may well be that the developments of the 1980s described above will be temporary and will produce no long-lasting changes in the nature of financial crises. However, there are a number of secular trends and institutional changes that have taken place over the course of the 1966–82 period that point in the direction of a possibly more permanent and qualitatively different financial environment in the post-1982 period. These include the following:

1. *Continued Financial Fragility.* The financial system has continued to become more fragile over the recent period. Figures 11.1–11.4 indicate in detail the increase in financial vulnerability of the corporate sector since the mid-1960s.[7] The problems of the thrift institutions have been discussed earlier. Figure 11.18 indicates the increasing asset-quality problems of the commercial banks (which of course have contributed to the record number of bank failures).

2. *A Secular Decline in Corporate Profits.* Figure 11.7 indicates the decline in corporate profits since the mid-1960s. Although profitability has increased sharply in the recent expansion, the improvement in relation to trend is due only to the favorable tax treatment of corporate profits in recent legislation. Profits before tax have increased, but before-tax profitability has not reached the previous peak recorded in 1977. A decline in profitability in the corporate sector clearly makes it more difficult for corporations to meet debt payment commitments, and encourages the increased use of debt to compensate for reduced internal funds.

Although the theories of Karl Marx that were considered in Chapter 2 were discussed in the context of the business cycle, his views, like Minsky's, can be interpreted to apply over a longer period of time. His view of a declining rate of profit is thus one hypothesis that can be used to explain changing financial developments in the postwar period.[8]

3. *The Success of the Federal Safety Net.* It was mentioned above that federal deposit insurance, lender-of-last-resort actions, and government policies to minimize recessions have lessened the severity of financial crises during the 1966–82 period (in comparison with the early twentieth century). At the same time, though, the very success of these policies has had unwanted side effects.

In particular, the attitude has developed that government authorities will not allow a very large bank to fail, for fear of the repercussions on the financial system. This attitude has probably encouraged some additional risk-taking that otherwise would not have occurred.

Deposit insurance has most likely had similar effects. Although deposit insurance has clearly played a crucial role in preventing bank runs, it has, particularly in conjunction with the placement of deposits by brokers, allowed banks to finance unusually risky operations with funds that depositors consider risk-free. Penn Square Bank is a case in point. Depositors who invested their money with Penn Square paid no attention to Penn Square's lending policies because their deposits were federally insured.

Finally, the prevention of the severe repercussions of crises by lender-of-last-resort actions, and the use of monetary and fiscal policy to mitigate recessions, have also had unwanted side effects. As in the earlier postwar period, they have allowed the distortions in the debt structure to keep on building.

Minsky points out that lender-of-last-resort actions by the Federal Reserve have had the effect of protecting various sources of debt-creation:

> By extending central bank protection to particular assets and
> institutions, the Federal Reserve 'endorses' the continued
> use of that instrument and the viability of institutions. Thus
> the spectrum of financing forms that are available increases.[9]

He contends that such lender-of-last-resort actions are inflationary: "This intervention by the Federal Reserve both helps stop the plunge to a deep depression and assures that the subsequent recovery from the rather mild depression that does take place will be inflationary."[10]

4. *Financial Innovation and Deregulation.* Albert M. Wojnilower also has a long-term theory that was not considered in Chapter 2. He contends that the financial system has become much more prone to excessive credit creation and inflation. His explanation traces an interactive process between financial innovation and deregulation.

Wojnilower's view, as discussed above, is that credit crunches have come about in the postwar economy because of unexpected interruptions in the supply of credit. To avoid such interruptions in the future, after each episode both government authorities (via deregulation) and private market participants (via financial innovations) have taken steps to eliminate the credit bottlenecks. By such a process interest-rate ceilings have been eliminated, floating-rate loans have proliferated, and the financial futures market has been created. Wojnilower contends that the removal of all credit supply "speed limits" has been harmful because of the excessive credit creation that it has encouraged.

Although banks have seen deregulation as a way to respond to competitive pressures, the general trend toward deregulation has raised new problems for them. The effect of interest-rate deregulation on thrift institutions has been discussed in an earlier chapter. Geographic and, in particular, product deregulation have also taken place. Banks are now attempting to move into the fields of securities underwriting, insurance, and real estate development. While these new activities hold open the promise of new opportunities for financial institutions, they also carry with them substantial risk.

5. *The Inappropriateness of the Institutional Structure.* The institutional structure affecting financial intermediaries is currently in a state of flux. Institutional structures that were appropriate for the early postwar period are no longer appropriate. Yet no new structures have taken their place.

For example, several proposals for modifying the deposit insurance system have been put forward, with the purpose of reducing the incentives that deposit insurance provides to increased risk-taking. Yet none has yet been agreed upon. Changes in financial technology have broken down barriers that have existed for years and forced increased competition among financial institutions, and also between financial institutions and other businesses such as Sears Roebuck. However, new institutional structures to define the basis for this new competition have not been created. Inflation has destroyed the viability of interest-rate ceilings, but the resulting deregulation of interest rates has created new problems.

A promising line of analysis has placed institutional mismatches like these into the general context of a "social structure of accumulation."[11] In general, economic growth can proceed when the institutional structure is supportive of growth, as it was during the early postwar period. But when secular trends and institutional change make that structure inappropriate, as they have in the later postwar period, a new institutional structure is required. The future functioning of the financial system in a way that is supportive of further growth, and financial stability, will depend largely upon the ability of economic and financial groups to fashion a new institutional structure appropriate for the current period.

Notes

Notes to Chapter 1

1. Allen Sinai, "Discussion of Papers on The American Financial Environment," in *Financial Crises: Institutions and Markets in a Fragile Environment*, ed. Edward I. Altman and Arnold W. Sametz (New York: John Wiley and Sons, 1977), p. 187.

2. For a collection of many of Minsky's important articles, see Hyman P. Minsky, *Can "It" Happen Again?* (Armonk, New York: M. E. Sharpe, Inc., 1982).

3. Charles P. Kindleberger, *Manias, Panics, and Crashes* (New York: Basic Books, 1978).

4. In addition to the contemporary writers discussed later on in the book, some other quite recent work includes the following: Andrew Carron, "Financial Crises: Recent Experience in U.S. and International Markets," *Brookings Papers on Economic Activity*, 1982, No. 2, pp. 395–418; *Crises in the Economic and Financial Structure*, ed. Paul Wachtel (Lexington, Massachusetts: D. C. Heath and Co., 1982); *Financial Crises*, ed. Charles P. Kindleberger and Jean-Pierre Laffargue (Cambridge: Cambridge University Press, 1982); Jack Guttentag and Richard Herring, "Credit Rationing and Financial Disorder," *The Journal of Finance* 39 (December 1984): 1359–82.

5. The particular writers discussed in this book were chosen with two aims in mind: to include writers from both the past and present, and to represent the different theoretical perspectives within economics. Nonetheless, any choice of authors remains arbitrary to some extent. Other important theorists, e.g., Irving Fisher, could easily have been included.

6. Joseph A. Schumpeter, *Business Cycles*, Vol. I (New York: McGraw-Hill Book Company, 1939), p. 30.

7. John Robinson, "What has become of the Keynesian Revolution?" in *After Keynes*, ed. Joan Robinson (Oxford: Basil Blackwell, 1973), p. 5.

Part I

Notes to Chapter 2

1. Thorstein Veblen, *The Theory of Business Enterprise* (New York: Charles Scribner's Sons, 1904), esp. Chapter VII, "The Theory of Modern Welfare."

2. Ibid., pp. 177–78, 92.

3. Ibid., pp. 96–97. See also Chapter V, "The Use of Loan Credit."

4. Ibid., p. 186 and Chapter VI, "Modern Business Capital."

5. Ibid., pp. 199–200.

6. Ibid., p. 197.

7. Ibid., pp. 200–201.

8. Ibid., p. 191.

9. Wesley Clair Mitchell, *Business Cycles* (Berkeley: University of California Press, 1913). The theoretical part of this volume was reprinted as *Business Cycles and Their Causes* (Berkeley: University of California Press, 1941).

10. Milton Friedman, "Wesley Clair Mitchell as an Economic Theorist," reprinted in *Wesley Clair Mitchell, The Economic Scientist*, ed. Arthur F. Burns (New York: National Bureau of Economic Research, 1952), p. 244.

11. Mitchell, *Business Cycles and Their Causes*, p. vi.

12. Ibid., pp. ix, xi.

13. Ibid., pp. 1–2.

14. Ibid., p. 153.

15. Ibid., pp. 39, 43–44.

16. Ibid., pp. 155 and 45.

17. Ibid., pp. 154–55.

18. Ibid., pp. 47–48.

19. Ibid., p. 157.

20. Ibid., p. 158.

21. Ibid., p. 72.

22. Ibid., p. 73.

23. Ibid.

24. Ibid., pp. 73–74.

25. Ibid., p. 70.

26. Ibid., p. 158.

27. Ibid.

28. Ibid., pp. 123–124.

29. Karl Marx, *Capital*, Vol. III (New York: International Publishers, 1967), p. 360.

30. Karl Marx, *Theories of Surplus Value*, Part II (Moscow: Progress Publishers, 1968), p. 514. Emphasis in original.

31. Ibid., p. 515. Emphasis in original.

32. Marx, *Capital*, Vol. III, pp. 481–82.

33. Ibid.

34. Marx, *Theories of Surplus Value*, Part II, p. 514. Emphasis in original.

35. Ibid., p. 516. Emphasis in original.

36. Marx, *Capital*, Vol. III, p. 490.

37. Ibid., p. 513.

38. Ibid., p. 516.

39. Ibid., p. 408.

40. Hyman P. Minsky, *John Maynard Keynes* (New York: Columbia University Press, 1975), pp. viii, ix.

41. Ibid., p. 57.

42. Hyman P. Minsky, "The Financial Instability Hypothesis: An Interpretation of Keynes and an Alternative to 'Standard' Theory," *Nebraska Journal of Economics and*

Business 16 (Winter 1977), reprinted in *Challenge* 20 (March-April 1977):22.

43. Minsky, *John Maynard Keynes*, p. 61.

44. Minsky, "The Financial Instability Hypothesis," p. 24.

45. Hyman P. Minsky, "A Theory of Systemic Fragility," in *Financial Crises: Institutions and Markets in a Fragile Environment*, ed. Edward I. Altman and Arnold W. Sametz (New York: John Wiley and Sons, 1977), pp. 139–40. Emphasis in original.

46. Ibid., p. 142.

47. Ibid., p. 143.

48. Minsky, "The Financial Instability Hypothesis," p. 24.

49. Minsky, *John Maynard Keynes*, p. 119.

50. Minsky, "A Theory of Systemic Fragility," p. 146.

51. Hyman P. Minsky, "Finance and Profits: The Changing Nature of American Business Cycles," in U.S. Congress, Joint Economic Committee, *The Business Cycle and Public Policy, 1929–80*, Joint Committee Print (Washington, D.C.: Government Printing Office, 1980), p. 221.

52. Minsky, "A Theory of Systemic Fragility," p. 146.

53. Minsky, "Finance and Profits," p. 222.

54. Minsky, "A Theory of Systemic Fragility," p. 149.

55. Hyman P. Minsky, "Capitalist Financial Processes and the Instability of Capitalism," *Journal of Economic Issues* XIV (June 1980):517.

56. Minsky, *John Maynard Keynes*, pp. 121–22.

57. Hyman P. Minsky, "The Federal Reserve: Between a Rock and a Hard Place," *Challenge* 23 (May-June 1980).

58. Hyman P. Minsky, "Financial Resources in a Fragile Financial Environment," *Challenge* 18 (July-August 1975):11.

59. Minsky, *John Maynard Keynes*, p. 114.

60. Hyman P. Minsky, "The Financial Instability Hypothesis: A Restatement," reprinted in *Can "It" Happen Again?* by Hyman P. Minsky (Armonk, New York: M. E. Sharpe, Inc. 1982), p. 107. Hereafter referred to as "Restatement."

61. Minsky, "Financial Resources," p. 22.

62. Minsky, "The Financial Instability Hypothesis," p. 25.

63. Hyman P. Minsky, "The Financial Instability Hypothesis: Capitalist Processes and the Behavior of the Economy," in *Financial Crises*, ed. Charles P. Kindleberger and Jean-Pierre Laffargue (Cambridge: Cambridge University Press, 1982), p. 13. Hereafter referred to as "Capitalist Processes."

64. Minsky, *John Maynard Keynes*, p. 143.

65. Minsky, "The Financial Instability Hypothesis," p. 25.

66. The capitalization factor is not the interest rate itself, but is positively correlated with it. See Minsky, *John Maynard Keynes*, Chapter 5, "The Theory of Investment," esp. pp. 99–104.

67. Hyman P. Minsky, "Financial Markets and Economic Instability, 1965–1980," *Nebraska Journal of Economics and Business* 20 (Autumn 1981):12.

68. Minsky, "Capitalist Financial Processes," p. 516.

69. Minsky, "A Restatement," pp. 107–108.

70. Minsky, "A Theory of Systemic Fragility," p. 140.

71. Minsky, "Capitalist Processes," p. 33.

72. Hyman P. Minsky, "Policy Pitfalls in a Financially Fragile Economy," in U.S.

Congress, House Committee on Banking, Finance and Urban Affairs, *Employment Risks from Present Credit and Business Liquidity Conditions, Hearings before the Subcommittee on Domestic Monetary Policy of the House Committee on Banking, Finance and Urban Affairs*, 97th Cong., 2d. sess., 1982, pp. 75–76.

73. Minsky, "Financial Markets," p. 14.

74. Minsky frequently refers to Fisher's article, "The Debt-Deflation Theory of Great Depressions," *Econometrica* 1 (October 1933):337–57.

75. Minsky, "Policy Pitfalls," p. 79.

76. Albert M. Wojnilower, "The Central Role of Credit Crunches in Recent Financial History," *Brookings Papers on Economic Activity*, 1980, No. 2, pp. 277–326. An updating of this article was presented by Wojnilower at the annual meeting of the American Economics Association in Dallas, Texas, on December 28, 1984. It was published in the proceedings of the conference as "Private Credit Demand, Supply and Crunches: How Different are the 1980s?" *American Economic Review* 75 (May 1985):351–56.

77. Wojnilower, "The Central Role of Credit Crunches," p. 277.

78. Ibid., p. 324.

79. Ibid., pp. 277–78.

80. Ibid., p. 278.

81. Ibid.

82. Ibid., p. 278.

83. Allen Sinai, "Credit Crunches—An Analysis of the Postwar Experience," in *Parameters and Policies in the U.S. Economy*, ed. Otto Eckstein (Amsterdam: North-Holland, 1976), pp. 244–74.

84. Ibid., p. 244–45.

85. Allen Sinai, "Discussion of Papers on The American Financial Environment," in *Financial Crises: Institutions and Markets in a Fragile Environment*, ed. Edward I. Altman and Arnold W. Sametz (New York: John Wiley and Sons, 1977), p. 187.

86. Ibid., pp. 194–95.

87. Sinai, "Credit Crunches," pp. 245–46.

88. Ibid., p. 246.

89. Ibid., p. 244.

90. Ibid., p. 246.

91. Ibid., p. 245.

92. Ibid.

93. Milton Friedman and Anna Jacobson Schwartz, *A Monetary History of the United States, 1867–1960* (Princeton: Princeton University Press for the National Bureau of Economic Research, 1963).

94. Milton Friedman, "A Theoretical Framework for Monetary Analysis," *Journal of Political Economy* 78 (March/April 1970):193–238.

95. Milton Friedman and Anna Schwartz, "Money and Business Cycles," *Review of Economics and Statistics* 45 (February 1963):32–64, reprinted in *The Optimum Quantity of Money and Other Essays*, by Milton Friedman (Chicago: Aldine, 1969), pp. 189–235.

96. Milton Friedman and Anna J. Schwartz, *Monetary Trends in the United States and the United Kingdom* (Chicago: The University of Chicago Press, 1983), Chapter 2, "The General Theoretical Framework."

97. Milton Firedman, *An Economist's Protest* (Glen Ridge, New Jersey: Thomas

Horton and Co., 1972), p. 38. Friedman expresses this opinion in many of his other writings as well.

98. Friedman and Schwartz, *A Monetary History*, p. 35.

99. Ibid., p. 352.

100. Ibid., p. 676.

101. Ibid., p. 354.

102. Ibid., p. 298.

103. Ibid., pp. 307–8.

104. Friedman and Schwartz, "Money and Business Cycles," p. 218.

105. Friedman and Schwartz, *A Monetary History*, p. 355.

106. Friedman and Schwartz, "Money and Business Cycles," p. 218.

107. See Friedman and Schwartz, *A Monetary History*, pp. 407–19, for further discussion.

108. Ibid., p. 393.

109. Ibid., p. 394.

110. Ibid., pp. 167–68.

111. Ibid., p. 163.

112. Milton Friedman, "Why the American Economy is Depression-Proof," a lecture delivered in Stockholm in April 1954. Printed in *Dollars and Deficits*, by Milton Friedman (Englewood Cliffs, New Jersey: Prentice-Hall, Inc., 1968), pp. 72–96.

113. Ibid., p. 77. Emphasis in original.

114. Milton Friedman, "The Changing Character of Financial Markets," in *The American Economy in Transition*, ed. Martin Feldstein (Chicago: The University of Chicago Press, 1980), pp. 78–86.

115. Ibid., pp. 79–80.

116. Milton Friedman, "Current Monetary Policy," in *Dollars and Deficits*, pp. 153–64.

117. Ibid., pp. 156–57. Emphasis added.

118. Ibid., p. 161.

119. Ibid. Emphasis added.

120. Milton Friedman, "Monetary Policy," in *Dollars and Deficits*, p. 171.

Notes to Chapter 3

1. For further discussion, see Minsky, "Finance and Profits," pp. 217–18.

2. Milton Friedman, "The Monetary Theory and Policy of Henry Simons," *Journal of Law and Economics* 10 (October 1967), reprinted in *The Optimum Quantity of Money and Other Essays*, by Milton Friedman (Chicago: Aldine, 1969), pp. 81–93.

3. Ibid.

4. Ibid., pp. 85, 89.

5. Ibid.

Notes to Part II

1. Henry Kaufman, Foreword to *Financial Crises: Institutions and Markets in a Fragile Environment*, ed. Edward I. Altman and Arnold W. Sametz (New York: John Wiley and Sons, 1977), p. vii.

Notes to Chapter 4

1. For the sake of the readability of this descriptive summary of financial crises, data that would support a number of statements made in Part II are not included. The interested reader desiring more documentation at this point can consult the charts in Part III or the flow of funds tables in my Ph.D. dissertation, "Financial Crises: Theory and Evidence in the Postwar U.S. Economy," The American University, 1984.

2. In fact, since the financing gap measures the difference between *actual* investment spending and internal funds, it is a result of the interaction of the demand for funds for investment with the supply. When combined with other relevant data (such as the COPE series), though, it probably provides a reasonable approximation of the demand.

3. Historical data for specific growth rates of the monetary aggregates and bank credit are also presented in the dissertation referred to in note 2.

4. Board of Governors of the Federal Reserve System, *Annual Report, 1966*, p. 140.

5. Ibid., pp. 147–48. Emphasis added.

6. Ibid., p. 30.

7. Ibid., p. 247.

8. Ibid., p. 232.

9. Ibid., pp. 168, 174.

10. Ibid., p. 103.

Notes to Chapter 5

1. Federal Reserve Bank of New York, *Annual Report, 1969*, pp. 14–16.

2. Board of Governors of the Federal Reserve System, *Annual Report, 1969*, p. 3.

3. The data reported in the flow of funds tables understate the significance of this source of funds, however. The vast majority of the activity in the federal funds market is interbank borrowing and lending which is netted out in the flow of funds accounts. Typically it is the large banks with loan opportunities that borrow fed funds from smaller banks with excess reserves. Therefore the banking system as a whole is able to utilize its reserves more efficiently and expand its lending.

4. Ibid., p. 11.

5. Sherman J. Maisel, *Managing the Dollar* (New York: W. W. Norton and Company, Inc., 1973), p. 254.

6. William C. Melton, "The Market for Large Negotiable CDs," *Federal Reserve Bank of New York Quarterly Review* 2 (Winter 1977–78):28.

7. Albert M. Wojnilower, "The Central Role of Credit Crunches in Recent Financial History," *Brookings Papers on Economic Activity*, No. 2 (1980), pp. 291–92.

8. Board of Governors, *Annual Report, 1970*, p. 97.

9. Flow of funds data indicate that nonfinancial corporations issued commercial paper at a seasonally adjusted annual rate of $3.8 billion in the first quarter of 1970 (or $0.95 billion during the quarter). The overall reliance of nonfinancial corporations on commercial paper is underestimated by the flow of funds data, however. The primary reason is that big nonfinancial issuers of commercial paper (like Chrysler Corporation) do so through financial subsidiaries, and these financial subsidiaries are excluded from the nonfinancial corporate business sector in the flow of funds data. Also, the primary buyers

of commercial paper are other corporations. As these intercorporate transfers are netted out, the reliance upon commercial paper by some corporations is missed.

10. Evelyn M. Hurley, "The Commercial Paper Market," *Federal Reserve Bulletin* 63 (June 1977):531–32.

11. Board of Governors, *Annual Report, 1970*, p. 137.

12. Ibid., p. 18.

13. Thomas Timlen, "Commercial Paper—Penn Central and Others," in *Financial Crises: Institutions and Markets in a Fragile Environment*, ed. Edward I. Altman and Arnold W. Sametz (New York: John Wiley and Sons, 1977), pp. 233–34.

Notes to Chapter 6

1. Federal Reserve Bank of New York, *Annual Report, 1974*, p. 4. See also Norman N. Bowsher, "Two Stages to the Current Recession," *Federal Reserve Bank of St. Louis Review* 57 (June 1975):1–8.

2. Board of Governors of the Federal Reserve System, *Annual Report, 1974*, pp. 39–40.

3. Brian M. Neuberger, "The Exposure and Financial Involvement of Bank Holding Companies in the Real Estate Investment Trust Industry," in U.S. Congress, Senate Committee on Banking, Housing and Urban Affairs, *Real Estate Investment Trusts, Hearings*, 94th Cong., 2d sess., 1976.

4. Wyndham Robertson, "How the Banks Got Trapped in the REIT Disaster," *Fortune*, March 1975, p. 113.

5. See "Changes in Bank Lending Practices, 1974," *Federal Reserve Bulletin* 61 (April 1975):223.

6. Andrew F. Brimmer, "The Federal Reserve and the Failure of Franklin National Bank: A Case Study of Regulation," in *Business and the American Economy, 1776–2001*, ed. Jules Backman (New York: New York University Press, 1976), p. 115.

7. Joan Edelman Spero, *The Failure of the Franklin National Bank: Challenge to the International Banking System* (New York: Columbia University Press, 1980), p. 108.

8. Sanford Rose, "What Really Went Wrong at Franklin National," *Fortune*, October 1974, p. 225.

9. Brimmer, "The Federal Reserve and the Failure of Franklin National Bank," p. 131.

10. Dwight B. Crane, "Lessons from the 1974 CD Market," *Harvard Business Review* 53 (November-December 1975):75.

11. Spero, *The Failure of the Franklin National Bank*, p. 117.

12. Ibid., pp. 114–15.

13. Brimmer, "The Federal Reserve and the Failure of Franklin National Bank," pp. 109–110.

14. Ibid., p. 133.

15. Joseph L. Sinkey, Jr., "The Collapse of Franklin National Bank of New York," *Journal of Bank Research* 7 (Summer 1976):117.

16. Ibid.

17. Brimmer, "The Federal Reserve and the Failure of Franklin National Bank," p. 136.

Notes to Chapter 7

1. Data Resources, Inc., "Chrysler and the U.S. Economy: A Simulation Study," in U.S. Congress, Senate Committee on the Budget, *Second Concurrent Resolution on the Budget—Fiscal Year 1980, Hearings before the Senate Committee on the Budget*, 96th Cong., 1st sess., 1979, pp. 98–105.

2. "Monetary Policy and Open Market Operations in 1979," *Federal Reserve Bank of New York Quarterly Review* 5 (Summer 1980):59.

3. "Changes in Bank Lending Practices, 1979–81," *Federal Reserve Bulletin* 67 (September 1981):679.

4. Federal Reserve Bank of New York, *Annual Report, 1980*, p. 3.

5. See Joseph F. Sinkey, Jr., "The Performance of First Pennsylvania Bank Prior to Its Bail Out," *Journal of Bank Research* 14 (Summer 1983):119–33.

6. U.S. Securities and Exchange Commission, *The Silver Crisis of 1980*, 1982.

7. U.S. Congress, House Committee on Government Operations, *Silver Prices and the Adequacy of Federal Actions in the Marketplace, 1979–80, Hearings before a Subcommittee of the House Committee on Government Operations*, 96th Cong., 2d sess., 1980, p. 281.

8. Ibid., pp. 339–45.

9. See Stephen Fay, *Beyond Greed* (New York: Penguin Books, 1983), pp. 81–102, for details.

10. U.S. Congress, Senate Committee on Agriculture, Nutrition, and Forestry, *Report of the Commodity Futures Trading Commission on Recent Developments in the Silver Futures Markets*, 96th Cong., 2d sess., 1980, pp. 48, 56–57.

11. Ibid., p. 65.

12. Fay, *Beyond Greed*, pp. 131–37.

13. House Committee on Government Operations, *Silver Prices*, pp. 12–17.

14. Ibid., p. 27.

15. Senate Committee on Agriculture, *Report of the Commodity Futures Trading Commission*, p. 72.

16. Fay, *Beyond Greed*, p. 108.

17. "Interim Report on Financial Aspects of the Silver Market Situation in Early 1980," in House Committee on Government Operations, *Silver Prices*, pp. 244–45. Emphasis in original.

18. House Committee on Government Operations, *Silver Prices*, pp. 342, 347.

19. Senate Committee on Agriculture, *Report of the Commodity Futures Trading Commission*, p. 87.

20. House Committee on Government Operations, *Silver Prices*, pp. 342, 348.

21. Senate Committee on Agriculture, *Report of the Commodity Futures Trading Commission*, pp. 82–83.

22. "Interim Report," p. 246.

23. Fay, *Beyond Greed*, p. 217.

Notes to Chapter 8

1. The answers to this and subsequent questions from the Survey of Bank Lending

Practices are available from the Board of Governors of the Federal Reserve System, Banking Section, Division of Research and Statistics.

2. Data are from the Reports of Condition and Income filed with the appropriate regulatory agency by all insured commercial banks.

3. Anthony G. Cornyn, "Financial Developments of Bank Holding Companies in 1982," *Federal Reserve Bulletin* 69 (July 1983):512.

4. Federal Deposit Insurance Corporation, *1982 Annual Report*, pp. 5, 31.

5. Michael J. Moran, "Thrift Institutions in Recent Years," *Federal Reserve Bulletin* 68 (December 1982):726.

6. Federal Home Loan Bank Board, *Annual Report 1982*, p. 19.

7. Ibid., p. 8.

8. See Moran, "Thrift Institutions in Recent Years," pp. 731–34, for a description of these new accounting techniques.

9. U.S. Congress, Senate Committee on Banking, Housing and Urban Affairs, *Disturbances in the U.S. Securities Market, Hearing before the Subcommittee on Securities of the Senate Committee on Banking, Housing, and Urban Affairs*, 97th Cong., 2d sess., 1982, p. 21.

10. Federal Reserve Bank of New York, *A Report on Drysdale and Other Recent Problems of Firms Involved in the Government Securities Market*, September 15, 1982.

11. Ibid., pp. 29–30.

12. Ibid., p. 30.

13. Richard L. Hudson and Kenneth H. Bacon, "How Agencies Helped Avert Drysdale Panic," *Wall Street Journal*, 1 June 1982, p. 29.

14. Federal Reserve Bank of New York, *A Report on Drysdale*, p. 32.

15. U.S. Congress, Senate Committee on Banking, Housing, and Urban Affairs, *Failure of Penn Square Bank, Hearing*, 97th Cong., 2d sess., 1983, p. 8.

16. Ibid., p. 15.

17. U.S. Congress, House Committee on Banking, Finance, and Urban Affairs, *Penn Square Bank Failure, Hearings*, Part 2, 97th Cong., 2d sess., 1983, pp. 9–10.

18. U.S. Congress, House Committee on Banking, Finance, and Urban Affairs, *Penn Square Bank Failure, Hearings*, Part 1, 97th Cong., 2d sess., 1982, p. 392.

19. "The Stain from Penn Square Keeps Spreading," *Business Week*, 2 August 1982, p. 60.

20. House Banking Committee, *Penn Square Bank Failure*, Part 2, p. 271.

21. *Business Week*, 2 August 1982, p. 60.

22. Ibid., p. 61.

23. Board of Governors of the Federal Reserve System, *Annual Report, 1982*, p. 113.

24. Federal Financial Institutions Examination Council, "Country Exposure Lending Survey: June 1982," Statistical Release E.16, December 16, 1982.

25. Ibid.

26. David P. Dod, "Bank Lending to Developing Countries," *Federal Reserve Bulletin* 67 (October 1981):654.

27. Alan Riding, "Mexican Outlook: Banks are Wary," *New York Times*, 17 August 1982, p. D13.

28. Robert A. Bennett, "Mexico Seeking Postponement of Part of Debt," *New York Times*, 20 August 1982, p. A1.

29. Edward Cowan, "Loans and Credits for Aiding Mexico are Mapped by U.S.,"

New York Times, 21 August 1982, p. A1.

30. Art Pine, "Banks Avert World Financial Crisis Over Defaults, but Dangers Remain," *Wall Street Journal*, 31 December 1982, p. 13.

Notes to Chapter 9

1. For a description of this process, see Irving Fisher, "The Debt-Deflation Theory of Great Depressions," *Econometrica* 1 (October 1933):337–57.

2. Victor F. Zonana, "Seafirst Corp. Suffers Because of Unit's Links to Penn Square Bank," *Wall Street Journal*, 17 August 1982, p. 1.

3. John P. Forde, "Seafirst Shares Drop on News of Loss, Credit Agreement," *American Banker*, 24 January 1983, p. 1.

4. "Moody's Lowers Seafirst Rating," *American Banker*, 25 January 1983, p. 15.

5. Andrew F. Brimmer, "The Federal Reserve as Lender of Last Resort: The Containment of Systemic Risks," a paper presented before a Joint Session of the American Economics Association and the Eastern Economics Association, Dallas, Texas, December 29, 1984, pp. 19, 20.

6. Ibid.

7. U.S. Congress, House Committee on Banking, Finance and Urban Affairs, *Inquiry into Continental Illinois Corp. and Continental National Bank, Hearings before the Subcommittee on Financial Institutions, Supervision, Regulation and Insurance of the House Committee on Banking, Finance and Urban Affairs*, 98th Cong., 2d sess., 1984, p. 201.

8. Ibid., pp. 245–46.

9. Ibid., pp. 250–51.

10. Continental Illinois Corporation, Continental Illinois National Bank and Trust Company of Chicago, *1982 Annual Report and Form 10-K*, p. 27.

11. U.S. Congress, House Committee on Banking, Finance, and Urban Affairs, *Inquiry into Continental Illinois Corp.*, p. 459.

12. Ibid., p. 286.

13. Ibid., p. 460.

14. Ibid., p. 288.

15. Jeff Bailey and Tim Carrington, "Run Continues on Continental Illinois Deposits," *Wall Street Journal*, 2 July 1985, p. 3.

16. Ibid.

17. Leon E. Wynter, "Continental Illinois Daily Bank Borrowing Jumped by $2 Billion," *Wall Street Journal*, 3 July 1984, p. 2.

18. John Helyar and Leon E. Wynter, "Continental Illinois Fed Borrowing Rises; FDIC Mulls Change in Bank Management," *Wall Street Journal*, 9 July 1984, p. 5.

19. Office of the Comptroller of the Currency, Federal Deposit Insurance Corporation, Federal Reserve Board, Joint Press Release, "Permanent Assistance Program for Continental Illinois National Bank and Trust Company, Chicago, Illinois: Comprehensive Statement," p. 7.

20. Patrick I. Mahoney and Alice P. White, "The Thrift Industry in Transition," *Federal Reserve Bulletin* 71 (March 1985):153.

21. Ibid., p. 140.

22. Ibid., pp. 145–50.

23. *Savings Institutions Sourcebook* (Chicago: United States League of Savings Insti-

tutions, 1984), p. 10.

24. *Revitalizing America's Savings Institutions, 1983 Federal Home Loan Bank Board Annual Report*, December 1984, p. 35.

25. Mahoney and White, "The Thrift Industry in Transition," p. 148.

26. Nancy L. Ross, "S&Ls Told to Curb Fast, Risky Growth," *Washington Post*, 31 October 1984, p. A1.

27. Monica Langley, "Bank Board Seeks to Limit Activities of U.S.-Insured, State-Chartered S&Ls," *Wall Street Journal*, 7 May 1985, p. 3.

28. "What's Behind the Run on America's Biggest S&Ls?" *Fortune*, 17 September 1984, p. 133. The estimate was made by Jonathan Gray, an analyst at Sanford C. Bernstein & Co.

29. For FCA's explanation of its accounting procedures, see its amended 10-Q Quarterly Report to the SEC for the quarter ending June 30, 1984 (dated August 15, 1984).

30. Thomas C. Hayes, "Thrift Unit Reports Big Loss," *New York Times*, 16 August 1984, p. D1.

31. Frederick M. Muir, "Financial Corp. of America Net Declines by 97%," *Wall Street Journal*, 26 October 1984, p. 3.

32. Frederick M. Muir, "Financial Corp. of America Gave U.S. Policy Veto," *Wall Street Journal*, 10 October 1984, p. 3.

33. "Snatching Two Financial Giants from the Brink," *Institutional Investor*, December 1984, p. 177.

34. "The Rise and Fall of Marvin Warner," *Business Week*, 6 May 1985, p. 104.

35. Martha Brannigan, "ESM Group Unit Apparently Hid Losses of as Much as $300 Million, Auditors Find," *Wall Street Journal*, 6 March 1985, p. 6.

36. Clare Ansberry, Lynda Schuster, and Martha Brannigan, "Ohio Moves to Bolster Thrift Guarantees as Losses Mount from ESM Unit Failure," *Wall Street Journal*, 12 March 1985, p. 3.

37. Ibid.

38. "Closing of Ohio S&Ls After Run on Deposits is One for the Books," *Wall Street Journal*, 18 March 1985, p. 6.

39. "The Rise and Fall of Marvin Warner," p. 106.

40. David La Gesse, "SEC is Scrutinizing Home State's Link with ESM Failure," *American Banker*, 18 March 1985, p. 3. This article contains a good discussion of the transactions between ESM and Home State.

41. Ansberry et al., "Ohio Moves to Bolster Thrift Guarantees as Losses Mount from ESM Unit Failure," p. 3.

42. Quoted in *Business Week*, 8 April 1985, p. 34.

43. James L. Rowe, Jr., "Regulators Fear More Failures," *Washington Post*, 12 April 1985, p. F1.

44. R. H. Melton and Tom Kenworthy, "S&L Crisis Surfaced 3 Weeks Ago," *Washington Post*, 18 May 1985, p. A8.

45. "Old Court's Books Reveal Extensive Real Estate Position," *American Banker*, 23 May 1985, p. 23.

46. Nina Easton, "Run on Thrift Challenges Maryland Fund," *American Banker*, 13 May 1985, p. 2.

47. Steve Swartz, "Maryland Names Conservator for Two Thrifts," *Wall Street Journal*, 14 May 1985, p. 3.

Part III

Notes to Chapter 11

1. The debt-equity ratio in the text is the traditional one based on the actual values reported by the nation's corporations. This historical cost data, though, overstate the debt burden when inflation reduces the current real value of obligations incurred in the past. However, outstanding debt-equity ratios based on either the market value of corporate equity or the replacement cost of corporate assets also show an increase as the cyclical peak is approached. In addition, ratios based on flows rather than outstandings, such as quarterly flows of debt to internal funds, demonstrate a similar cyclical pattern.

2. The level of depreciation is also included in the numerator of the interest coverage ratio. However, since depreciation has continually increased throughout the entire period considered here (see Figure 11.15), it would not contribute toward a decline in the ratio itself.

3. There are a number of possible approaches that could be used in defining an empirical measure of the profit rate. The measure used here includes the capital consumption and inventory valuation adjustments in order to remove the distortions that inflation produces in reported profits. After-tax profits are used because they are more useful in assessing the contribution made by profits to internal funds (although the cyclical movement of the before-tax profit ratio is the same as that of the after-tax ratio). Total nonfinancial corporate domestic income was used in the denominator, rather than a measure of the capital stock, partly because a quarterly rather than an annual series was needed, partly because of the conceptual problems of estimating the value of the capital stock independently of the profit rate itself, and partly because the nonfinancial corporate domestic income series and the nonfinancial corporate profits series are drawn from the same data base. Using gross domestic product of the nonfinancial corporate sector in the denominator instead of domestic income again changes the level of the ratio but not its cyclical movement.

Notes to Chapter 13

1. Minsky mentions the role of government deficits in most of his articles cited in Chapter 2. For example, see Minsky, "Finance and Profits," pp. 243–44.

2. Sinai, "Credit Crunches."

3. Minsky, "Finance and Profits," p. 244.

4. Hyman P. Minsky, "Longer Waves in Financial Relations: Financial Factors in the More Severe Depressions," *American Economic Review* 54 (May 1964):324–25.

5. See Paul M. Sweezy and Harry Magdoff, "The Long-Run Decline in Liquidity," *Monthly Review* 22 (September 1970).

6. With debt-equity measures based on the market value of corporate equity or the replacement cost of corporate assets, the pattern is somewhat different but the geneal conclusion remains the same. Although values of these two ratios were somewhat higher in the early 1970s than they were in 1984, the average ratio for the years 1966 to 1984 was significantly greater than for the years 1945 to 1965. For the debt-equity measure based on the market value of corporate equity, the average ratio for the later period was .690

compared to .506 for the earlier period; for the replacement cost ratio, the comparable averages were .448 and .348.

7. A recent study by Robert Pollin examined three different explanations for the recent secular increase in debt-dependency of the corporate sector: Minsky's financial fragility hypothesis, inflation, and declining profits. He found the last explanation to be the most persuasive. See Robert Pollin, "Corporate Financial Structures and the Crisis of U.S. Capitalism," unpublished Ph.D dissertation, The New School for Social Research, 1982.

8. The appropriateness of attributing a declining rate of *corporate* profitability to Marx might be questioned, since his average rate of profit is based on a concept of surplus value which also includes returns to money lenders and landlords. In particular, a declining corporate profit rate might be compatible with a rising or stable rate of profit in Marx's terms, since interest payments have increased so rapidly in the postwar period. However, a recent study has found that the broader measure of profitability has also declined. See Robert Pollin, "Distribution of Capital Income and the Falling Rate of Profit in the U.S. Postwar Economy," mimeo, June 1984.

9. Minsky, "Financial Markets and Economic Instability," p. 9.

10. Minsky, "Finance and Profits," p. 244.

11. See, for example, David M. Gordon, Richard Edwards, and Michael Reich, *Segmented Work, Divided Workers: The Historical Transformation of Labor in the United States* (Cambridge: Cambridge University Press, 1982), pp. 22–32.

Selected Bibliography

Altman, Edward I., and Sametz, Arnold W., eds. *Financial Crises: Institutions and Markets in a Fragile Environment.* New York: John Wiley & Sons, 1977.

Beman, Lewis. "How It All Came Apart in the Eurodollar Market." *Fortune*, February 1975, p. 85.

Board of Governors of the Federal Reserve System. *Annual Report.* Various years.

Brimmer, Andrew F. "The Federal Reserve and the Failure of Franklin National Bank: A Case Study of Regulation." In *Business and the American Economy, 1776–2001*, pp. 108–40. Edited by Jules Backman. New York: New York University Press, 1976.

———. "The Federal Reserve as Lender of Last Resort: The Containment of Systemic Risks. A Paper Presented Before a Joint Session of The American Economic Association and The Eastern Economic Association. Dallas, Texas, December 29, 1984.

Business Week. "The Stain from Penn Square Keeps Spreading." 2 August 1982, pp. 60–62.

Crane, Dwight B. "Lessons from the 1974 CD Market." *Harvard Business Review* 53 (November-December 1975):73–79.

Dod, David P. "Bank Lending to Developing Countries." *Federal Reserve Bulletin* 67 (October 1981):647–56.

Fay, Stephen. *Beyond Greed.* New York: Penguin Books, 1983.

Federal Reserve Bank of New York. *Annual Report.* Various years.

Federal Reserve Bank of New York. *A Report on Drysdale and Other Recent Problems of Firms Involved in the Government Securities Market.* 15 September 1982.

Fisher, Irving. "The Debt-Deflation Theory of Great Depressions." *Econometrica* 1 (October 1933):337–57.

Friedman, Milton. "Wesley C. Mitchell as an Economic Theorist." In *Wesley Clair Mitchell, The Economic Scientist*, pp. 237–82. Edited by Arthur F. Burns. New York: National Bureau of Economic Research, 1952.

———. *Dollars and Deficits.* Englewood Cliffs, New Jersey: Prentice-Hall, Inc., 1968.

———. "Why the American Economy is Depression-Proof." In *Dollars and Deficits*, pp. 72–96. Edited by Milton Friedman. Englewood Cliffs, New Jersey: Prentice-Hall, Inc., 1968.

———. "The Monetary Theory and Policy of Henry Simons." In *The Optimum*

Quantity of Money and Other Essays, pp. 81–93. Chicago: Aldine Publishing Co., 1969.

————. *The Optimum Quantity of Money and Other Essays*. Chicago: Aldine Publishing Co., 1969.

Friedman, Milton, and Schwartz, Anna Jacobson. *A Monetary History of the United States 1867–1960*. Princeton, New Jersey: Princeton University Press, 1963.

————. "Money and Business Cycles." In *The Optimum Quantity of Money and Other Essays*, pp. 189–236. Edited by Milton Friedman. Chicago: Aldine Publishing Co., 1969.

Kaufman, Henry. "Financial Crises: Market Impact, Consequences, and Adaptability." In *Financial Crises: Institutions and Markets in a Fragile Environment*, pp. 153–59. Edited by Edward I. Altman and Arnold W. Sametz. New York: John Wiley & Sons, 1977.

————. Foreword to *Financial Crises: Institutions and Markets in a Fragile Environment*. Edited by Edward I. Altman and Arnold W. Sametz. New York: John Wiley & Sons, 1977.

Kindleberger, Charles P. *Manias, Panics, and Crashes: A History of Financial Crises*. New York: Basic Books, 1978.

Kindleberger, Charles P. and Laffargue, Jean-Pierre, eds. *Financial Crises*. Cambridge: Cambridge University Press, 1982.

Light, J. O. and White, William L. *The Financial System*. Homewood, Illinois: Richard D. Irwin, 1979.

Maisel, Sherman J. *Managing the Dollar*. New York: W. W. Norton & Company, Inc., 1973.

Marx, Karl. *Capital*. 3 vols. New York: International Publishers, 1967.

————. *Theories of Surplus Value*. 3 parts. Moscow: Progress Publishers, 1968.

Melton, William C. "The Market for Large Negotiable CDs." *Quarterly Review of the Federal Reserve Bank of New York* 2 (Winter 1977–78):22–34.

Minsky, Hyman P. "Longer Waves in Financial Relations: Financial Factors in the More Severe Recessions." *American Economic Review* 54 (May 1964):324–35.

————. "Financial Resources in a Fragile Financial Environment." *Challenge* 18 (July-August, 1975):6–13.

————. *John Maynard Keynes*. New York: Columbia University Press, 1975.

————. "The Financial Instability Hypothesis: An Interpretation of Keynes and an Alternative to 'Standard' Theory." *Challenge* 20 (March-April 1977):20–27.

————. "A Theory of Systemic Fragility." In *Financial Crises: Institutions and Markets in a Fragile Environment*, pp. 138–152. Edited by Edward I. Altman and Arnold W. Sametz. New York: John Wiley & Sons, 1977.

————. "Finance and Profits: The Changing Nature of American Business Cycles." In U.S. Congress, Joint Economic Committee, *The Business Cycle and Public Policy, 1929–80*, pp. 209–44. Washington, D.C.: Government Printing Office, 1980.

————. "The Federal Reserve: Between a Rock and a Hard Place." *Challenge* 23 (May-June 1980):30–36.

————. "Capitalist Financial Processes and the Instability of Capitalism." *Journal of Economic Issues* 14 (June 1980):505–23.

————. "Financial Markets and Economic Instability, 1965–1980." *Nebraska Journal of Economics and Business* 20 (Autumn 1981):5–16.

————. "The Financial-Instability Hypothesis: Capitalist Processes and the Behavior of the Economy." In *Financial Crises*, pp. 13–39. Edited by Charles P. Kindleberger and Jean-Pierre Laffarge. Cambridge: Cambridge University Press, 1982.

————. "The Financial Instability Hypothesis: A Restatement." In *Can "It" Happen Again? Essays on Instability and Finance*, pp. 90–116. By Hyman P. Minsky. Armonk, New York: M. E. Sharpe, Inc., 1982.

————. *Can "It" Happen Again? Essays on Instability and Finance*. Armonk, New York: M. E. Sharpe, Inc., 1982.

Mitchell, Wesley Clair. *Business Cycles and Their Causes*. Berkeley, California: University of California Press, 1941.

Moore, Geoffrey. *Business Cycles, Inflation, and Forecasting*. Cambridge Massachusetts: Ballinger Press for the National Bureau of Economic Research, 1980, p. 444.

Moran, Michael J. "Thrift Institutions in Recent Years." *Federal Reserve Bulletin* 68 (December 1982):725-38.

Pollin, Robert. "Corporate Financial Structures and the Crisis of U.S. Capitalism." Ph.D. dissertation, New School for Social Research, 1982.

Robertson, Wyndham. "How the Bankers Got Trapped in the REIT Disaster." *Fortune*, March 1975, p. 113.

Rose, Sanford. "What Really Went Wrong at Franklin National." *Fortune*, October 1974, p. 118.

Sinai, Allen. "Credit Crunches—An Analysis of the Postwar Experience." In *Parameters and Policies in the U.S. Economy*, pp. 244–74. Edited by Otto Eckstein. Amsterdam: North Holland, 1976.

————. Discussion of Papers on The American Financial Environment. In *Financial Crises: Institutions and Markets in a Fragile Environment*, pp. 187–203. Edited by Edward I. Altman and Arnold W. Sametz. New York: John Wiley & Sons, 1977.

Sinkey, Joseph F., Jr. "The Collapse of Franklin National Bank of New York." *Journal of Bank Research* 7 (Summer 1976):113-22.

Spero, Joan Edelman. *The Failure of the Franklin National Bank: Challenge to the International Banking System*. New York: Columbia University Press, 1980.

U.S. Congress. House. Committee on Banking, Finance, and Urban Affairs. *Penn Square Bank Failure. Hearings before the House Committee on Banking, Finance, and Urban Affairs*, Part 1, 97th Cong., 2d sess., 1982; Part 2, 97th Cong., 2d sess., 1983.

U.S. Congress. House. Committee on Government Operations. *Silver Prices and the Adequacy of Federal Actions in the Marketplace, 1979-80. Hearings before a Subcommittee of the House Committee on Government Operations*, 96th Cong., 2d sess., 1980.

U.S. Congress. House. Committee on Banking, Finance, and Urban Affairs. *Inquiry into Continental Illlinois and Continental Illinois National Bank. Hearings before the Subcommittee on Financial Institutions Supervision, Regulation and Insurance of the Committee on Banking, Finance and Urban Affairs*, 98th Cong., 2d sess., 1984.

U.S. Congress. Senate. Committee on Agriculture, Nutrition, and Forestry. *Report of the Commodity Futures Trading Commission on Recent Developments in the Silver Futures Markets*, 96th Cong., 2d sess., 1980.

U.S. Congress. Senate. Committee on Banking, Housing, and Urban Affairs. *Real Estate Investment Trusts. Hearings before the Committee on Banking, Housing and Urban Affairs*, 94th Cong., 2d sess., 1976.

U.S. Congress. Senate. Committee on Banking, Housing, and Urban Affairs. *Disturbances in the U.S. Market. Hearing before the Subcommittee on Securities of the Senate Committee on Banking, Housing, and Urban Affairs*, 97th Cong., 2d sess., 1982.

U.S. Congress. Senate. Committee on Banking, Housing, and Urban Affairs. *Failure of Penn Square Bank. Hearing before the Senate Committee on Banking, Housing, and Urban Affairs*, 97th Cong., 2d sess., 1983.

U.S. Securities and Exchange Commission. *The Silver Crisis of 1980*, 1982.

Veblen, Thorstein. *The Theory of Business Enterprise*. New York: Charles Scribner's Sons, 1904.

Weeks, John. *Capital and Exploitation*. Princeton, New Jersey: Princeton University Press, 1981.

Wojnilower, Albert M. "The Central Role of Credit Crunches in Recent Financial History." *Brookings Papers on Economic Activity*, No. 2 (1980), pp. 277-326.

————. "Private Credit Demand, Supply and Crunches: How Different are the 1980s?" *American Economic Review* 75 (May 1985):351-56.

Index